35⁰⁰

26307

D0081066

LIBRARIES DESIGNED FOR USERS

Libraries

Designed

for Users

A Planning Handbook

by Nolan Lushington & Willis N. Mills, Jr. AIA

Hamden, Connecticut   *1980*
LIBRARY PROFESSIONAL PUBLICATIONS

©Nolan Lushington and Willis N. Mills, Jr.
First published in 1979 by
Gaylord Professional Publications
and reprinted in 1980 as
a Library Professional Publication,
an imprint of
The Shoe String Press, Inc.
Hamden, Connecticut 06514

Library of Congress Cataloging in Publication Data

Lushington, Nolan, 1929-
  Libraries designed for users.

  Originally published in 1979 by Gaylord Professional
Publications, Syracuse, N.Y.
  Bibliography: p.
  Includes index.
  1. Library planning—Handbooks, manuals, etc.
2. Library architecture.   3. Libraries—Space
utilization.   I. Mills, Willis, 1933-   joint
author.   II. Title.
Z679.5.L87   022'.3   80-24928
ISBN 0-208-01892-1

Contents

The measurements within this book are given for the most part in inches and feet. This table is included for the convenience of those readers wishing to convert these measurements to metric equivalents.

metres			approximate U.S. or English equivalent
0.001	(millimetre)	mm	0.04 inch
0.01	(centimetre)	cm	0.39 inch
0.1	(decimetre)	dm	3.94 inch
1	(metre)	m	39.37 inches
10	(decametre)	dkm	32.81 feet
100	(hectometre)	hm	109.36 yards

U.S. or English measurement	approximate metric equivalent
1.0 inch	25.4 mm or 2.54 cm
12.0 inches or 1 foot	30.48 cm or 0.3048 m
36.0 inches or 1 yard	0.9144 m

Preface and Acknowledgments

I have been interested in the planning of physical facilities for libraries ever since I first read an American Library Association pamphlet entitled *Dear Mr. Architect* in the 1950s and began planning a small school library at St. Andrew's School in Middletown, Delaware. When I became a public librarian at the Free Library of Philadelphia in the 1960s, I began to understand Emerson Greenaway's efforts to make libraries information centers in addition to their traditional function of circulating books. I was enthralled with the delight with which so many different kinds of people used the public library. Later, as a reference librarian in a suburban community, I saw an information media center, with many kinds of library subjects and media specialists all working together to meet a wide range of user wants tried out under Jack Bryant's enthusiastic and intelligent leadership. It worked, and in 1969 an addition to the Greenwich (Connecticut) Library made it possible for me to work with a perceptive architect, Willis Mills, Jr., in designing an information center that would focus user attention on the tremendous range of information and media resources available in a modern library.

This new concept of information center design was reinforced for me by a Council on Library Resources fellowship that permitted me in 1972 to visit many recently designed libraries in the British Isles. Talking with British librarians, such as John Chapman of Doncaster, I began to see that peoples' need for all kinds of information resources to satisfy the demands of a complex society and better shape their lives was international and was bound to result in some significant changes in library design.

During the past five years, I have had the opportunity to participate in the planning of more than 25 new or remodeled library buildings, all of which utilized this concept of a multistaffed information center. In the course of such projects, I have learned much from other librarians, from library boards and library users, and from architects that is worth sharing with my colleagues. A prominent library educator has said that library building consultation is a cottage industry. This may be one of its most exciting attributes! Technical innovations— such as computerized circulation control with its capability to diminish the size of circulation desks, on-line touch terminal catalogs to replace card catalogs, and information bank terminals accessing dozens of data bases—make library planning a constantly changing art and science. The planning process itself, based on new public library goals and purposes, must be experimental and empirical as concepts are more firmly linked to community analysis and quickly shifting community wants and needs.

This book is an effort to summarize some of the things I have learned that may be of help to others, especially to those planning medium-sized libraries serving 200 to 2,000 people a day in communities of 10,000 to 100,000. It is intended to be somewhat more detailed than Rolf Myller's excellent *The Design of the Small Public Library* published in 1966. It is certainly not intended to replace the great Wheeler and Githens book, nor is it intended for the planning of large city or university libraries.

We have included a chapter by Dr. Gwendolyn Wright of Southern Connecticut State College on the design of school library media centers because these library resources, serving the same community in general as the medium-sized public library, are important units in the library network. It was the hugely upgraded and innovative school library media facilities and programs of the 1960s that helped shape the library expectations and use patterns of today's most active public library users.

An essential point made in this book is that libraries designed for towns are not scaled down versions of big city libraries. Libraries of 30,000 square feet or less can be designed as single story structures with most public services concentrated in a single multistaffed information media center from which a variety of services can conveniently and effectively be delivered. Larger libraries cannot do this because of the necessity for vertical traffic and service on a greater scale. There are some indications that future library designs may utilize this 30,000 square foot scale even in larger communities; micro materials and networking require less space for housing materials and equipment and permit access-to-resources on a more human scale.

I hope that this book will stimulate dialogue among library users, librarians, architects, interior designers, and researchers. Initially, we will examine the way people experience libraries and the way in which library design has evolved. We will then look at the design process—collecting information, communicating about library design, and the roles of the consultant, the architect, the staff and the community leadership. We will discuss various functional areas in the library, how they are related, and what their requirements are. There is a section in chapter 5 on planning facilities for the handicapped, legally mandated for all public buildings under Public Law 533, and a chapter on library planning from the architect's view of challenges and solutions. The last chapter contains critiques of specific library plans.

Acknowledgments for this book terrify me. I am indebted to so many people for help in its preparation, that I'm sure to forget someone—please forgive me.

My great thanks to:

My wife, Brooks, and children—Christopher, Nancy, and Michael—all participated in the library planning game, with Brooks compiling the index; my publishers, Walter Curley and Virginia H. Mathews for their confidence that I could produce; and to Virginia for cheerful encouragement and careful editing; my collaborator, Willis Mills, Jr., a sharp and helpful critic; Dr. Gwendolyn Wright of Southern Connecticut State College, who wrote the chapter on school library media Centers; Emerson Greenaway, for showing me what libraries are all about; many clients—librarians and trustees: Gretchen Hammerstein, Richard Robbins, Grace Birch, Lawrence Eaton, Bill Kasius, Marie Mersky, Virginia Carter, Roberta Cairns, Joan Turner, William Deakyne, Marian Wade, Barbara Gibson, Claris Cahan, Martha Strickland, Marcella Finan, Ken Blaisdell, Beth Long, Anita Daubenspeck, Bonnie O'Bryan and Jill Smith; architects with whom I have worked: Willis Mills, Jr., Marshall Christenson, Richard Schoenhardt, Dana Newbrook, Bob Stillings, Bob Miller, Arnold Gustafson, Tom Lyons, Joseph Beretta, Jim Walden, Jim Flynn, Bruce Falconer, David Presbrey, Dale Cutler, Mo Finegold, Aaron and Elaine Cohen, Gus Franzoni; library colleagues from whom I have learned a great deal: Keyes Metcalf, Ellsworth Mason, Alan Clark, Ray Holt, Faith Hektoen, and the Connecticut Environments for Children Committee; June Shapiro (who contributed the first section of Chapter 8 on planning the design of childrens' rooms), Sam Molod, Dave Smith, Ozzie Joerg, Dick Waters, Jack Bryant, Joseph Ruef, Meredith Bloss, Dorothy Garey and John Kernan.

Very special thanks are owed to the staff, trustees, and Friends of the Greenwich Library who gave me the opportunity to work out ideas in practice. I owe a debt to the expectant, sometimes difficult to please library user, personified by Bob Carrol, Ed Keefe and George Leavens.

And a special "thank you" to Marie Cole, whose positive and progressive attitude toward libraries and fund raising for them made possible the addition to the Greenwich Library.

The drawings for this book were prepared by Roz Levine. Some photographs are by George Leavens (Byram Library). What little I am able to impart about lighting comes from the patient explanations of Ellsworth Mason, Keyes Metcalf, Elaine Cohen, Sy Shemitz, and Sven Bruun. My students at Southern Connecticut State College helped by questioning—everything.

Greenwich, Connecticut   Nolan Lushington
April 1978

1 Library Design and User Experience

Libraries designed as community resource centers can play a useful role in human communication. As informational and cultural switching stations, they help to meet the needs of individuals for information required to maintain a satisfying life style. Informational and cultural needs must draw upon an increasingly wide range of traditional published materials—books, magazines, newspapers—as well as a great variety of new media of the audio-visual type—videodiscs, computer data banks, micro-media, audiotapes and film. Information in all these formats grows in cost, quantity, variety and complexity, so libraries have rapidly evolved as highly structured institutions operated by professionals attempting to forge this mass of materials, equipment and techniques into an orderly instrument for satisfying individual needs, one by one.

Libraries are one of the few institutions designed to facilitate individually received information and communication, yet the volume and complexity of materials make the ideal of individual responsiveness increasingly difficult to attain.

Design for Individuals

This book is an effort to describe how the design of physical facilities can help achieve the goal of tailored service to each library user. The problem of size and scale is critical. How can a large building serving thousands of people each day offer good service that must be, in many cases, self-service? Recent studies have shown that more people use materials inside libraries than take materials out of libraries, so it is no longer possible to design libraries as if they were primarily for the circulation of books. Libraries with strong film collections report that more of their patrons watch films than borrow books, yet book circulation in these libraries has increased too. Libraries must be designed for the widest possible spectrum of taste, inquiry, and informational or cultural need, and to provide assistance in utilizing materials in all formats. To make a large and complex service function like an intimate and personalized one is an objective that requires careful design and use of space, as well as tremendous flexibility.

Community Needs

The professional teamwork required for such a design must be firmly based on the needs and wants of the community. Continuous assessment of needs and desires by a variety of means provides library management with its most valuable tool for the budget process and for setting service priorities and objectives. A community information and referral service that is constantly collecting and disseminating specific information relating to the community can serve as a basic source of information about many community needs and about the extent to which they are perceived as informational needs. This service can and should be integrated into the total spectrum of library reference services and, in combination with them, become the core of the library's service facility. Combine these informational services with the full array of media for client use, including video production facilities, and individuals can fully experience library media service geared to today's complex, shifting society.

A major barrier to library use lies in bad design of facilities and buildings, that is, faulty symbolization and visualization of what the library is really offering. What aspects must be examined if we are to change the stereotypes that still linger among the majority of the population?

Location

Performance objectives related to increased use by a greater percentage of the population require a location exactly where a large proportion of the people go—market areas, primarily, situated on busy roads—*not* in civic centers, schools, or parks.

Identification

Hours of availability should be announced on signs visible to non-library users and meaningful to them, with mention of popular services. Lighted signs can be read at night from moving automobiles.

Circulation checkout area showing individual user pockets and machine height/transaction height counter.

Convenience

There should be parking close to the building; a highly visible, easy entrance (with automatic doors like those at the supermarket); simple arrangement; large directional signs; and immediate access to books, magazines, films, newspapers, as well as projectors, copiers, and microform readers.

Quality of the Library Experience

A welcoming staff, comfortable seats, and a place to talk and meet people and enjoy a snack; colorful, well-lighted displays that suggest what to read, look at, or listen to; control of sound; lighting that encourages behavior suitable to a variety of activities; books that look attractive; and machines for use with other media that *work*—these are some of the things that enhance the library experience.

Properly designed graphics, furniture, lighting, and functional relationships can create the library environment we seek and avoid—inaccessible building and materials, long waits, put downs by the staff, and bewilderment about where to go.

Educators have begun to understand that there are many human capabilities in addition to verbal and mathematical skills, and that libraries can help to foster them. The visual skills of artists and cameramen, craft skills, and communication skills can be related to the library as a unique community communications center. The key to interpreting and operating the needed services has to be a new kind of librarian generalist with some knowledge of communications, psychology, film and video potentials, as well as the essentials of bibliographic control and the use of printed materials.

In urban areas, which have many people using a variety of kinds of libraries, there are some exciting library buildings designed and operated to provide a maximum of specialized services of a limited nature. The Chicago Regional Media Service Center is one example of a library geared to heavy use and circulation of audiovisual materials and equipment. Its auditorium is fully equipped for any type of sight and sound presentation; its study carrels are equipped for use of TV and AV; and there are facilities for production and reproductions of such media materials as slides and audiotapes. The Lincoln Center Library in New York City is another example of a public library devoted to the arts. The design features of such centers should be studied carefully for adaptation in general public libraries that want to offer such specialties on a more limited scale. It may be unnecessary to build in such facilities for the enjoyment of special services once interconnections and networking make it possible for highly specialized services to be delivered to users through smaller outlets, using distant expert assistance and materials in combination with terminals and locally available equipment.

Less is More

How small can a library be and still give adequate service? With building and maintenance costs increasing and transportation limited by the energy shortage, we must constantly question the need for more and more library space in which to provide good services. Technology is gradually giving librarians more control over their operations and processes and gradually interlocking libraries in computer-based networks that provide marvelous alternatives to the insatiable need for more space. An interesting management tool for limiting space needs is the computerized circulation control system, which is increasingly capable of reporting useful information on library use by subject, client category, and other characteristics. Such systems help to retrieve needed books more quickly, thus reducing the need for duplicate copies, and they report on title inactivity so that deadwood can be cleared from the shelves. Networked computers can make independent libraries act like a single system for the users and for cooperative acquisitions.

Complexity and Individuality

How can such an array of services be made and kept responsive to individual needs? Much exploration of this desirable intent is under way. Recent pilot programs in several public libraries have, for instance, attempted to define the role of the library in self-paced education. Such programs have based learner's advisory services on assessment of each individual's learning needs and style. Library and other community resources may then be fitted to these personal requirements. New library designs should frame such independent, individualized learning processes with spaces and facilities both for private study and for learning consultation.

Design Characteristics

What design characteristics are required by the new functions and uses of libraries?

1. Integrated design to accommodate a wide range of media.
2. Centralized service center location of professional staff from which various services can radiate.
3. Flexibility of facilities and equipment to make change easy and possible.
4. Spaces of various shapes and sizes to assure user choices.
5. Compact storage for materials arranged for rapid and convenient retrieval.
6. Material and services planned for access with the greatest possible economy of effort for staff and public user.

Conflicting Objectives

Many paradoxes and conflicting objectives are inherent in these design characteristics. Thorough understanding of these paradoxes is the key to good design. How, for example, can a library provide centralized, integrated services and individual spaces? How can detailed design be accomplished while retaining flexibility? How can change be accommodated with massive quantities and varieties of materials to shift around? How can staff control be maintained while assuring individual privacy and freedom?

The Flexibility Fallacy

Many recent library designs, recognizing the need for flexibility, have featured open, modular designs with movable partitions, masses of electrical outlets, expensive clouds of fluorescent lighting and quantities of ventilating outlets. The theory has been that the architect's role was to provide a flexible, universal space, so the librarian could then do whatever he or she wanted in it.

A visit to such a library reveals a banal desert of space—lifeless, mindless, bland—without any apparent understanding of the varied requirements of different library service areas. A universal space can be the beginning of a useful design, but it must be followed with careful selection of furnishings, equipment, lighting and graphics to breathe life and color into the specific library activities that will take place there.

It may be that flexibility requires the retention of an architect, designer or space planner on a continuing basis, so that design changes can become a way of life for a library along with changes in program and priorities. Several university libraries have staff with this assignment—Nancy McAdams at the University of Texas, for example. The work of Andrew Kostanecki at the Darien (Connecticut) Public Library is an example of planning for continuing change in a library of completely different scale.

How Do Users Experience Libraries?

To illustrate some problems encountered as users experience libraries, let us look at the hypothetical experience of a family making its first trip to the community library.

The Carters have just moved into a house in a suburban town. One Saturday afternoon, on their way to the shopping center, they pass a Georgian style brick building on a side street. It could be a bank, town hall or telephone exchange, but the Carters see small children coming out with books tucked under their arms, so they guess that the building is the local library. They hunt for a parking space, drive around the block and park in a one-hour metered space. Walking back toward the library, they have to scramble up a ten-foot hill to arrive at the rear door. They tug open the heavy door and find themselves in a dimly lit concrete stairwell; paper signs indicate that adults are UP, children DOWN. The Carters decide to take seven year-old John to the children's area, and plunge down the stairs and through another heavy door into a low-ceilinged cellar, lit with glaring bluish fluorescent lights and furnished with massive oak chairs and tables. Around them is a confusing welter of shelves crammed with books of every size, condition, and age. Near the entrance is a high counter and an impatient line of children waiting to have their books stamped. Staff members are behind the counter, or in a glassed-in office area smoking, and there doesn't seem to be anyone available to help the newcomers.

Several children and adults, too, surround the card catalog, which is a 60 tray unit, 5 trays wide. John squeezes between patrons at the catalog and manages to extract a drawer holding cards on tennis books with numbers in the 700s. Looking around at the bookstacks, he sees 500s and 600s, but no 700s. His mother does find a display of tennis books in a corner, and they pick out a book for a beginner. Mrs. Carter finally succeeds in borrowing the book for John, after an argument with the clerk about proof of residence.

Then the Carters climb the stairs to the adult area—another large, cluttered room with masses of bookstacks interspersed with more golden oak tables and spindly wooden chairs. Mr. Carter browses through the material on the new book shelf, then goes over to the busy check-out desk and asks for the new Erica Jong novel. The clerk gives him a doubtful look and suggests that he try looking in the card catalog. Before he can ask where it is, she returns to stamping books. Mr. Carter wanders around the room until he finds a huge pile of drawers in an alcove. Searching for Jong, he finds only a reference to *Fear of Flying*. Bewildered, he looks around for a librarian, and spotting a desk in another alcove labeled REFERENCE, he waits there for several minutes until a woman walks briskly up and asks what he wants. He repeats his request for the Jong book and is told that the book has been received, but not processed, and already there is a waiting list two-months long.

Mrs. Carter's search for books on macrame has proved to be equally frustrating, because she did not understand that oversize art books were shelved in a special location. The Carters decide to find out about library programs. After asking again

Fiction book
catalog

at the check-out desk, they are referred to a bulletin board in the reference room where a hand-lettered sign tells them that *Gunga Din* is being shown that evening. Having seen this classic film on television the previous week, they decide to pass it up and inquire about future films. The reference librarian produces a dog-eared folder, and they thumb through a sheet listing future library programs and copy down the dates of some old movies and a local string quartet concert. Asking where the programs are held, they are referred to a hall on the third floor with folding chairs, some cases filled with stuffed birds, and a badly curled and yellowed movie screen. Struggling back downstairs, they emerge into a crashing thunderstorm and run back to their car only to find it being towed away by the police.

Improving the Library Experience

Basic library improvement objectives designed to help the user could have improved this experience. Obviously, many of the worst elements in the experience relate to library operational practices, but physical improvements are closely related to operational procedures.

Some ways in which this experience could have been improved include:

1. Convenient library location:
   a. Ample parking.
   b. On a major road.
   c. Near where people go for other purposes, for example, a shopping center.
   d. Level entrance from parking lot into the building.
   e. Sign identifying the library to passing motorists.
2. Easy opening doors.
3. Building directory at entrance.
4. Functional relationships delineated at entrance by graphics and inside by lighting, furniture arrangement, and colors.
5. Information center visible from the entrance; one single multistaffed location for all reader inquiries, with card catalog, bookstacks, reference materials, audiovisual services grouped around it, and a large double-sided service counter for staff and library users.

6. Comfortable seating and convenient task-oriented lighting.
7. Sufficient duplicate copies of popular materials.
8. Library communication about programs by displays, flyers, and publicity.
9. One story services or elevators/escalators.
10. Attractive meeting or program room with well-kept equipment.

Many of these objectives can be accomplished within existing structures, but all require a dedication to the policy of *user convenience* and an understanding of the relationships of library functions to design solutions. Libraries are used by individuals and should be designed with the individual in mind. Building size and scale, furnishings, equipment, and individual building experiences should emphasize the convenience and enjoyment of the individual.

Leadership in library improvement must be based on the support of library boards dedicated to locating and building a library structure and financing services with user convenience as the first priority.

Norman O. Brown in *From Politics to Metapolitics* talks about "an environment that works so well that we can run wild in it." In our desire to create an institution uniquely responsive to the needs of the individual, we must strive for this kind of unobtrusive order.

Back in 1931, that greatest of all library philosophers S. N. Ranganathan said it as well and as concisely as it can ever be said in his Five Laws of Library Science:

1. Books are for use.
2. Books are for all.
3. Every book its reader.
4. Save the time of the reader.
5. A library is a growing organism.

Performance Objectives for Readers of This Book

Be able to prepare a library improvement program based on community wants and library use.
Be able to recognize library functional relationships.
Be able to critique an existing library building.
Be able to interview and select an architect and consultant.
Be able to direct and evaluate the work of a library design team.
Be able to evaluate proposed library sites.

Be able to critique schematic designs for libraries from
the point of view of User Convenience and Staff
Effectiveness

Be able to improve energy conservation, graphics, seating and lighting in existing libraries as well as in
library plans.

2   Library Designs of the Past and New Concepts of Design

Everyone dreams of the perfect library. Aldous Huxley in *Brave New World* envisioned an environment that would assault all our senses at once. The strong media-centered school of the late 1960s envisioned individual study carrels where each student could plug into an array and totality of experiences by twirling a telephone dial.

Architecture is a social art. Societies build for the needs particular to their time and place. Library architecture has evolved from the storage of a few rare manuscripts in a cabinet (or *armium)* to be used by the few learned individuals in a monastic order. Books were rare and carefully protected. Today, libraries try to provide information of all kinds to a public of all sorts in a free and open manner. (The history of library architecture is fully presented in Nicholas Pevsner's *A History of Building Types* pp. 91-110.)

With the Renaissance and the age of humanism, it was natural that libraries should become accessible to the reading public. Monasteries had been not only the place where books were collected and preserved, but also the place where books were produced. But the invention of movable type made it possible to publish a greater number of volumes than could be copied by hand. University libraries or national collections replaced the monastic libraries as the main depositories of printed material.

Books were still rare and were protected by being

chained to lecterns or tables. Michaelangelo's Laurentian Library (1523–71), built in Florence for the Medici, followed this tradition. The relationship between the individual reader and the collection was simple—man, a room, benches, tables, and books, illuminated by windows along the outside wall. Presumably, the librarian and the architect decided which books should be chained to which table.

It soon became apparent that chaining books to reading tables was wasteful of space. The further development of printing decreased the value of books, so they no longer needed to be chained. They could be stored in cases along the perimeter wall. Christopher Wren's Trinity College Library (1676), Oxford, was typical of the "wall system" libraries. Window sills higher than the shelves permitted a continuous wall of books. Each college at Oxford and Cambridge universities had its own library, often the gift of learned or wealthy collectors. In addition to books, statues, globes and scientific instruments were stored and used in these long, high rooms.

As the flow of printed material increased, the one room library with books along the perimeter wall and reader seats in the center became an obsolete architectural solution. Multilevel bookshelves made an appearance. Shelves were extended vertically to the ceiling—accessible first by ladder and later by gallery. Other solutions developed, such as a central reading room surrounded by rooms filled with books. These forerunners of "peninsula" bookstacks required a staff of librarians and pages to locate the book and bring it to the central reading room for the reader. The central reading room's importance was often expressed by a dome with a skylight to provide illumination.

Thomas Jefferson's design for the library at the University of Virginia (1822–26) was based on the Pantheon in Rome. Jefferson's library was sited at the end of an academic mall formed by a series of pavilions dedicated to the various branches of learning. As an academic community, the University of Virginia is a landmark in public education. The library occupied the central position of importance. It was both the focal point and crossroads of university life.

The Rotunda at the University of Virginia was designed by Thomas Jefferson to be the university library and the focal point of the campus.

Perhaps the most significant development of the nineteenth century was the emergence of truly *public* libraries. After the French and American revolutions, it was again natural that libraries should become more democratic institutions. Just as libraries had moved from the monastery to the university, they now moved to serve a widening circle of people. Ironically, it was Frederick the Great who established the first truly public collection, which was open daily for the people of Berlin. His intention that the library should be public was indicated in its inscription " . . . nutrimentum spiritus."

Not only were national collections open to the public, but community libraries became an important feature in nineteenth century life. Pevsner believes that the first public library in the United States was located at Peterboro, New Hampshire, in 1833. In England, Parliament extended the act permitting raising of taxes for local museums to provide taxes for local libraries in 1850. During this same decade of the 1850s, a number of American cities began allocating a portion of tax monies to the support of libraries. This advanced the cause of community libraries. Still later, in the United States, the Carnegie Libraries funded through a private trust eventually brought nearly 2,500 community libraries into being.

Size and Scale

As libraries grew to 1,000 books or more, shelving was placed against the walls and readers were seated in the center of the room. The basic elements remained the readers and the books, with little requirement for organizational systems or circulation control, since books did not circulate.

When libraries grew to the 10,000 book size, there began to be a need for a catalog to help readers identify and locate a particular book. It became important for users to see the catalog and to be able to find the book. These libraries often used free-standing bookstacks (shelves) instead of wall shelving. The free-standing stacks held more books because they used both sides of each stack. As the number of stacks increased, it became important to arrange them in a precise relationship so users could stand in front of a section and search for a book from left to right and top to bottom, then proceed to the next range of stacks and continue the sequential

search. Most architects understood the relationship between the catalog and the bookstacks, positioned them so
that they could be seen from the library entrance, and
placed them together for easy access. Readers' seating
was usually placed in one large area contiguous with the
bookstacks and rigidly geometrical in design. Although
the furnishings were stiff and uncomfortable, lighting
was carefully considered; readers' stations often had
individual lamps in addition to natural light from windows and skylights.

Architecturally, several developments were note-
worthy. A few libraries were designed with a radial
layout plan. Either bookstacks or reader seats radiated
from a central control point. This provided optimum
supervision, although some space was lost because the
aisles increased in width toward the perimeter. The
library at the British Museum (1854–56) in London featured radial seats with a multilevel perimeter stack at the
circumference of the room. A glazed dome provided
illumination by day, with reading lights on the tables for
evening use.

The Industrial Revolution brought new building
materials such as steel to libraries. The steel cable driven
elevator, which made possible the multistory building,
was also developed. Artificial light, central heating, and
air conditioning brought new technologies to all architecture, including the architecture of libraries. The Bibli-
othèque St. Genevieve in Paris (1843–50) by Henri La
Brouste is one of the more dramatic examples of the new
technology, with exposed steel framing, a glazed barrel
vaulted roof, and metal bookstacks.

Later in the nineteenth century, H. H. Richardson
of Boston designed a series of libraries with asymmetrical plans and freely designed exteriors that were particul-
ary appropriate to their suburban settings. Often these
libraries were donated by successful business leaders as a
civic gesture. The informality of their sloping roofs,
turretted stair towers, rusticated masonry walls, and
heavy arches fulfilled the dreams of the donors for an
architecture of civic importance without the formalism
of neoclassical "temples of learning." The interiors of
these Richardson libraries were as romantic as their
exteriors. They possessed the vertical space and grandeur of the nineteenth century supported on sturdy

stone walls. The collections they housed were often divided into rooms of human scale, reflecting a romantic linkage of books, masonry, and steeply pitched dark wood ceilings. Such rooms are difficult to service and supervise by today's functional standards, nevertheless, these libraries, and some of the Carnegie libraries, do exude a rich architectural character difficult to duplicate today.

Carnegie Libraries

In the Carnegie building era libraries were considered as "monuments of learning." The buildings were themselves learning experiences. Monumental stairs required users to look up at one of the classical-copy styles of architecture in stone or brick that were common to most institutional architecture before 1930. Ornamentation—pediments, friezes, cornices, stone incised names of classical authors—set a tone of dignity and permanence. Heavy carved doors required substantial physical effort for persons who wished to open them and enter the enormous lobby. Marble check-out counters and hard stone floors contributed to a feeling of solidity and unyielding grandeur, while at the same time symbolizing mind-shrinking concepts of archival austerity. Chairs were back-breakingly straight and tables enormous and open, so that patrons could be in full view of a librarian at a desk and chair suspiciously like a teacher's. Bookstacks lit by an occasional 30 watt bulb formed canyons of steel and glass, which often imparted a painful static electrical shock to users. Hard-edged spaces and furnishings constantly impinged on the soft roundness of the human form.

This physical hardness was reinforced by the guarded firmness of the quality of service. These libraries were not places to idle away a few spare hours, but purposeful centers of traditional wisdom. Library users were expected to enter knowing what they wanted, to state their business, and to know how to use books efficiently.

Libraries as Monuments

Most libraries built well into the twentieth century adopted classical designs with huge open spaces designed to do homage to the educational value of books. Many great architects still try to express the monumentality of book storage design dramatically. Gordon Bunshaft of Skidmore, Owings & Merrill designed a magnificent exterior translucent marble shell many stories high for his interior glass-encased, open-framed bookstacks at the Beinecke rare book library of Yale University in New Haven, Connecticut.

In order to accommodate an additional floor of bookstacks in the same cubic area as in McKim, Mead, and White's original building, Philip Johnson designed a bridge-truss suspension system for his bookstacks in the addition to the Boston Public Library. Unfortunately, this fascinating design is, unlike Bunshaft's, hidden from view. However, the immense central hall of the Boston Public Library addition, devoid of any library activity, represents Johnson's effort to go back to the traditional view of the library as architectural monument.

Universal Space

In the 1940s and 1950s, the Bauhaus concept of universal space brought little comfort to the marble palaces. Concrete and glass boxes were created in the International style, with identical large open spaces and masses of flourescent lights in the ceilings. Large glass sides brought the outside into the building whether it was a busy, noisy street or a crowded parking lot. Readers wanting to sit near the glass would roast in the morning sun, shielding their eyes with dark glasses, or freeze in the night cold, squinting at pages with inadequate light when the sun set. Artificial lighting in these buildings was often inadequate because engineers had calculated on using natural light most of the time, forgetting that libraries are most used on dark winter afternoons. Lights installed in 20-foot high ceilings required scaffolding to replace burned out bulbs; if the bulbs were incandescent and burned out frequently, they were not always quickly replaced. Low hung ceilings were sometimes worse because of the extreme glare from the lamps; plastic diffusers yellowed with dirt and age, further reduced the light. Universal space required that lighting, heating, and ventilating ducts be recessed into ceilings, where they were expensive to install and difficult to service. These libraries at their worst gave little clue to users as to whether they were gyms, airplane hangars, or parking garages.

Function Expressed

In the 1960s, universal space gave way to a new concept dubbed by some architectural critics the "New Brutalism," in which lighting, ducts, fire extinguishers— all the mechanical paraphernalia of builders—were revealed in bright colors. Concrete formed with rough boards and butcher block counters became decoration that sought to emphasize the natural textures of materials. During this era, some perceptive and thoughtful architects sought to understand and design spaces that differentiated and stated library functions.

In the case of John Johansen's landmark, the Goddard Memorial Library at Clark University, Worcester, Massachusetts, this effort extended to expressing each particularized interior function in the exterior form of the building. The contrast between the random asymmetry of external form and the regular geometric order of the central interior bookstack creates an artistic tension. It is an expression of individualized learning at the perimeter of the building near the light, in contrast to the collective knowledge symbolized by a multistory bookstack at the center of the building where natural light is less important.

Inside, each function is open to and flows directly into every other function—but lights, furnishings, and mechanical systems clearly separate and emphasize the uniqueness of each activity.

The Mechanics of Libraries

How libraries function is going to be increasingly important as librarians and library users begin to understand how the wide variety of media fit into the patterns of user needs. Books are fantastically useful things—*The Whole Earth Catalog* called a library "a handy, handy, handy, thing"—and books can supply a wide range of answers, understanding, inspiration, and pleasure.

A library retrieves information for a user and is uniquely concerned with the *individual choice* of that user. Unlike other educational institutions, a library makes no effort to impose its value systems on its users. Individual choice can best be exercised through opportunities to choose freely. Once a library staff member begins a dialogue with a user, institutional and sociocultural influences may begin to intrude. The worst thing the librarian can do, according to a recent inteview with Ivan Illich, is to try to mediate between the person and the book. However, as libraries grow in size and complexity, as do user's needs, more assistance rather than less may be needed.

Library design should recognize this duality of library use and function by making self-service easy while at the same time providing quick and convenient access to professional librarians. Within the last 25 years, many trends have complicated this need to provide for both self-service and rapid staff accessibility. These trends include:

1. The exponential growth of information, which has doubled in less than ten years. This is reflected to a lesser extent in the publishing of popular books. Twice as many trade or general book titles were published in 1977 as were published in 1952.
2. Higher levels of education, which have equipped a larger percentage of the population to want and use more of this information.
3. A technological revolution, which has provided an increasingly complex array of delivery systems in a vast nationwide network of loosely organized information sources.

By the 1960s, it was apparent that grouping large masses of people into reading rooms was not the best way to facilitate the individual's ability to choose among a wider range of media nor to use this material in a variety of environments. Many new design relationships were tried:

1. Open-design libraries pioneered by Alvar Aalto in Finland in the early 1930s attempted to make all library elements visible and accessible to all users as they entered the library building by grouping functional elements on terraces within a large open space.
2. Split-level designs encouraged a variety of environments related to a central control station.
3. Individual study carrels scattered throughout the stacks provided privacy in smaller areas.

4. Dial access arrangements—costly and installed with technical difficulty—provided remote access to materials lodged in some cases in buildings other than the library.
5. The resource center concept arranged a variety of materials and machines in subject groupings distributed throughout the building.
6. The information center design concentrated a multi-staff location with a variety of machines and terminals in the middle of a range of user and materials environments.

A split-level library design with an information center.

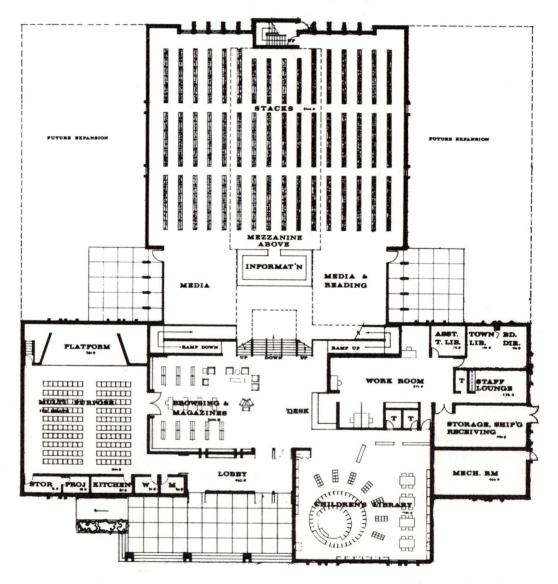

TRUMBULL PUBLIC LIBRARY
Trumbull, Connecticut

A. J. Palmieri, Architect

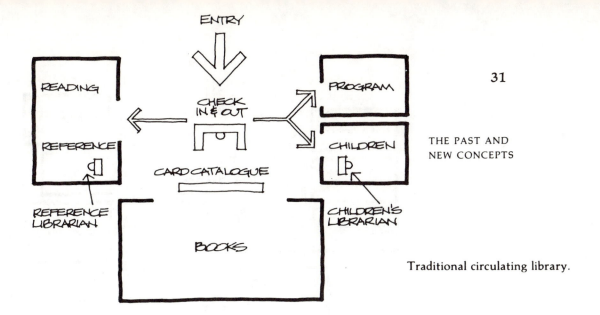

Traditional circulating library.

These design variations offer three major functional relationship alternatives:

1. Staff/users and materials to be borrowed centered on a check-out desk. This may be thought of as the *circulating library alternative.*
2. Staff/users and materials divided into resource centers each with a particular subject focus, with staff-public interaction sites, user seating, and materials in each. This resource media design is found in many school library media centers and large libraries. It may be thought of as the *media resource center* alternative.

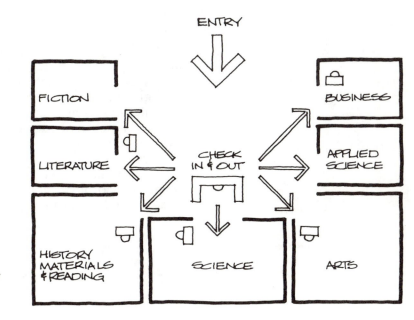

Resource/Media Center

ENTRY

BROWSING

CHECK
IN & OUT

CHILDREN

READING

INFORMATION

MEDIA

REFERENCE

PROGRAM

CARD
CATALOGUE

BOOKS

Information Center.

3. Staff/users interaction site in a central location for reference books, data terminals, and other user machines that require staff assistance. This alternative features several staff/user services in one location. It may be thought of as the *information center* alternative.

Functional relationships must recognize the more sophisticated user's self-service capability while also recognizing the key role of the librarian in assisting all users to take advantage of the wide range of new technology. Buildings designed in the 1980s should recognize all these trends:

1. All major library functions identifiable at entry by one or more of the following methods:
   a. Variety of lighting methods: spots, light clouds, task lighting.
   b. Large lighted signs.
   c. Characteristic furnishings.
   d. Color selection.
2. The information service center identifiable from the entrance, easily accessible, and in a position to offer staff control of other functional areas, but not perceived as a barrier to self-service library use.

3. A wide variety of media experiences—films, micro materials, public computer terminals, stock ticker, telephones, video, slides—should be visible to the public and controllable by staff.
4. Children's and adult service areas identifiable from the entrance and easily accessible one from the other.
5. Program facilities accessible to children and adults and controllable when other library services are in use or when the library is closed.

The librarian has evolved from being a caretaker to being the most essential element in the information retrieval process—an interpreter and guide.

Basic Functional Relationships

Each area of the library should have its special functions reflected in its design.

Entrance, Browsing, and Check-in, Check-out Area.

In this area, quick self-service functions should "pop out" at the library user immediately upon entering the building. Lighting, color, and furnishings set the feeling of happy welcome. The check-in and check-out desk must be near the entrance for public convenience in dropping off returned books and for staff control in preventing theft, but it should be unobtrusive, since public service here is minimal in comparison with the information service area. About 30 percent of the people entering library buildings are there to see new materials. This quick in and out clientele should be served near the entrance with this combination of materials:

1. Community bulletin board and flyer display.
2. Recent books; there are never enough of these, so nearby should be—
3. Paperbacks displayed with spine and covers showing.
4. Magazines and newspapers, including titles being considered for subscription by the library.
5. Media display on rear-view screen of stills from various library media—films, video, film slides.
6. Recently returned books on book trucks to enhance reader convenience and lower reshelving costs.

Display methods in this area should employ the concept of friendly objects—some materials should be casually scattered on long tables, some displayed on slanted shelving to show covers. This area can never be completely orderly, but every few hours it should be changed for an interesting and lively appearance.

Information Media Center

Library functional relationships are reflected by placing the *information-media center* in the middle of the building, easily visible and accessible from the entrance. It should include ready reference materials, computer terminals, and a micro center media counter, film/video viewers. Nearby should be catalog indexes, reference materials, carrels, and study rooms.

Bookstacks

The bookstack with its large size and highly regular arrangement should be near the Information Center and the aisles should be visible from the Information Center. Graphic signs on end panels, and shelves should lead the reader to the book. Regular, geometric orderly arrangement results in ease of self-service use and requires seating close by. Seating should be near but not in the stacks. Placing seating in stacks requires more space and results in readers being disturbed by people searching for books. Staff control requires aisles easily visible from the check-in desk and from the information center. A librarian helping a user in the stacks should be able to glance back at the information center to see if another person is waiting there for assistance. Circulating and reference (non-circulating) materials need to be differentiated by graphics, location, and color. In most libraries, many information questions will require the use of circulating books.

Reading and Study Areas

Individual study rooms; individual and ganged carrels with low privacy shields; individual comfortable lounge chairs with back, shoulder, and head support; group study tables; and group study rooms: all should be available in a quantity mix determined by community needs and budget. They should be convenient to the bookstacks, but broken into small groupings supervisable by staff and other users. Ideally, lighting and temperature should be controllable by the individual and there should be a choice of enclosed or open, natural environments.

Nearness to the check-out area is important, but not nearness to the Information Center, from which they should be carefully differentiated and sound isolated. The children's area should provide for free individual activity as well as group story/film experiences and quiet study and browsing. Young adults need space for noisy social gathering—with music, group tables, near a place for soda and candy, and with smoking facilities. However, they will also want to study quietly in a neat and orderly environment. Defining these different kinds of spaces with lighting, colors, furnishings, and equipment must be done carefully.

THE PAST AND
NEW CONCEPTS

Information center and bookstack in Bristol, Ct.

Program/Multipurpose Area

Access through the single controllable library entrance should be available, but this area should also be capable of operation when other library services are closed. It can be located near the children's area, but not near the information center.

Staff Work Areas and Offices

Clerical work and processing work areas should be near the check-in area for good supervision. The information-media center work area should be large enough for several staff and a wide variety of quiet and noisy activities, film inspection, bibliographic work. The delivery entrance should be near the check-in and processing work areas. Other staff work areas can be interspersed throughout the building for staff and user convenience.

Storage Areas

Custodial and supply storage should be remotely located, especially secure on a separate key system, with quantity distribution of supplies on a weekly basis. Other storage areas can be distributed throughout the building for staff convenience.

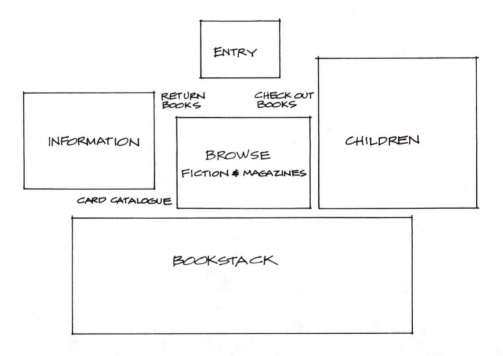

Functional relationships drawn to scale for a building program. Sequence of use:(1) Enter the building; (2) return books; (3) browse in fiction and recent books, look at a newspaper or magazine; (4) inquire at the information desk or look in the card catalog; (5) search for a particular book in the bookstack; (6) check-out a book, leave the building.

Because they are noisy, utilities should be sound-insulated from quiet library activities by location and by sound deadening materials. They should be located for easy servicing from outside.

Area Relationships within Library Buildings

Bookstacks occupy the largest single space within a library building. Many planners seek to split the bookstack areas and distribute them throughout the building. This has the disadvantages of requiring a planning decision concerning the eventual size of each area and of not permitting flexible change as the collection evolves. It also has the disadvantages of making it more difficult to find a particular book and of requiring the entire building to be built with the necessary strength to support books. A more flexible solution, and one that will make for easier use, is to place all books in one continuous stack area. This stack may occupy from 30 to 40 percent of the total building area. An alternative would be intershelving of nonbook media with books, but AV and other nonbook media come in a variety of sizes and shapes and often require machines in order to use them.

Reader seating will take from 20 to 30 percent of the total building area. Staff work and storage space not open to the public will require at least 15 percent of the total building, and nonassignable space required for corridors, elevators, heating, and air-conditioning equipment will take another 15 percent. Multipurpose areas are quite variable in libraries as a percentage of available space but may take as much as 10 percent of the total available space.

A multistaff information center library showing projection station, circulation and reference functions, as well as staff office, meeting room, and control. Manross Library, Bristol, Connecticut, SMS Architects, Willis N. Mills, Jr.

3 Starting to Develop a Library Improvement Program

Today's social needs demand change in the purpose and structure of public library services for three basic reasons:

1. The rapid increase in knowledge.
2. The greater need for more people to know.
3. Everyone's right to expect and receive information.

These points were included in a recent statement prepared by the ALA-Public Library Association Committee on Goals for briefing citizen groups who were participating in the White House Conferences on Library and Information Services during 1977-1979. They reinforce Ranganathan's law, quoted in chapter 1, "A library is a growing organism."

If libraries are to be essential elements in community efforts to satisfy everyone's need to know, they must be planned with easy access, convenience, and flexibility. The planning process must follow a pattern of *expectation of change* related to shifting community needs. The necessity for changes in priorities, scope, and operation of programs is often signalled by needed changes in facilities.

How does a librarian and/or a library board determine that physical changes are needed? Overcrowded conditions in the library are certainly a major signal. If there is insufficient public and staff space to use books and other media and if existing space is being properly utilized, it becomes apparent that an addition or a new building is needed to hold more books or readers or to provide better services. Techniques for judging the adequacy of physical facilities are given later in this chapter.

Before the Consultant Comes

Before a consultant is retained, library improvement objectives should be defined. Although we list here sequential steps in planning, some of these steps can be carried out concurrently. Many can be performed by the library staff, the board, or community volunteers:

1. Describe the community.
2. Measure present library use.
3. Examine physical facilities.
4. Set tentative objectives.
5. Organize community resources.

The best approach is to create a *facilities improvement planning team* with members who represent the library staff, the library board, the library's community, and add to them the architect or interior designer and the consultant. Architects and consultants can provide a wide range of experience and can bring to the analysis of data already gathered both perspective and objectivity as well as a choice of solutions.

The consultant is asked for a proposal to study community needs and other data and turn them into library requirements and a plan. A good consultant will visit the library, obtain information, and interview the library board. He will define the problem, but this will be more difficult or ineffective if the preparation by the staff and the board has been insufficient. Poor preparation and input for the consultant can result in a library improvement program (LIP) that is less than the community needs and deserves.

Although a consultant can bring useful experience and knowledge to a particular library task, his effectiveness will be many times increased and the job completed sooner if staff and board work carefully together before he comes.

The steps the community portion of the team must consider are:

1. Community Analysis	Staff and Board
2. Library Improvement Program: Goals and Objectives Recommended LIP	Staff and Board Consultant
3. Library Use Analysis	Staff
4. Facilities Analysis: Obsolescence Report	Architect and Consultant
5. Final Library Building Program: complete description of each functional area in the new facility.	Library Consultant and Staff
6. Architect Selection: meeting with consultant and staff. Analysis of the library building program from an architectural point of view.	Library Board
7. Site Search: analysis of various sites from library location and architectural points of view.	Architect and Consultant
8. Proposed Site Analysis: showing of location of building on a particular site for board approval.	Architect, Consultant, and Board
9. Schematic Design: architect presents several schematic solutions to the library building program; consultant critiques these solutions from a functional point of view and presents recommendations for approval.	Architect, Consultant, and Board
10. Design Development: architect develops one or more schematics, including furniture plans, lighting, graphics, HVAC, traffic flow, equipment locations. Models and presentation drawings. Consultant critiques design details, works with interior designer and engineers.	Architect and Consultant

11. Working Drawings: architect develops working drawings for construction of the building.   Architect

12. Construction Supervision   Contractor, Architect, and Staff

13. Post Occupancy Analysis   Architect, Consultant, and Staff

Community Analysis

Efforts at community analysis have been a part of library surveys for decades. Ruth Warnke wrote a very useful article about community analysis more than 20 years ago. The University of Syracuse has run seminars on this technique, and the University of Denver has formed a Community Analysis Institute to teach librarians how to analyze their communities in a way that will be helpful in library planning. Demographic statistics derived from U.S. Census reports provide a profile of the economic, ethnic, age, and geographic distribution in the community.

The steps in performing a community analysis are:

1. Collect information from the census, from local government reports, and from local organizations.
2. Interview community opinion leaders outside the library. Discuss their general information needs; do not limit this discussion to specific library matters.
3. Evaluate existing library services by using available statistics and sampling techniques and by interviewing library staff members and library users.

These steps should result in answers to these questions:

Who are the people?
What do they do for business and recreation?
What do other community agencies do?
What are community wants and needs for information services? Do people relate their information needs to library services and capabilities?
What has been and is being planned by other community agencies to meet these needs?
How does the library reflect community interests and satisfy community needs?

How can the library plan to improve its services and facilities to better satisfy community needs?

Community characteristics, such as the following, are also considered in a community analysis:

Transportation patterns.

Interviews with organizations likely to have an impact on future library use.

Patterns of employment, development schemes for retail and industrial purposes.

Political framework within which the library operates.

History.

Topography and climate.

Educational facilities and levels of attainment.

Recreation.

Communication: radio, TV, and newspapers affecting the community.

Library history and organization.

Library financial support.

Library services, hours of operation, programs, and special services.

Circulation, registration, borrowing index, location of borrowers.

Library materials.

In collecting community data, it is important to have a communications framework for the information closely related to library needs. For example, a chart showing how present library use relates to the present location of the library must be related to a map of geographic population distribution if it is to be a valid part of a library community analysis. If the library draws 50 percent of its patrons from within a one mile radius of the building, this information has interest in regard to present use; but if we also know that 50 percent of the population lives within a mile of the library, then we have a clearer picture of the appropriateness of the location.

In many cases, community analysis and library use relationships may provide a discouraging statistical description. They should always be interpreted in light of future potential library use demonstrated by comparison with other demographically similar communities with better library use patterns. Community analysis factors must be related to library use patterns.

Consideration of goals and objectives should be accomplished in the light of answers to questions such as the following and in conjunction with a new analysis of the community, its use of library facilities and services, and the facilities now available.

Is the library working in the community to promote the use of library services and media for education, recreation, and cultural enjoyment?

Is the library reaching out to unserved groups, including minority and non-English-speaking groups?

Is the library a cultural center for the arts, crafts, and exhibitions?

Is the library presenting new and controversial ideas and events?

Is the library involved in programs of adult independent study and continuing education?

Is the library involved in literacy training and/or the use of bilingual materials?

Is the library the first agency that comes to the minds of most community residents when they need information on *any* subject?

Discussion and redefinition of long-term goals and objectives will indicate directions for program change and assist in determining if a consultant is needed and what he or she will do. This is the basis and first step in development of the LIP.

When this analysis has been completed, it will then be possible to set performance objectives for a new facility and to examine community resources to accomplish these objectives.

The initial task of defining community goals and objectives in regard to library services requires clearly organized data about the community and an understanding of how this data relates to a library facilities program. This phase can be accomplished by (1) identifying the data needed, (2) collecting and organizing the facts, and (3) determining how the information relates to library improvement.

The library consultant, with experience of various library buildings and with a knowledge of library functions and the latest applications of technology in libraries, is often far more knowledgeable in these areas than a library staff, which may have had minimal experience in library building, or an architect who has worked on just a few library buildings and never worked as a librarian. Even architects with considerable library design experience may continue to make the same design mistakes over and over again because of a lack of understanding of how users and librarians actually work, together or independently.

In the give and take of design development, it is often difficult for the library staff to establish the credibility necessary to get a building committee to make a design change necessary to improve the functioning of a building. The ideal combination is a knowledgeable staff and building committee, an experienced consultant, and an architect with strong design ideas but with willingness to listen and a desire to create a service-oriented building, rather than a monument to his own preconceived idea of "library."

Library Use Analysis

Library users can themselves explicitly or implicitly tell librarians how libraries need to be improved. We are all familiar with carefully laid out and paved rectangular paths that are ignored by walkers who create their own diagonal paths through the grass. Most libraries already have more formal communication systems so that members of the public can say what they need. These include:

Reserve systems, which permit library users to fill out a card indicating that the book they looked for in the library was not available.

Replacement systems, which require librarians to determine frequency of use of books and other materials. Additional copies are ordered and books are discarded or rebound according to these checks.

Circulation-Subject analysis systems, which determine the use of various broad subject areas and books owned and books purchased in those subjects.

A staff and public *suggestion book* prominently displayed can be used to find out how the public and staff think that library facilities might be improved, but the staff must show how they respond to each suggestion. The library's response to user suggestions needs to be communicated back to the public.

In addition, there may be in-depth interviews of a

variety of people who use the library. For example, a high school student coming to use reference books needs a carrel desk with good lighting near reference shelving; while a retired person coming to browse in magazines needs a comfortable lounge chair easy to get in and out of, with individually controlled lighting near magazine display shelving. Interviews with people in the community who do not now use the library may be helpful, too, in pointing out physical or psychological barriers.

Performance measures for public libraries as set forth in a recent ALA publication provide some useful indicators for determining library building requirements. One performance measure is *maximum facilities use*. This is an effort to measure the number of people using a particular area or function at a given time so as to determine the peak periods for facilities use. This technique can determine during what percentage of library hours most facilities are in use, thus indicating the urgency of the need for additional facilities. Performance measure studies conducted in libraries all over the country have shown that there is an increasing trend toward use of the library's resources *within* the building. In most library systems, more than 50 percent of the people entering a library do not borrow books to take out, but instead use the books and other materials within the library. Therefore, library planning groups should bear in mind that the provision of seating for people and other work and study spaces is as important, at least, as provision for housing and circulation of library materials.

A basic quantitative measure in library use study is library *entries*—that is, the number of persons entering the library premises. An electronic counter or a turnstile is the best instrument for measurement, but a hand or desk counter can also be used. *Book circulation* by total and by subject breakdown is an almost universal library use measure. *Reference/information* questions are a significant means of measuring professional library services since they are a unique service combining materials use and staff services available *only* in a library.

Book Collection Size

Requirements may be estimated by the community LIP team.

There are several methods for determining how large a book collection a community needs. These methods relate to:

Population Size: Three to five books per capita is the most frequently quoted figure. According to this "rule," there should be 150,000 books minimum for a population of 50,000 people. If the population is expected to grow in 20 years to 70,000, there should be provision for at least 210,000 books.

Net Book Additions: This is a second way to determine the required size of a library collection. Most libraries buy and discard a relatively constant number of books each year. By determining the average net book additions for a given year, one can judge how many spaces will be needed for the next 20 years.

Circulation per Capita: For many years, the figure of ten circulations per capita (per year) has been considered a very good book circulation; thus a community of 50,000 people in which 500,000 books a year are circulated has been considered to have a very active library. Such a community may require a slightly larger book collection than a community circulating only five books per capita. However, as circulation increases, the amount of book space needed may not necessarily increase, since more books will be out in the community and fewer on the shelves.

Circulation per Volume: ALA standards in the 1960s called for a book collection size of three to five volumes per capita—the smaller the population, the larger the per capita. Thus libraries serving 10,000 people were thought to require 50,000 books, while libraries serving 200,000 people would hold 600,000 volumes. If the ten per capita circulation figure is applied to the 10,000 population community, we then derive a ratio of 100,000 circulations from a book collection of 50,000, or two circulations per volume held. In the 200,000 population area with a ten per capita circulation of 2 million volumes and holdings of 600,000 books, the ratio of circulation per volume would be more than three to one for an even more intensive use. Communities may want to monitor and improve their library's performance in this area.

Frequency of Book Use and Weeding: If the shelves are overcrowded, an obvious first question should be—are these books necessary? The cost of building shelf

space approaches $10 per volume. The purpose of
a library is to have books that people use. Giving
shelf space to books that have not circulated in five
years is not only costly but it also discourages
many readers who are seeking popular newer and
more useful material. The books that just sit on
the shelves are predominantly older, less attractive books. It is important that many of them be
available to the infrequent reader, but the extent
and speed of interlibrary loan networks make it
highly questionable for individual local libraries to
retain them.

Methods of Weeding: One method of weeding a library
collection is the Slote system of colored self-stick
dots applied under the plastic covers just above the
call number on the spine of each book as it is
circulated. Soon books without colored dots stand
out on the shelves as uncirculated and possible
candidates for discard. Colors are changed each
year. Slote's recent book on library weeding has a
rigorous mathematical method of determining
what percentage of these books should be discarded.
Another method of identifying little used books is
incorporated in the computerized circulation control systems now on the market. These systems
can be programmed to generate monthly reports
on book titles that have not circulated for the prior
12 months, so librarians may make an individual
determination on whether or not to discard these
materials. Initial setting up of these systems requires that book titles are input into the computer
as they are checked out so that all materials without computer labels can be identified as not having
been checked out.

Another relatively accurate sampling method to
determine frequency of use is:

1. Estimate the number of books on the shelves
   (say, for example, 100,000).
2. Divide this number by 400 to derive an interval number (in this case, 250).
3. Starting with a randomly selected book from
   the shelves, look on the book card to find out
   when it was last used.

4. Count books sequentially and, using the interval number (250), check the next book to determine when it was last used; and so on.

Building Size

Even before a consultant is retained, it may be necessary to arrive at a rough estimate of building size. In most cases, it is inadvisable to guess at building size because this should be a function of community needs and library use based on careful projections of population and use. However, rough estimates can be derived from empirical standards based on many library buildings. These standards range from, for example, Connecticut's population/area relationships to building block standards of book and seating needs.

Population/Area Relationships. A 20-year projection of population growth applied to a sliding scale of area determines the population/area relationships. For a population of 10,000 or less, allow 1 square foot of building area per person. For a population of 100,000, .6 square feet per person would be sufficient.

Building Block Standards. The 20-year population projections are applied to books and reader seats to determine the building block standards. Book requirements are estimated at the rate of three to five per capita for populations of 10,000 to 100,000. These books can be easily fitted into a public stack at the rate of 15 books per square foot. For example, a city of 50,000 requiring 200,000 books needs a stack area of approximately 13,600 square feet (200,000 divided by 15). Readers seats are estimated at the rate of five seats per 1,000 people in towns of 10,000 or more. Thus, a city of 50,000 would require 250 seats, which would take up 30 square feet per seat including traffic space around the seat for a total of 7,500 square feet. Thus, books = 13,600 square feet; seats = 7,500 square feet.
In addition, staff/work space at an estimated 15 percent of total building area would require about 4,500 square feet; nonassignable space for heating and ventilating equipment, corridors, stairs, walls, entryways, and such will take up at least 20 percent of the building, or 6,000 square feet. We thus have:

Books	13,600
Seats	7,500
Staff/work	4,500
Nonassignable	6,000
Total	31,600 square feet

This total does not include such essentials as a multipurpose public meeting room requiring 10 square feet per seat and media facilities. However, this building block method of estimating size will establish a minimum parameter for a building planning committee to begin working on a program and to initiate the planning process.

Facilities Analysis: Obsolescence Report

An especially effective and easily understood technique for use in judging physical facility needs is that of the *Library Obsolescence Report* used by Aaron and Elaine Cohen in their seminars. The Cohens are concerned about how people behave in buildings and how this behavior can be improved by good design. (See the bibliography for the particulars on their recent book.)

The librarian looks carefully at the physical aspects of the library. Here are some areas to look for:

Too many books on shelves.
Readers crowded into seating areas.
People waiting to use the card catalog.
Dark, depressing colors.
Peeling paint.
Barriers to access by the handicapped.
Homemade signs.
Worn woodwork or upholstery.
Uncomfortable temperature or humidity.
Overcrowded rooms—too much furniture.
Poor lighting, not aimed at tables or shelves and giving
off glare and reflections.
Insufficient lighting.

Physical facilities problems can best be expressed by a photographic analysis of the building as a part of a library obsolescence report. These photos show overcrowded conditions, uncomfortable furnishings, shabby materials, poor lighting, inconvenient entrances and stairs, and other discouragements to library use.

With the photographs and a simple description of functional and physical problems, library authorities can begin to define behavioral objectives for a new or renovated building.

Developing Criteria and Objectives

In order to evaluate the present and future performance of a library, it is necessary to establish user-oriented criteria. Several years ago the American Library Trustee Association in its *ALTA Newsletter* issued a set of questions to help trustees evaluate libraries. Recent trends toward accountability through program budgeting in industry and government have encouraged establishment of objectives that are measurable within a given time frame and that directly relate to clientele. This method of thinking about libraries can establish useful communication bridges among librarians, trustees, funding authorities, and citizens. Here are some clientele-oriented performance objectives that could serve as points of discussion in drafting community objectives prior to hiring a consultant or architect. The library user should:

Be able to sit in a chair with back and shoulder support without waiting, for 90 percent of the hours the library is open.

Be able to read easily without direct or reflected glare at a table or individual study carrel.

Be able to enter the library with an armload of books or other materials without having to open a door by hand.

Be able to use the library during most holidays and Sundays, when the majority of people have free time.

Be able to reach the library in no more than 15 minutes driving time.

Be able to park within 200 feet of the library during 90 percent of the time it is open.

Be able to obtain 90 percent of the books owned by the library in no more than 30 days reserve waiting time.

Be able to see a film at the library 90 percent of the time the building is open without waiting more than 15 minutes.

Be able to read quietly without disturbance 90 percent of the time the building is open.

Be able to obtain a discussion room in the library within a maximum reservation time of two weeks.

Be able to see and communicate with a professional library staff member within 15 minutes of entering the building.

Be informed of all library programs by display flyer or sign within 50 feet of the entrance to the building.

Be able on behalf of a community organization to use library meeting facilities and be constantly informed of their availability.

Be able to utilize video and other AV production facilities as an individual or a community organization within one week of seeking such use.

Be able to come to a children's program at least twice a week.

Be able to find a book, film, or tape of interest within 15 minutes of entering the building whether child, young adult, adult, or senior citizen.

Be able to obtain adult learning program consultation within one week, and be able to enter a sequential learning program of choice.

All this means that the library or library system should:

Be able to satisfy 85 percent of the users' information requests.

Be able to seat 90 percent of library users coming to film shows.

Be able to supply 90 percent of users requests for books in the library, 5 percent in a regional system on 72 hours waiting time, and the additional 5 percent in less than a month.

Be able to supply copies of published books within one month of publication date (not in the catalog, but to the patron).

Be able to satisfy every library user with some sort of useful service and material even if not with the actual material requested.

Encouraging Community Support for Change

Library boards and building committees can be problems to improvement oriented librarians. They can destroy initiative by failing to support improvements and prevent change because their vision of the library's mission and potential is too narrow. They, as well as the wider community, need to be aware of user expectations and what they require of the library. If the librarian reports to the board by means of pictures, words, and statistics the changes that are needed, the interest of the members may be won. Perhaps board members might be asked to hold an open house at a busy time to hear and see library users in action. An aware and enthusiastic board can be an exceedingly effective way of hastening change.

The composition of a building committee, usually appointed by the board, can be of crucial importance. The librarian can enter into the appointing process by suggesting criteria for selection of committee members. There should be no more than five members, and they should be available for weekly luncheon meetings during the entire improvement project. Committee members should be regular—perhaps monthly—library users. A member with building design and construction expertise an be especially useful if this knowledge is coupled with frequent library use. Business and financial management expertise is useful, but it can be a problem if interest is confined to the bottom line aspects of the project. Staff members and board members can often supply a variety of points of view on physical facilities. Ask staff members to report on additional materials or equipment needed. Ask board members to comment on the comfort and appearance of specific library functional areas.

Economic Considerations: Communication with Municipal Officials

Community planning is a broad town responsibility involving town officials, institutions such as libraries, state and regional agencies, and a broad spectrum of community groups. Library staff members and trustees must seek to open useful, credible means of communication with all these planning groups and to demonstrate the library's awareness of community long-term planning and financing. Library trustees can be especially effective in discussing bonding requirements and in fitting library financing into the town's financial structure. One way of doing this is to demonstrate the library's understanding of the need for multiphased economic planning. In terms of library improvement these phases are:

Phase 1: a community analysis of library needs at minimal cost.
Phase 2: the hiring of a consultant and architect to express library needs in the form of a library improvement program and design of an addition or new building.

Phase 3: the basic building construction.
Phase 4: the purchase of furnishings for basic services.
Phase 5: the purchase of furnishings for new services.
Phase 6: the implemention of the long-range improvement and renovation plan with additional staff related to additional public use.

These library improvement planning phases could be related to a variety of funding sources—public funding for phases 2 and 3 and perhaps private, state and federal funding for other phases. A wide involvement, with clearly delineated responsibilities, of many community resources in this planning function can result in early financial commitment to library improvement.

Library Visits

Recommendations for layout and equipment are made by the consultant based on a wide range of experience, but the community team can feel most secure in these recommendations if they are aware of the many alternatives. Library visits can provide this direct experience of a variety of solutions that other communities have chosen.

Touring libraries and sharing experiences with board members, staff, architect and community officials can be an effective way of creating a climate for change.

Select libraries to visit that will be reasonably comparable in size and that offer the widest range of choices in layout and furnishings. *Library Journal* in its annual building issue, and several architectural journals, publish information on new buildings.

Before visiting a library, meet with the committee that is going to visit; invite trustees and town officials to join the tour. Telephone the librarian to arrange for the visit; offer to help with refreshments; arrange for a morning hour when the library will be least busy.

Follow up the tour with a slide show and analysis sheet presented to board members and local officials who did not go on the tour. Make certain that these post-tour showings are attended by people who went on the tour so that positive aspects of the library visits will be reinforced by a variety of points of view. Make a record of library visits in a notebook or file that will eventually include listings of the best furniture, lighting, and equipment as well as functional relationship ideas and conceptual program ideas. Take similar pictures of your own library to show the contrast in physical facilities.

Here are some things to look for in visiting libraries:

Exterior

Does it fit into the site and neighborhood?
Is it satisfying to look at?
Does it look like an inviting building to enter?
Is the entrance identifiable to people in cars as well as to pedestrians?
Is there a large exterior sign showing the hours and visible from passing cars at night?
Is it near retail stores?
Is there sufficient parking? Convenient to entrance?
Is it near mass transportation?
Is it convenient to get from the car to the entrance?
Is there a covered walkway and pick-up point?
Is there a public telephone outside?
Is there handicapped parking—12-feet wide stalls clearly marked?
No more than 1 in 20 slope from parking to entrance?
Are all curbs ramped?
Are there handrails?
Are there automatic opening doors?
Are the doors easy to operate by the frail, elderly, or handicapped?
Is the building lit at night—visible from vehicles?
Are the library's hours of service prominently displayed on sign *and* at entry?

Interior

When you enter the library, do you know where to go?
Are all service elements of the building easily and immediately visible and accessible from the entrance?
Do these areas pop out at the user—distinguished by signs, lighting, furnishings?
Are directional signs easy to see and logical to follow?

Children/Adults	Card Catalog
Books/Other Media	Reference/Information

Is there easy access to public telephones (low for handicapped) and copy machines?
Does there seem to be sufficient and appropriate space available to offer a full range of programs?

Is there a small conference room space near the reference room to seat about ten people?
Is there an auditorium/multipurpose room, an art gallery, a projection booth, a film theater?
Is there a story-telling area adjacent or contiguous to the children's room but out of traffic flow?
Are there display and exhibit areas?
Are they highly visible with accessible, special lighting?
Are they secure and controlled from the staff station?
Does this library seem to relate to the people of this particular community?
Does the staff seem aware of serving this unique community?
Does there appear to be effective traffic flow?
Where is the card catalog? Is it easily accessible to staff and public?
Is it near reference and nonfiction? Is it accessible from both the circulation desk and the reference desk?
Are all public areas accessible to handicapped users through use of ramps or an elevator, wide aisles, easy doors?

Community bulletin board.

Circulation Area

Examine this area carefully, as it is a major contact point between the staff and the library user. Its location should provide visual and functional control of public areas. Notice carefully which functions or routines are located here.

Are the functions logically arranged and identified?
Is the arrangement convenient for the user?
Are returns and check-out separated or identified?
Is there a registration and inquiry area?
Are returns made immediately at the entrance?
Do the books and other library materials circulate with minimal fuss?
Are the materials transferred easily to their correct locations?
Can they be immediately checked out again?
Is the space allocated to this central function too large, too small?
Is there room to expand if/as circulation of materials increases?

There should be smooth handling of all user requirements, even during maximum use periods. This requires several flexible staff locations.

Reference Information Area

Is it near the card catalog?
Is it near the reference books?
Is there seating for public and staff consultation?
Is lighting adequate for small type and glossy pages?
Are there provisions for future terminals, micro-readers, and other machines?
Is there an audiovisual media area nearby?
Can individuals readily use media?
Are there adequate electrical receptacles?
Are indexes, reference periodicals, micro-readers and materials grouped conveniently and near current periodicals?
Is there carrel seating for users right near the reference materials?
Is there acoustical treatment to dampen sound in this area—acoustical ceilings and partitions, carpeting?
Is there a quiet study area?
Is there a small meeting room in this area?
Is there a staff work area nearby so that staff can work privately yet be available to help with public services at busy times?

Is there a discernible warmth and welcome in the children's room?

Is there a welcoming, comfortable section that is instantly perceivable, yet aside from the main "hurly-burly" traffic flow, for the picture book age child?

Is there furniture for this size child?

Is there a comfortable place also for an adult to sit while sharing with the young child?

Are there touchable objects to attract the young child? Are they sturdy enough for touching?

Are there toys, games, realia? Display bulletin boards with lighting?

Is there an eye-catching story-hour or other pro-gramming space?

What evidence do you find of children's sharing of their interests and needs that reflect this particular community?

Shelving

Are the books in good condition?

Are they competently shelved? Sequentially?

Is the progression by subject clear? Number?

Are audiovisual materials in evidence? Equipment to use them with?

Are there paperbacks? Is it made easy to borrow them?

What is the relationship of the stack area to seating space?

Depressing	vs. Inviting
Open	vs. Crowded
Top-heavy	vs. Well-spaced

Seating

Is there a variety of types of seating?

Does the seating appear to be adequate: comfortable back support, upholstery, light? Are the chairs easy to get out of? Or do the chairs and tables snag clothing?

Bookstacks

Are the books well maintained? Plastic covers, rebound?

Have stacks been planned for approximately 7–8

books per linear foot, with top and bottom shelves allowed to remain empty for future expansion?

Are the stacks arranged in one numerical sequence so that the user can find the material without having to ask?

Are there end signs and shelf labels?

Are the bottom shelf books well-lighted without glare?

Are the most popular materials (new books and such) conveniently located?

Are special collections identified?

Are conditions appropriate for adequate care and maintenance of rare materials?

Climate control?   Humidity control?
Space for growth?   Natural light control?

Is this collection made available to the public? How are control and access managed?

Noise Control

Is there acoustical separation of public areas from staff work areas? (Essential for noise control.)

Are areas designated for quiet study (reference area, study carrels) away from main traffic patterns, but accessible? (Bookstacks are excellent noise absorbers.)

The circulation desk area is the noisiest. Maximum communication between staff and users at this service point should be encouraged.

Is there acoustical ceiling tile? Acoustical enclosures for machines?

Is there carpeting?

Convenience Facilities

Are toilets adequate? Are they easy to find—without asking? Are they controllable, well-lighted?

Do they have rails and wide doors for the handicapped? Do they have stainless mirrors?

Are light refreshments available for public purchase as well as for the staff?

Nonpublic Areas

Is the major staff workroom located near the circulation desk? Is the workroom for processing and AV work near the information center and /or card catalog?

Is there adequate space for smooth function of current activities?

Has space been reserved for staff and/or services expansion?

Is there good storage and variety of storage near activities?

How is it used? Is it needed? Have future storage needs—of gifts and duplicate periodicals—been anticipated?

Mechanicals

Is the wiring adequate? Is there extra electric service capacity?

Are there empty conduits available for phones, speakers, electronics?

Is service sufficient for basic AV functions? For cable TV?

Is there computer capacity in a cool location free of static?

Is there humidity control?

Are all windows functional, especially in New England, where weather conditions might permit shutting off both heat and air-conditioning for 4–6 months of the year for good conservation of energy?

Where are the thermostats?

Can lighting be moved?

Notice particularly stack lighting and lighting level in the reference area, as to variety, controls, color.

Are areas defined by their lighting?

Be aware that different intensities of lighting are appropriate to different areas of the library.

The Future

Is expansion on the present site possible?
Who has title to the land?
Is adjacent land available for future purchase?
Expansion *inside* the building?
Floor load for compact shelving?

After you have completed these steps,—Community analysis, facilities analysis and objectives development—briefly outline what you need to have the consultant do. Can any of these things be accomplished by you before the consultant arrives? Can any of these things be accomplished by you with some guidance from the consultant?

4 Developing the Library Improvement Program

Selecting the Consultant

In addition to having experience with library planning and building programs, the library consultant should be familiar with all types of library services in many different libraries. He or she should have visited and analyzed a variety of library buildings and be thoroughly familiar with costs and performance records of many different furnishing lines and equipment. The effective consultant has kept up to date on both library professional developments and management techniques such as program planning and budgeting, management by objectives, and building program writing.

The American Library Association's Library Administration Division (LAD) maintains a list of library building consultants who have some experience working on building projects. State library agencies also maintain lists of consultants who have worked in the state. The best source of information, however, is a recommendation from a librarian in a new building that works well.

Consultant fees can range from $100 to $250 a day depending on the complexity of the job and the experience of the consultant. Upset fees (the maximum to be billed for a complete job) can range from $2,000 to a fractional percentage of the project construction cost. It is preferable to relate fees to the need for specific consultant tasks to be performed and to the value of those tasks in reaching library goals, and *not* to the overall cost of the job. The consultant should set hourly and daily rates for a given period of time needed to accomplish a particular task. There should be a maximum upset fee and a minimum for the amount of time spent on-site meeting with board and staff.

A review of goals and objectives by the consultant, board, and staff should result in a list of specific consultant tasks such as:

Examine alternative functional relationships within an
    addition and the present building.
Provide for increased bookstack and seating capacity.
Provide for nonbook media services.
Reduce lighting glare and improve visual comfort.

Evaluating a consultant can be accomplished by a 45-minute interview based on a discussion of library goals and objectives and some research into the consultant's performance on similar jobs, as verified by a telephone conversation or in person. Either of these are more reliable indicators than written references.

Now you are ready to consider consultants. Several consultants who have been recommended should be asked to prepare proposals based on a detailed description of the task as defined by the library trustees and staff. Ask for a phased plan with price breakdowns and review periods.

Consultant's Contract

A consultant's contract should indicate the scope of the work, for example:

1. Work with staff to organize information on:
    a. Community.
    b. Library use.
    c. Library materials and physical facilities already in place.
2. Work with board to shape library performance objectives.
3. Write a library program to state objectives and describe facilities, equipment and functional relationships. This should be done in close cooperation with the library staff.
4. Discuss a preliminary program with the library expansion committee.

5. Prepare a final report, with details on equipment, lighting, graphics, acoustics, timetable, payment.
6. Work with the architect to critique schematics and design development.
7. Indicate the number of site days planned.
8. Plan meetings with the building committee and board.
9. Identify person with sign-off approval, indication of project completion.
10. Interface with municipal officials concerning expenses, payments, and other finances.

A Consultant's Proposal (Sample)

Phase 1: Analysis

Community Analysis.

With the assistance of the library staff and community governing officials, the consultant will collect and tabulate the following information:

1. Present population and its relationship to the library location. Various population concentrations should be mapped.
2. Transportation and road net—percent of library users coming by car, on foot, and in public transport will be determined. Road network will be analyzed in relation to the library location.
3. Future population projections for a 20-year period will be obtained with age breakdowns if possible. Population shifts will be analyzed if possible in relation to library location.
4. Shopping areas and patterns will be analyzed in relation to library location.
5. Town businesses and institutions will be considered in relation to library needs.

Library Use Analysis.

Library entries; location of library users; annual, weekly, and daily patterns of use will be analyzed, with a view to determining size and growth pattern for new facilities. Library book circulation, reference, and media use will be analyzed. A brief frequency of use sample of books will be analyzed.

Budget and staffing will be briefly reviewed and analyzed in relation to community and national trends.

Library Facilities.

Each library functional area and its present use will be analyzed and its book service facilities will be listed and its relationship to other areas noted.

Future Library Use.

Based on the above information, a chart will be prepared showing present areas, future potential use, and broad recommendations on future functional area requirements, based on community growth, financial capabilities, and library standards.

A written report will be prepared in ten copies and delivered orally to an audience of your choice at a mutually convenient time within one month of the signing of this contract. This work will require three site days and will cost no more than $000. At the end of this work, the library expansion committee will be expected to meet with the consultant and make recommendations for changes and to give further direction for the work. At the end of Phase 1, both parties will have an opportunity to review the relationship and revise the contract or end the contract. Once Phase 2 has commenced, it is assumed that the entire project will proceed as outlined in the contract, and the client undertakes to retain the consultant for the remainder of the work and not to use another library consultant for a period of five (5) years. Once this phase has been accepted by the library expansion committee, Phase 2 can commence.

Phase 2: Program Definition

Prepare Building Program.

Based on Phase 1, with modifications suggested by the library expansion committee, prepare a detailed description of each functional area in the expanded library facility. This work will be carried out in close consultation with selected staff members.

Discuss Program Advantages and Disadvantages.

Determine if the program should be carried out in a new building or in an addition to the present building. This work will require two site days and can be completed in one month at a cost not to exceed $000. A written report will be prepared and discussed with an audience of your choice.

Phase 3: Site Selection and Schematic Design

1. Working with an architect, discuss the building program and analyze five possible library sites suggested by the library expansion committee.
2. Critique several schematic plans prepared by the architect for a particular site and/or a building addition. These drawings should show scaled relationships among library functional areas and how they relate to entrances, parking, stairs and site.
3. Design development. Meet with the architect to discuss functional area relationships and details such as lighting, graphics, heating, air conditioning, furnishings and equipment. This meeting should take place before the architect commences work on these aspects of the design.
4. Critique architect recommendations on lighting, graphics, heating, air conditioning, furnishings and equipment. Phase 3 will require one site day and several days at the architect's offices and will cost no more than $000. Payments will be made monthly as work progresses. Travel will be reimbursed at 15¢ a mile.

How the Library Consultant Works with the Team

The library consultant is an expert in how people use libraries, in how libraries work, and in the wide range of alternatives available in library design. The consultant is not coming primarily to tell the board and architect what to do. Rather, the consultant's function is to make them aware of the variety of ways in which library buildings can operate and the consequences of a particular mode of operation. In many cases he will have a specific recommendation and should be able to explain and defend that recommendation against alternatives.

Unlike the architect, the library consultant is not primarily concerned with aesthetic preference, but he should be prepared to have functional explanations for his recommendations.

Communication.

The first task of the consultant will be to open up many avenues of communication with the staff and the expansion or building committee. He should seek a pleasant, communicative relationship with these groups and quickly acquire essential information about the community and the library.

Preliminary Report

Once community and library information are analyzed, and the library operation is observed, broad tentative recommendations should be submitted and discussed with the staff and board. This brief written document should include analysis and recommendations. After it is discussed, and revisions made, it should be accepted in writing by the building committee as the basis for the final program.

Final Report

The preparation of the final program should involve conversations with many staff members at all levels and considerable communication and revision before it is finally approved by the board.

Technological Recommendations

The library consultant develops a program by understanding the community and its pattern of library use and making recommendations to the library staff and building committee based on the latest library improvement trends.

For example, a community may have developed a library book circulation of ten per capita (relatively high) and may have begun to show films in the library occasionally. Now it is faced with more success than it can handle: increasing circulation and enthusiastic response to films, with a budget restraint that prevents the hiring of additional staff. Community analysis shows an increasing and better educated population with a high degree of interest in film experiences. The consultant might recommend a one-time investment in a computerized circulation control system that limits the need for additional circulation staff; the use of a mobile movie-mover with headphones to make films available without a special room; and an in-service training program to alert staff members to film opportunities and the careful design of a combined information/media center that can make available a wide range of film and book resources while providing for the future addition of video. Graphics, lighting, and sound absorbent materials can make these combined services possible while limiting the need for additional staff. The detailed design of this system will require close collaboration of consultant, staff and architect to design a wide range of services in a compact space, but the result will be staff effectiveness and public convenience without budget busting.

Working with the Architect

After the final library program is prepared and adopted by the library expansion committee and library staff, the consultant begins to work with the architect. At this early stage in a delicate communications relationship, it would be useful to discuss architectural style, community needs, economic constraints, and broad concepts of library service—recognizing that there will inevitably be conflicts among these factors. It is probably not wise to mail the program to the architect, but instead to engage in a conversation about it taking nothing for granted. The peculiar requirements of a library that must be carefully explained and considered are:

> User convenience.
> Variety of user needs and expectations.
> Community wants.
> Economic constraints.
> Library material requirements.
> Flexibility in planning.

Although these requirements will be covered in general in the program and in detail in the descriptions of library functional areas, they must constantly form the framework for discussion with the architect by building committees. Achieving credibility with the architect by recognizing the conflicts that will now begin to occur between library needs and aesthetic and mechanical considerations is a fundamental requirement for an effective consultant. The consultant contract should require that the consultant be present during meetings with the building committee to critique schematic and design development plans. These critiques will be covered in Chapter 12, as they are properly part of the architectural planning process. Now we will look in detail at the various parts of the building program.

Data Collection and Analysis

Obviously, the consultant will use the factual material prepared by the staff and board. Thus it is useful to look at this data collection and analysis phase of program preparation from the consultant's point of view.

Community information in the library improvement program should be a brief but essential part of the initial problem definition. As stated earlier, community analysis will reveal basic information on:

Present and future population and age trends for 20 years.
Traffic and shopping patterns and zoning and population distribution.
Community organizations and educational institutions that might affect library planning.

The consultant will relate library use information and growth in library use and materials to these community patterns:

1. Geographic pattern of library use established by a study of library registration files with a map prepared showing comparative use of the library by people residing in the different census tracts and within a one or two mile radius of the library building.
2. Demographic characteristics of each census tract compared to show educational and economic differences.
3. Library users and nonusers analyzed to determine their varying characteristics.

This information can be useful in determining possible library sites and in fashioning public information programs to reach nonusers. It can also help to define where libraries may need to plan bookmobile stops or branch library facilities and what services these facilities should offer.

The collection and interpretation of this information requires close cooperation among library staff, community leaders, and the library consultant. Much of it can be prepared and used to define the problem before the library consultant is retained. Once this information is collected and expressed, it will become realistic to define the community's future library needs and to discuss these needs with the staff and the building committee. This discussion can be used to set program objectives, which become the basis for a detailed description of library facilities.

How does the consultant go about determining the size of the facility needed? One way is to base size on "library standards" relating the library being studied to regional, state, or national recommendations.

Library Standards

How were library standards derived?

Traditionally, library building programs have been based on empirical standards derived from the size of the population. Library consultants have developed standards through practical experience, and these have been codified by the American Library Association or state library agencies. Standards based on population determine how many books a library should own, buy, and discard, how many seats should be provided for readers, and overall size of building in square feet. In most cases, there has been an assumption that as population increases, the amounts per capita could decrease, since as libraries grow in size they become more efficient in giving service and more people can share the same books and facilities. Thus, a smaller suburban library requires more books per capita than a larger urban library, to give reasonably adequate service.

Population	Books per Capita	Total Books
150,000	2	300,000
50,000	4	200,000

Beginning in the 1960s, ALA standards also urged smaller communities to group together into library systems serving a minimum of 150,000 people, so that all citizens could have access to a reasonably adequate variety of titles based on this larger population. These regional systems would have a large central library for full services and small branch outlets with a smaller range of services for convenience.

New Technology

Both library standards and system concepts are changing. Several technological breakthroughs in the 1970s, and the possibility of a national library network in the 1980s based on the new technology, make earlier systems concepts and methods of determining standards questionable. Computerized cataloguing, circulation control, and cooperative acquisitions coupled with telephone lines make it possible for regional and statewide library groupings to be created without a unified administration or geographic proximity. This opens the possibility of basing local library building programs on community needs only. Occasional or unusual requests can be handled quickly and effectively by the organization of resource networks, as, for example, through:

1. Distributed data bases that provide for disparate libraries to feed into a common computer bank.
2. Distributed processing of circulation and interlibrary loan through remote telephone-interconnected computer terminals.
3. Micro storage and transmission.
4. Facsimile transmission.
5. Truck delivery networks.
6. Publicly operated data terminals for querying in-library location and status of materials on order, as well as presently available, with the capability of using a terminal for reserving, interloaning, or supplying specific information from databanks such as that of the *New York Times*. Integrated computer programs will soon be available that will make it possible for a library user to locate books and information in any of a hundred regional or national resources.

Within the past decade, the library profession has begun to reject arbitrary professionally oriented standards in favor of a system that derives program size recommendations from careful analysis of library use and specific community population factors. This new method is particularly appropriate when determining the size of additions to existing buildings and/or renovations of buildings to improve the matching of facilities to program.

Performance Measures for Public Libraries

1974 provided library planners with an important new tool devised by Ernest de Prospo, Ellen Altman, and Kenneth Beasley to measure use of materials in libraries as well as circulation of materials outside of libraries. Several dozen public libraries of small, medium, and large size (measured by budget) were studied to develop use patterns. The *Performance Measures* study found that in-library facilities were used more than most people thought. In fact, over 50 percent of the people who used the libraries did not actually borrow books "to go", but used them in the library building. It was discovered that the larger the library, the smaller the percentage of book borrowers. This means that library space planners must pay increasing attention to in-library use and must understand that the complexity of modern information needs emphasizes both self-service and staff service requirements.

New Community-based Standards

Recent papers and articles emerging from the American Library Association Public Library Division Standards Committee under the leadership of Rose Vainstein and Meredith Bloss have emphasized community library use and analysis as the governing factor in determining library facilities expansion programs. They support the concept of studying library use in the community to tailor facilities to program.

The American Institute of Architect Researchitects Group recently published a book on community resource centers, emphasizing services and program as a community function, with the community resource center conceived as a place for a wide range of services for all ages and many purposes.

Constraints on Library Plans

In making program decisions based on present library use and community wants, it should be recognized that many public libraries are operating under such constraints that examination of present use may provide a distorted picture of future growth opportunities. Some existing constraints that should be carefully noted and allowed for by planners are:

1. Budget of less than 1.5 percent of the total town budget, including allocations to the schools. This will severely and artificially limit the library's service potential in personnel and materials. Because of budgetary constraints, a use pattern may have developed that attracts far fewer potential users than a larger budget would. Library budget potential should be based on tax base and grand list evaluation and on examination of the entire town budget. The political capabilities of the library team are an important factor in achieving improved budgeting. Communication with budgeting authorities and careful comparison with similar communities and standards may be helpful.

2. Problems described in Aaron and Elaine Cohen's library obsolescence report and discussed in their seminars on obsolescence of library facilities, include insufficient space; poor or insufficient lighting, inappropriate or poor painting; ineffective mechanical system (heating and cooling); and such physical use inhibitors as remote catalogs, multilevel stacks accessible only by stairs, closed micro-material facilities, poor acoustics. Internal facilities alterations, the possibility of additions, and budgetary capabilities for new and expanded facilities will also be affected by the political capabilities of the library team.

3. Ineffective management—poor communications among board, community, staff, and administration; insufficient staff development education so that newer techniques are not incorporated. Management capabilities can be improved by personnel shifts and/or education.

An elaborate study of English library use recently determined that one barrier to library development was that librarians were concerned with *needs* while library users acted according to *wants*. Librarians were trying to buy materials that would be helpful to their users, and the users were seeking materials that would give them pleasure. For example community analysis may reveal that users' educational achievement is high, but the users may be more interested in modern feature films than in studies of art and science. Recent studies of reading habits and readers both in America and Europe show that enjoyment is the objective for the majority of "regular" readers, and that recreation in its largest sense is a stronger motivation than those related to jobs, the need for facts, etc.

Needs or wants as expressed in community surveys may not always be accurate guides to the future success or failure of new programs because of limited perceptions about library service. A survey in a suburban library showed that less than 5 percent of the respondents felt the need for films at the library, yet film programs actually attracted over 25 percent of the citizens. Similarly, surveys of the need for Sunday openings revealed only 18 percent wanted Sunday opening, but many more used the library on Sunday. New programs and services properly publicized may *anticipate* community needs, or give expression and direction to unvoiced needs/wants.

Developing a library program should be a continuous, organic community process. Library use and community analysis monitored on a periodic basis should form the backdrop for experimental new programs and abandonment of old ones.

Community input to the consultant can be structured in the following ways:

1. Friends of the Library as a sounding board for improvement planning.
2. Library and community meetings, displays of library plans and presentation of proposed new program in a variety of community locations—service clubs, PTAs, Junior Chamber of Commerce, AAUW, neighborhood organizations.

3. A permanent planning group to discuss the broad range of new and old services, consisting of trustees, friends, staff, other librarians, consultants, local fiscal authorities.

We are all familiar with the difficulties of "planning by committee." It is necessary to delineate responsibilities so that planners do not become designers or programmers. *Planners* evaluate program alternatives presented by the library staff in order to determine their relationship to community wants. *Designers* then implement these programs by expressing functional relationships and requirements in drawings and specifications.

The complex process of continuing communication and orchestration of disparate concerned groups must be the main objective of the alert library director. New technological library capabilities should be monitored by professional librarians who then keep the public carefully informed.

The consultant is primarily a library planner. His role is to support and guide the library director, and focus the library improvement program on the specific objectives developed by the community.

Steps in Program Formulation

Program formulation should be based on:

Library use analysis.
Community analysis.
Library standards, based on past building experience.
New technology.
Constraints.

Studies of these factors should result in a community-based program emphasizing library user wants. An example of how these user wants might be related to physical facilities is as follows:

To find and read an interesting book.
To look at a magazine or newspaper.
To view a film or slide show.

Multimedia browsing area. An informal, serendipitous "friendly object" arrangement of flat and sloping lighted display shelves, counters, comfortable lounge chairs, occasional tables, rear projection screens with headphones, cassette players.

To find factual information on jobs, education, consumer questions, investments, sex, medical problems, crafts, beauty culture, fashions, gardening, taxes, community events, community services.

Information center organized for self-service and staff service with ready reference books, computer terminals, card catalogs, indexes, business services, carrels and chairs, and a multistaff double-sided counter.

To have Media experiences—strong image-filled vicarious experiences for recreation, fantasy, information, deeper life enhancement. These experiences may overlap with user wants in the information area that can be satisfied by art, music, or other media, and there may be some overlap with user wants that lead people to the browsing area.

Browsing, information, and media should be used with staff members trained to serve in all areas, but some effort will be needed to sound isolate and identify varying functions by graphics, lighting, and furnishings. This area should be contiguous to the information area. The media center should provide individual and group viewing areas for video disc, film, and audio-cassette. A production area, well-staffed for assistance in use of video portapaks, cameras, and editing equipment for the production of community communications to be used in meetings and organization work should be provided.

To share group experiences in a wide variety of films, music, art, lectures, and drama. Quality in these direct experiences is often related to cost and careful economy, for the community will often dictate a large quantity of seating to lower unit costs and offer good quality to a wide segment of community participation. A piano recital costing $1,000 should be experienced by at least 500 people.

A large auditorium equipped for art display, films, music, lectures, and drama, with dressing rooms, stage, and storage areas.

To have an opportunity for interpersonal communication with other users and the library staff. Independent learning is a lifetime process involving staff and users in a continuing dialogue. Users coming to the library with a community of interests should have an opportunity to share those interests and learn from one another.

Facilities should be provided for small group meeting places; coffee bar, conference rooms, lounge areas, and an art gallery.

To pursue independent learning. A small but important group of library users want to use a library regularly in some kind of sequential pattern for a long-range learning objective that may or may not be related to a structured educational objective. The availability in libraries of the superb film series *Civilization and Ascent of Man* for example, offers excellent opportunities in this sequential vein.

An adult learning center with individual study rooms equipped for audio and video.

To satisfy these user wants, library facilities must offer a different pattern of use opportunities than would probably be found in the traditional public library planned primarily to circulate books.

Having studied the community and its use of the library, and having communicated user wants within the informational and politico-economic structure of the community with a view to obtaining funding for library improvement, it may now be reasonable for the planning team to begin detailed program planning. Recognizing that each program is highly individual, here is an outline of what a library program might include.

A Library Improvement Program Outline (SAMPLE)

1. A statement of the library's long-term goal (existing statement): The promotion of useful knowledge; support of the social, economic, and educational goals of the community, and so forth.

2. Short-term objectives stated as performance objectives related directly to the library user, such as: Increase use of a a wider range of library media by 20 percent in year following LIP.

3. Community description, present and future: 20-year projection of the population and its geographic distribution; shopping and traffic patterns and transportation facilities; educational and economic profiles; communication structure.

4. Library use analysis: daily entries; percent of uses—children, adult, student, business, recreation. Maximum facilities use—seating, programs, media. In-library reference and information use. Book circulation, telephone reference, population frequency of use.

5. Library facilities analysis: obsolescence report (Cohens). Photos and slides of present use: crowded conditions, maintenance problems, materials use and storage problems.

6. Resources available: capital budget and operating budget; library as percent of town budget; town debt commitments; fund-raising potential; communication potential; state and federal financing? Timetable.

7. Site considerations: expansion, parking, zoning, shopping.

8. Space requirement analysis: for books, seating, media in various clientele and functional areas:
   Adult: Information-media
          Books and magazines
          User.
   Children: Information-media
          Books and magazines
          Activities and media production
          Story hour and group programs.
   Program: large group area for children and adults..
   Special collections: use and storage of local history media.
   Staff: technical services—circulation control, acquisitions, theft detection, cataloguing, interloan, media.
   Custodial: heating, ventilating, air conditioning, maintenance, and supply storage.
   Management: accounting, public relations, food, relaxation, public encounters in private areas.
9. Functional relationships of spaces.
10. Detailed analysis of each functional area including use, staff, area, juxtaposition, equipment, lighting, communications, ambience, colors, special requirements.
11. General comments on lighting, HVAC, architectural style, parking, landscaping, carpeting, handicapped access, coat racks, bicycle and motorcycle racks, exhibit and display requirements, graphics, telephone and computer systems.

Brevity results in improved readership. The library program is a means of communication, not an end in itself. It can be effective only if many people read it. For the architect, it must provide an outline for drawing a library plan, but for the community it must result in support for the building. This financial objective requires that the program be brief and readable. Avoid including all the facts. Include only those necessary to explain the need for improvement. Use arrangement to place detailed information at the end, so that the first few pages will really explain the need and motivate the community to act.

The final detailed planning analysis can be presented in the library functional area format. These forms are useful for:

1. Describing existing facilities.
2. Describing additions.
3. Combining descriptions of existing and additional facilities.

They should be prepared by the library consultant or experienced library staff planner. Each area description should then be discussed with each individual staff member (both supervisors and service librarians) and recommended changes considered before being compiled into a library program.

LIBRARY FUNCTIONAL AREA	
AREA DESIGNATION What function is performed Activities What library users and staff are meant to do in this area.	
Occupancy - Public (at one time)	Staff (at one time)
Furniture and Equipment Description Quantity Dimensions Area A detailed listing of each piece of equipment. Tables, chairs, counters, film projectors, micro-readers, desks, bookstacks, storage cabinets. These descriptions should include dimensions, materials (wood or metal), capacities, counter heights and widths, colors, lighting requirements.	
Close Proximity Desired other areas nearby	Close Proximity NOT Desired functions to be located far away
Area required (Total) in square feet	Proportions - Dimensions square, round, rectangular
Book Capacity	Seating Capacity
Other materials quantities of films, cassettes, magazines	
Architectural Features - Ambience - Environment How you want users to feel and act in this area. Comfort of furnishings, behavior patterns, lighting, signs, noise control.	

Although a 20-year population projection is the accepted basis for planning new library buildings or additions, experience has shown that actually the useful life of library buildings is often 40 years or more. It is therefore essential that library planners provide for the first stage of further expansion. How can this be done when we know so little about what changes will take place in the community and in library technology?

Many basic elements in the expansion planning, such as user accommodations, do not change. Human beings will presumably still be using the building in some way 40 years from the time it is built. If the population increase for the first 20 years were to be on the order of 10,000, the building should be sized for 50 seats in addition to its present capacity. The 20 years beyond that might bring the need for 15 additional seats to satisfy a further increase in population. Thirty square feet each, for a total of 450 square feet of additional seating space, would be needed.

Book space expansion may be more modest because of such trends as:

DEVELOPING THE
IMPROVEMENT PROGRAM

Hanging graphics
staff station and
phonorecord bins

Networking of libraries.

Compact micro storage and retrieval and miniaturization.

Computerization.

Format changes, such as videodiscs.

Electrical requirements will almost certainly increase, so there should be a surplus capacity in the electrical service and empty conduits supplied from outside the building to all staff and public service centers in the building.

Mass use areas, such as program rooms and group meeting areas, need additional capacity beyond the planning period because of population changes.

Although based on outdated traditional library building standards, the following library improvement planning (LIP) information sheet provides basic useful information to provide a rough planning outline.

LIBRARY IMPROVEMENT PLANNING ESTIMATES

PUBLIC FUNCTIONS

SEATS

>   5 seats per 1,000 population (Wheeler)
>   30 square feet per seat, as an average
>   15 square feet per reader seated at a table
>   10 square feet per reader seated in chair away from table
>   20 square feet per child reader, 30" per reader at table
>   Seat height - 15½" - 18"
>   Seat depth - 15" - 17"

TABLES

>   Aisle space - 5'
>   Height - 30" adult; 25", 28" children
>   Round - 48" or 42" for children
>   Rectangular - 36" x 60" for 4 readers, 78" for 6

BOOKSTACKS

Section rows of shelves between two supports 3'

Range - series of sections end to end, usually 18' or 6 sections.

Wall shelving is single-faced.

Free standing shelving is usually double-faced.

Steel shelving is 90", 72", 60" or 42" high.

Wood shelving is 84", 72", 60" or 42" high.

Shelf capacities are Double-faced 90" = 300 books per section Single-faced 42" = 75 books

Spacing: public - 6' center to center, 3' aisle closed stack - 5' or less, center to center

Area book capacity varies from 10-15 books/sq ft

Linear capacity - 1' for 7-8 books.

If collection is expected to double in 20 years, leave 1/3 of each shelf for future expansion.

Ratios within the book collection:

    Reference - up to 10%

    Children - up to 25%

    Adult - 80% (nonfiction, 55%; fiction, 25%)

Withdrawals - 5% of the total collection each year, as needed.

Additions or replacements - 1/5 volume per capita.

Book collection - 3-5 volumes per capita (minimum).

35,000 population - 3¼ volumes per capita.

CARD CATALOG

1 tray holds enough cards for 250 books,

5 trays holds enough cards for 1,250 books.

MAGAZINES

10 titles per 1,000 population

STAFF AREA

150 sq ft per staff member

1 staff member per 2,000 population (1/3 professional)

MISCELLANEOUS

Nonassignable, utilities - 15-20% of area

TOTAL BUILDING AREA

50,000 population - 0.6 sq ft per capita
For a lower population - higher square footage per capita

CARPET

9 square feet = 1 square yard

LIBRARY HOURS

For population of 35,000 - 65 hours/week.

5 Planning Library Buildings

This chapter concentrates on those aspects of planning related to major physical considerations that affect the library program, including general planning factors.

Economics of Building

Operating costs for the public library should constitute about 2% of the town's overall budget, including that large percentage allocated to the public schools. If wages are in many cases determined by union negotiation and book costs are subject to production inflation factors, then utilities and maintenance would seem to be one of the few places where an administrator might exercise some semblance of control, but they are in fact one of the fastest growing areas of library costs.

Estimates of cost vary, but in terms of percentages one can estimate that salaries account for 70% of the library operating budget, materials for 20%, and maintenance and utilities for 10%. Utilities include electricity, heat, cooling and telephone, and maintenance covers painting, repair and custodial cleaning.

With building costs, and all of the above costs skyrocketing, it is difficult to place dollar figures on the cost of building and maintaining a library building on a per square foot basis, but in the recent past one could peg the cost of a new building of up to 50,000 square feet (including site acquisition, furnishings and equipment) at about $3.75 per square foot if cost is amortized over a 20 year period. Added to the cost of maintenance and utilities this comes to nearly $6.00 per year per square foot.

Figures can be broken down to find the cost of the various elements in a library building. Books can be stored in open stacks at a ratio of 15 per square foot. Therefore, the cost of building, heating, lighting, cleaning, and maintaining a stack area is about 4 percent of the cost of the book. Reader seating takes 30 square feet per seat, or $180 per year for all costs. A community of 20,000 people with a 15,000 square foot library may include 80,000 books and 100 seats. Over a 20 year period, the building will cost $1,125,000 to build and $600,000 to maintain, for a total of close to 2 million dollars. If the benefit returned to the community by a well-planned building can be measured at 4 million circulations, 400,000 reference questions (and, it is hoped, answers!), 400,000 persons as members of an audience for films, and a variety of other such product objectives, the building can, at the end of 20 years, be considered to have returned the investment with interest, and be retired.

Criteria for a Library Site

Towns build libraries infrequently, on the average about once in 40 years, yet the library will be used by more citizens than any other building in town. Libraries are used by children, students, business people, do-it-yourselfers, artists, writers, taxpayers, people learning new skills, professional people updating their knowledge. The library must be in a location where it can be constantly visible to all these people:

1. On a major road used by most citizens.
2. Near a shopping center that is open nights and Saturdays when the library will be open.
3. Convenient to parking and mass transportation. Ninety percent of present library use is by automobile. One parking space for every 300 square feet of net usable building area (excluding stairs, hallways, mechanical spaces); one parking space for every two adult reader seats.
4. Easy for pedestrians and children on bicycles to find, and safe for them to come to (safe traffic control).
5. Convenient for the elderly and handicapped—no curbs, or at least depressed curb cuts, no hills from the parking lot to the library.

Locations to avoid:

1. Parks—dangerous at night, subject to vandalism.
2. Schools—closed at 3 P.M. Most residents do not attend school. Noisy, disruptive.
3. Offices—closed at night, crowded and noisy in daytime.
4. Town hall or civic center—often closed at night.

Site cost is usually a minor fraction of construction and operating cost, yet if the library is obscurely located, it will not be used and the people will be paying for a facility that is inconvenient for them.

A library is built for citizen *Use*—if people see it, they will use it. If 2 percent of the town budget annually is spent to operate a library, the facility will give a handsome return on investment if it is located properly.

Parking Lot

The function of parking is to make the library accessible to the 90 percent of users who come by car. If the library is properly sited near the most important shopping center in town, it will be a busy place and taxpayers will be receiving the maximum convenience and access for their tax dollar. Identification of the library building will result from a design that is natural to the town and its environment, yet symbolizes the distinctive function of the library as a useful and informative individual service. A large lighted sign indicating the hours that the library is open will be an essential part of residents' experience of this building. The sign should be

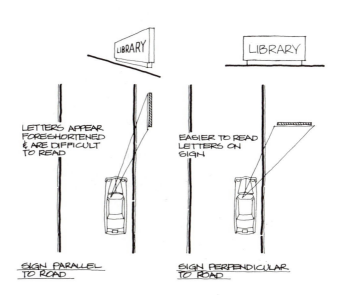

Proper placement of the library sign is essential to its effectiveness.

placed perpendicular to the road and should be of sufficient size to be seen by motorists passing at the speed limit. The sign may have to be even larger if it is competing with commercial signs in this location.

Parking convenience is essential. Commercial establishments have known this for years, and libraries must be able to compete with other retail centers. Parking lot design considerations include:

1. A full-size car stall is 9 feet wide and 20 feet deep. Small car stalls are 7½ feet wide and 16 feet deep.
2. Angled parking may increase lot capacity in unusual site configurations. However, perpendicular parking is generally the most efficient layout.
3. Handicapped parking should be located near the building, and the curb near the building should be ramped for wheelchairs—a 12 to 1 slope.
4. An area for stacking snow (in climates that have it) should be provided with a curb cut so that snowplows can shove snow completely off the asphalt.
5. Lighting should be low to avoid shining in neighbors' houses.
6. Trees can be honey locust or nondeciduous to avoid leaf raking problems.
7. Parking should be near the building but concealed by a stone wall or berm to soften the hot asphalt appearance.
8. A covered area near the building with a waiting lane and public telephone should be provided for patron pickup. Outside, but near the entrance, there should be a covered area for waiting for transportation. This should be located with both cars and bus transport considered.
9. There should be a lockable book drop for people to return materials when the library is closed. This slot should be large enough for books but *not* for records, which will be damaged if mixed with returns of books. Above the book drop on the inside should be a CO_2 fire extinguisher with a fusible link to put out fires that may be caused by dropping flammable material into the book slot. Under the book slot should be double carpeting or a durable foam material to cushion the books. The book drop should be a large open space rather than a container that could be rapidly filled and would then cause damage to books being forced into the slot.

10. Chains and power for a control gate should be considered if non-library use is likely.
11. In heavy snow areas, covered parking should be considered.
12. Bicycle racks with full front wheel support and locking capabilities should be provided in a covered location.
13. A motorcycle rack with full support for the wide front wheel and with locking capabilities should also be in a covered area. If motorcycle racks are not provided, bikers will use car spaces.
14. Small car markings and signs should delineate small car areas.
15. If the library is built on top of tiered parking, the entrance from the garage should be well-lighted and inviting and there should be a book return location.

The Entrance

Entering the library should be an attractive, inviting, and orienting experience. When patrons leave their cars, they should be able to immediately identify the library entrance and walk directly to it. Their hands will be filled with books, films, records, and equipment, so they will need to be able to enter the library through doors that open automatically. The entrance door should be protected from the wind by its location or by a wind baffle of some kind. As the library grows in use, the doors will tend to remain open longer. If 3,000 people or more enter the library each day, and these entries are reasonably distributed over all the time the library is open, it may be feasible to consider an *air curtain* rather than a door, since with this volume of use the doors will be open most of the time anyway. To protect staff and patrons from drafts, the vestibule or entryway will have either to be very long or to employ a wind baffle or offset entrance. It may also be useful to install what is commonly known as a "hair-dryer" over the entrance. This device cools or heats the air that comes into the building when the doors open. It includes a very powerful fan and a high temperature coil and may have some effect in conserving energy since it prevents very cold or very hot air from entering the building.

Entrance mats to clean snow and moisture off people's feet are very useful. A Pedi-Mat, incorporating carpet strips mounted on aluminum and separated by narrow openings for dirt to drop down through the mat, is unusually effective and easy to clean and maintain.

Material Return Location

Once inside the doors of the library, it is natural for users entering the building to want to drop materials and equipment as soon as they enter, and it is also probably natural for them to enter on the right of the exit and to look to their right upon entering for a return area. If the library is small and there is only a single check-out and return area, it is most economical to place this between the entrance and exit, so that the same staff member can easily help with both returns and check-outs.

Theft Detection.

Devices for theft detection have specific entry design requirements. Ideally, entrance and exit doors should be separated with some device to prevent the entry door from being used as an exit. This device must incorporate a shear pin so that in panic emergency situations the entrance door can be used as an exit. The exit path must be narrow enough for the theft detector to work and the exit locking device must be visable from and connected by an electrical conduit with the check-out desk.

Entry POP!—Independent Self-Service

When patrons enter the library, they should recognize all the library functions. Lighting, graphics, and furnishings should make the information center, card catalog, media stations, book and media storage, magazines, micro area, and browsing areas immediately visible and identifiable. A display area near the entry should include a lighted, keyed map that would lead a user to all library functions—especially if they are not on the main floor. This display area should also include notices of library programs, and exhibits. A large bulletin board and pamphlet dispenser for community events for the current and future month should also be provided. A community calendar for future months should be available at the information center.

Rather than presenting the user who is entering the building with a high counter barrier where clerical check-out operations are being performed, the modern library should invite the user to work directly with a librarian who is carefully trained to analyze and satisfy information needs. The information area, immediately accessible to but sound isolated from the entrance, should invite the user to be seated at a low desk-height counter where he or she can browse through pamphlets on library services and can see the complete array of services available while waiting for an intelligent service interview with a trained professional librarian. Surrounding this double-sided information counter should be all these services:

1. *Media:* rear projection screen, 16 mm projectors, slide projectors, video-cassette players, audio-cassette players.
2. *Computer terminals* providing access to *New York Times* Info Bank, Lockheed, and other data bases.
3. *Micro materials center:* film and fiche reader-printers.
4. *Public access catalog* in computer terminal or card form, including information on interlibrary loan procedures.
5. *Ready-reference materials:* encyclopedias, indexes, dictionaries, town and library information, book location materials, maps, pictures, calendar.
6. *Fiction and nonfiction bookstacks.*
7. *Reference bookstacks.*
8. *Magazine display,* with back issue storage and indexes nearby.
9. *New materials display,* a multimedia browsing area.

Handicapped Access Requirements

Barrier free design is now mandated nationally by Public Law 533. Here are some basic considerations in making a library accessible to the handicapped:

Building Approach

At least one *primary* entrance at a grade floor level shall be accessible by means of a walk uninterrupted by steps or abrupt changes in level, not less than 5'-0" wide, with ramp slope less than 1' in 20'.

Off-street Parking

Location close as possible to primary entrance.
Parking spaces 12'-0" wide.
Reserved parking signs 6'-0" high.
Curb cut between parking area and approach walk.
Curb cut slope is 1' in 12' or less.
Curb cut 4'-0" wide.
Directional signs to accessible entrance.

Total Parking in Lot	Required Number of Accessible Spaces for Handicapped
Up to 25	1
26 to 50	2
51 to 75	3
76 to 100	4
101 to 150	5
151 to 200	6
201 to 300	7
301 to 400	8
401 to 500	9
501 to 1,000	2 percent of total
Over 1,000	20 plus 1 for each 100 over 1,000

Telephone

If public or pay phones are installed, 5 percent or no less than one shall be accessible to and usable by physically handicapped persons.
Coin slot 54" or less in height. Telephone equipped for hearing disabilities.

Elevators

Required if there are four or more levels.
Cab size 25 sq ft minimum, least dimension 48" or more.
Elevator door 36" clear opening.
Corridor call button less than 55" high.
Metal braille numbers less than 48" high.
Cab handrail 30"-33" high.

Automatic door operation with safety and light ray reverse.
Audible signal at grade level.

Toilets

(2 percent or 1 fixture of each type/floor).

Water Closets

Stall 3'–6" × 6'–0" (front entry).
Stall 3"–6" × 7'–0" (side entry).
32" clear stall opening/outswing door.
48" × 48" clear space in front of stall.
Handrails each side of stall. 48" long, 33" high, 1½" diameter and 1½" clear from wall.

Seating Accommodations

Fixed seating in places of assemby shall provide the following number of viewing positions accessible to wheelchairs by the easy removal of other seats:

Capacity of Assembly Space	Number of Viewing Positions
Up to 25	1
26 to 50	2
51 to 75	3
76 to 100	4
101 to 150	5
151 to 200	6
201 to 300	7
301 to 400	8
401 to 500	9
501 to 500	2 percent of total
Over 1,000	20 plus 1 for each 100 over 1,000

Circulation Control

The purpose of a library circulation control system is to retrieve books from circulation as quickly as possible with maximum convenience for the library patron and minimal staff, material, and equipment costs. This operation should be efficient and unobtrusive.

Small Library Systems.

(Up to 30,000 circulations per year.) In these libraries, one or two staff members can easily handle the daily volume of circulation without delay to patrons and accomplish all the necessary routines with an inexpensive manual system such as the *Newark staff charge.* This system requires the following manual procedures:

1. Registration of library patrons—Rolodex.
2. Book card marking with patron number.
3. Book card filing by date due.
4. Book card slipping when books are returned.
5. Overdue notice, typing and mailing.
6. Delinquent notice, typing and mailing.
7. Delinquent flagging of patron file.

Medium Library Systems

(Up to 300,000 circulations per year.) In these libraries, slow check-out and return systems requiring considerable manual routines such as are used in small libraries would be both expensive in terms of staff time and inconvenient in terms of patron delay.

In these cases a *transaction card system* should be used, which eliminates the need for patron files and book card filing and slipping but which requires T-card files or numbered sheets. Either a photographic or other sequential numbered system would be economical. When books are checked out, a sequential transaction card is recorded—with patron number and date due—often by microfilm camera. When the book is returned, the sequential transaction card is removed, matched, and the book discharged. All transaction cards *not* returned are recorded as *not* matched, and the microfilm is searched for patron overdue information. A computer terminal linked by telephone to a host computer such as the Gaylord System may be a solution at this level of use.

Large Library Systems

(Above 300,000 circulations per year.) A computer-based automated system offers lowest cost and most effective service. These systems require extensive input time, but once they are set up they require minimum staff time compared to the book card system and vastly improved control over the sequential transaction card system. The automated system matches book and patron number when books are borrowed by means of an automatic number reading device. This device also discharges the book when it is returned. If the item is not returned, the system automatically generates overdue notices. Branched, indexed programs make it possible to search the random-access disc file by author, book number, or patron number.

Not too long ago, librarians thought it was necessary for a circulation control system to provide the location of a book at any moment, the number of times each book had circulated, retrieval of overdue books at all costs, and circulation count by classification. Registration files were kept up to date with many hours of labor.

Recently, some of these aspects of circulation work have been dropped because of their increasing costs. Some libraries have abandoned registration files completely. Under some systems, work that used to be done by the staff is done by the borrowers. In some systems, slipping of returned books is not necessary; prestamped date due slips have replaced the stamping of books.

Now computerized circulation systems are bringing a return to the kind of detailed control that the book card file systems used in smaller libraries can provide. These computerized systems require borrowers' cards and are expensive to purchase for the small library.

According to the *Study of Circulation Control Systems,* (1962) by George Fry and Associates, any circulation system for a public library should provide the following:

1. Identity of materials charged out.
2. Identity of borrowers.
3. Means for securing the return of the materials if they are not returned within a reasonable period of time after due date.
4. A total number count of all materials charged out.

The minimum characteristics of a circulation system should be:

1. Simple for the public to use and for the library staff to operate.
2. Economical in relation to the total budget.

Circulation Counter Configuration

Patron side:

> 39″ transaction height for user convenience
> 29″ height—childrens area

Staff side:

> 30″ high work counter so that materials can be swept off patron top area and easily isolated for processing. Terminals for check-in by light pen and for theft detection sensitizing should be located here concealed from the public for quick, easy staff operation. CRT (cathode ray tube) TV-like device for querying computer to answer patron questions on their delinquency status should be on a turntable for patron access.

Book Trucks:

> for quick easy sorting of returned materials.

Corrals:

> for filled book trucks on the patron side so recently returned books may be borrowed *before* they are shelved.

Reserve:

> book storage to hold reserved returns for other patrons.

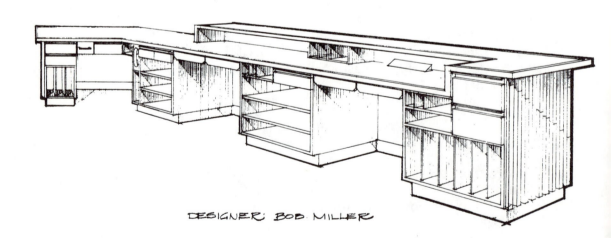

DESIGNER: BOB MILLER

A thoughtfully designed circulation counter for adults and children with 39″ high transaction top and lower 30″ high staff work counter. Machines fit on top of the work counter and underneath the transaction top. *(Groton, Connecticut Library.) Designer: Bob Miller of Lyons, Mather and Lechner.*

Program: Circulation Control Area
Goal: Convenient, rapid, easily understood, controlled, cost effective handling of material returned to
and checked out from the library.

Public Service Objectives

Return:

Provide a convenient location for users to
quickly and easily return a maximum of 2,000 books,
400 phonorecords, and, 50 films each day.

Reshelve:

Provide a quick and cost effective method for
the staff to return these materials into circulation *or*
reshelve them in proper sequence.

Reserves:

Make available to the staff a maximum of 200
books, 50 phonorecords, and 20 films in an easily
accessible reserve area. Hold 100 reserves for tele-
phoning.

Check-out:

Check-out by computer light pens (3) and
desensitize (2 machines) a maximum of 2,000 books
and 400 records a day.

Delinquent:

Make available to the public staff-accessed
CRT-displayed information on delinquent status.

Fines and Fees:

Accept and record payment of $300 a day in
cash and checks for fines and lost materials.

Renewals:

Process 100 telephone renewals each day by
staff using CRT.

Registration:

Register 20-25 new or renewed users each
day. Clerical and professional staff cooperate in this

important task of welcoming and orienting new library patrons.

Photocopier:

Make change for photocopiers and assist patrons in their use. Load paper and toner and phone for service.

Magazine check-in:

Check-in and service 100 magazines and newspapers each day.

Mail Receipt and Sorting:

Sort and make available for quick, easy pickup 500 pieces of mail to 40 separate locations.

Telephones:

Answer 200 daily telephone calls. Forward 180 calls a day. Monitor and act upon calls received on phone answering cassettes when library is closed.

Directional and Reception:

Answer and direct 400 people a day to various building locations. Accept and hold for pickup 20 large packages to 10 separate locations.

Supply Storage:

Provide easily accessible storage for 120 shelf feet of supply items used weekly.

Deliveries:

Provide orderly, accessible storage for 200 items to be delivered to 10 branch and town locations.

Bindery Discards:

Store 200 books waiting to be processed for rebinding, repair, and replacement.

Pickup:

Store 100 books and mail awaiting pickup.

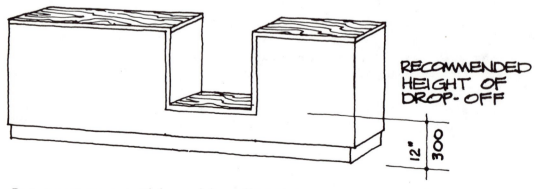

Projector return area with lowered drop-off counter

ADULT-HEIGHT COUNTER

39" - 42"
975 - 1050 MM.

HEIGHT OF COUNTER SUITABLE FOR CHILD & FOR STAFF WORK

29" - 32"
725 - 800 MM.

USEFUL AREA FOR ISOLATING RETURNED BOOKS QUICKLY & FOR SCREENING COMPUTER TERMINAL

Circulation Counter.

Mail Posting:

Store 100 items to be weighed on the postal scale, run through the meter, and mailed. Pencil sharpener and stamping area.

Coin Sorting:

Sort 2,000 coins a day, wrap and deliver to administration office.

Letter Typing:

Type 5 letters a day.

Paperbacks:

Sort, label, and stamp 200 paperbacks a day.

Interlibrary Loan:

Keep records on interlibrary loans for one year (2,000 - 4 × 9 slips) arranged alphabetically by title.

Part-time Employees:

Provide sign-in and sign-out sheets.

Custodial Paging:

Broadcast (beeper) device.

The circulation center of a library for a town of 5,000 (*Byram, Connecticut*).

Lost and Found Area:

Space for 50 items.

Interview Patrons:

Respond to complaints about services. (Private area).

Interview prospective clerical and page employees:

(Private area).

Compile daily, weekly, and monthly statistics.

Coat Storage for Staff:

15 coats and small lockers at desks.

Library pamphlet display for Public:

Provide bulletin board and displays on library activities.

Overdue Sorting:

For about 100 books a day.

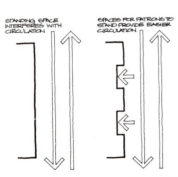

STANDING SPACE
INTERFERES WITH
CIRCULATION

SPACES FOR PATRONS TO
STAND PROVIDE EASIER
CIRCULATION

CHARGE DESK WITH
STRAIGHT FRONT

CHARGE DESK WITH
INDENTED FRONT

Up to 20 percent of the total floor area of a library building may be given over to staff work, office, and storage spaces not accessible to the public. But staff work areas for staff members who spend a good deal of their time working with the public must be close to the areas where they work with the public so that staff members can be in their offices working on nonpublic tasks yet available to come out and assist as soon as public service is required. This usually means glass enclosed offices.

Administrative offices, those of library directors, business managers, bookkeepers, and secretaries, may be located outside of public areas and even on a different level than public services in libraries serving populations of 75,000 or more.

However, it is useful for the director to have at least visual surveillance over public service areas.

Technical services, including purchasing, processing, and cataloging of library materials as well as the technical aspects of book circulation control, tend to be located so as to give convenient accessibility to delivery of large quantities of materials and access to the public card catalog. These two requirements are often in conflict, since the catalog should be in the center of the public service space while the delivery entrance should be remote from the public. Access to the catalog is the more important consideration.

However, as libraries grow in size, perhaps one of the most logical areas to move to another level are the technical services since the remote location of a public service would result in greater inconvenience for library users. Recent impressive technical developments, such as on-line circulation control systems and catalogs, may lead to a reduction in the space required for technical services and increase the feasibility of locating technical services remote from the public catalog.

Multipurpose Room

Even the smallest libraries require multipurpose rooms, because in most communities the library building is used by such a large percentage of the population over such a wide range of hours that it soon becomes the informational and cultural center of the town. It is one of the few town buildings designed for *all* the people, providing services to all of them for most of their active lives.

It is obviously more economical for a town to build a multipurpose room in a library centrally located for the entire community than to try to adapt assembly rooms in school buildings throughout the town that are often closed in the evening. The multipurpose room in the library uses the already operating library heating and cooling system, the centrally located library parking lot, and the staff of the library, which is already active and knowledgable about community wants.

Flexibility in design for multipurpose rooms is a problem just as it is in other parts of the library because a room designed ideally for one purpose will not be quite as satisfactory when used for another purpose. A level floor limits the number of seats that can be used to about 15 rows before the sight lines become restricted. A sloping floor is not much more expensive to provide than a flat floor, yet it will assure clear sight lines and comfortable angles of vision for media presentations. But a sloping floor makes the room unsuitable for use for exhibits and difficult to use for conference groups.

A room for a spoken presentation is ideally square, while film theaters tend to be long rectangles. Acoustics for films require a sound absorbent wall in the rear; music is best in a room with harder wall surfaces that produce more resonance and more overtones.

Community analysis to understand the program opportunities available to users and how the room fits into the pattern of other town facilities will determine size and program requirements. If the town has another meeting room—how large is it and what types of programs are scheduled? Are there commercial art galleries and concert halls in town? Are there a variety of film opportunities in town? In many cases, the library will want to compete with commercial establishments to bring another dimension of quality or variety to what otherwise might be a one-dimensional town exposure to commerical films. The library's commitment should be to quality and variety, as well as to bringing new and experimental art forms to the community. Some of the program uses that may be required for a single public room are:

The low cost of renting quality films and their wide degree of availability and popularity make films a top priority for library programming. A white wall or a fixed matte screen is ideal for projection. Pull-down screens are more expensive and tend to curl with age. Sound should come from behind the screen. This is possible with a single large speaker system permanently mounted behind a fixed perforated matte white screen. However, perforated screens reduce the brightness of the image and require more frequent replacement. The screen should be capable of being covered by drapes when it is not in use to protect it and the speaker from damage. The speaker does not have to be very expensive, since most 16 mm sound tracks will not deliver very low bass tones.

The amplifier should be mounted in a closed projection booth, but the volume and tone should be capable of being controlled from the rear of the room to assure correct sound levels. Drape controls and light dimming controls in the projection booth will be useful. The booth itself should be large, to provide maximum flexibility in projectors that may be used. A shelf will diminish this flexibility, projection carts are more useful. The window should go from 30 inches in height to the booth ceiling and should be of double glass to prevent noise leakage. Electrical receptacle and control conduits should come out at the 28-inch height on the front wall of the booth below the window. The booth should be equipped with several carefully shielded small adjustable lamps so that work in the booth with lights will not disturb viewers. The booth should include a sturdy table bolted to the side wall and equipped with motor operated rewinds for the rewinding of films. Radio, cable TV, and video conduit leads from the street should be considered in the design of the projection booth. Equipment racks for amplifiers, tape recorders, and phonograph should be designed to absorb sound.

Art Exhibits

A clear white wall with a homosote or cork backing and a light-track ceiling provides good flexibility, but the wall will have to be made sound absorbent for film purposes. Try to avoid vertical mullions or seams or textures that might clash with pictures, and try to have directional rather than general illumination. Picture wire molding, although it avoids constant puncturing of the walls, results in distracting wires holding the frames visible to the browser. Ceilings and floors in an art gallery should be in neutral colors to avoid competing with the artwork.

Musical Performances

Piano storage and delivery of pianos through doors with a 6-foot clear opening may be required. Some hard surfaces for acoustical resonance and overtones may also be required. Musical acoustics are more difficult problems than are film or speaker acoustics and require special consultation.

Forums

Loudspeakers distributed throughout the ceiling for best sound distribution without high sound levels are required.

Dramatic Presentations

Stage provisions are difficult to program. Wings on both sides, concealed from the audience, provide a minimum of dramatic effect—at least better than an open platform. Scenery fly and storage space can be exceedingly expensive and can encourage use by drama groups that may preempt the space from public use, and require hours or days of rehearsal time. Lighting for dramatic purposes can also be astronomically expensive, but some provision should be made for musicals, speakers, and readings. Rheostats for selective darkening of stage, aisles, and audience area are not too expensive. Dressing rooms are very useful amenities for speakers or any kind of musical performance. They should ideally include a lockable closet, mirror, dressing table, and a sink with hot and cold water.

Library Lighting

The function of lighting in a library is not only to help people find materials to borrow but also to provide good lighting that will limit eye fatigue in long-term use areas. In addition, *task lighting,* in which light fixtures are related to the work to be performed, can make the library easier to use by directing attention to various areas and activities. Since light is used only where necessary, energy is conserved. Ideal library lighting includes a variety of appropriate lighting levels with minimum glare and minimum brightness of light fixtures.

The three basic types of lighting available are:

Incandescent lighting. Bulb life is often less than 1,000 hours and is very expensive compared with other kinds of lighting available. However, this type of lighting presents good color and is comfortable for long periods of time. A point source of light is provided.

Fluorescent lighting. High lumen output per watt of electricity is provided, and the bulbs last over 20,000 hours. Careful selection of warm white fluorescent bulbs or balanced white (sunlight) will provide relatively good color rendition that will be comfortable for reading for a long period of time. Strip fluorescent lighting is the least expensive. The new General Electric F40 LW/RS/WM watt miser will deliver 3,050 lumens from less than 40 watts. Be careful to specify quiet ballasts. Fluorscent lamps often pulse light output and are therefore best used in tandem.

High Intensity Discharge (HID) mercury vapor or metal halide light bulbs. The advantages of these lights are that they will burn twice as long as fluorescent bulbs and provide high lighting levels per dollars of electricity consumed. On the other hand, color rendition is not as good as fluorescent or incandescent (3,500°/K), and it is important to keep ballasts which tend to be noisy, remote. This light is also intensely bright at the source. Bulb explosions, though infrequent, can be a problem.

The Illuminating Engineering Society library lighting standards have always been very high in lumen output. Just a few years ago, experts were recommending over 100-footcandles of initial illumination in libraries. Luminous ceilings were installed so that anywhere in the room lighting levels would be uniformly high. But at the same time, some distinguished library consultants, such as Keyes Metcalf, were pointing out that these high lighting levels produced glare which causes the pupil of the eye to contract, thus reducing visual acuity or the ability to see clearly. To cut glare, light must be made to strike the object to be read from many directions (inter-reflection).

Diffusion lenses control the glare caused by *direct artificial light*. These lenses are working effectively if the outlines of the lamps cannot be seen when looking at the fixture and if there is uniform light without bright spots and without reflected glare caused by light striking the viewing surface at an angle. Reflected glare hitting the viewing surface at a 45° angle can be reduced by directional louvers or lenses that limit the spread of light, but these louvers and/or lenses often reduce lumen output, requiring closer spacing of fixtures. The relative location of fixtures and reading surfaces can also reduce reflected glare.

Thirty-five-footcandles of *indirect light* on a viewing surface coming from a white dome would be an ideal for controlling glare. A Frank Lloyd Wright designed library in Marin County, California, has such a ceiling, but the lighting level is very low. Artificial light has to be delivered at very high lumen output to provide sufficient indirect light to make it possible to read for long periods of time without eye fatigue.

With *ambient lighting,* which is uniform, furnishings may be placed anywhere. Prisms—acrylic lenses—spread light, but it is hard to prevent direct and reflected glare and it is wasteful. Also it gives a dull appearance, without variety to highlight services or differentiate services from passageways and from reading and public service areas. *Light clouds,* consisting of strip fluorescent fixtures over high use areas, also permit flexible furniture arrangement.

Cove lighting provides a wash of light on wall shelves and could serve in a library to highlight materials of great reader interest. Fixtures should be placed a foot and a half from the walls so the light extends a good distance down the wall area. If the light is too close to the wall, it will light only the highest shelves.

Track lighting, although expensive, provides an interesting highlight of spots on walls and provides flexibility, since fixtures can be moved or removed when not needed. A wide variety of lighting and bulb types is available.

Parking lot lighting should consist of mercury vapor fixtures placed on high poles to minimize vandalism and provide maximum light from a single source. Care should be taken to shield the light source from neighbors. Careful arrangement of lights and light shields will be necessary to achieve this. An expensive but pleasing alternative is a large number of low vandal-proof high intensity discharge fixtures illuminating curbs & corners.

Graphics should be carefully designed to go with the lighting scheme of a library. It is usually impossible to light graphics properly if the graphics system is designed after the lighting is installed. Ideally, a graphics system for a library should be designed at the same time the lighting system is planned.

In planning library lighting, be sure to:

Avoid sunlight in long-term use areas. It is unpredictable and difficult to control. Ultraviolet light damages paper and bindings.

Select lenses carefully to diffuse light and prevent glare. Acrylic opalescent molded plastic lenses are desirable.

Locate fixtures to minimize ceiling brightness and veiling reflectance caused by light striking the viewing surface at a 45° angle.

Limit light intensity variation in small rooms or in contiguous areas. Use low intensity light in nonreading areas.

Install fixtures and lenses that burn cool and make cleaning and lamp replacement simple. Plan scheduled group relamping.

Avoid glare and reflection by careful selection of diffusers, louvers, and light locations.

Let users control lighting.

Other points to consider are:

Parawedge louvers, used with fluorescent lamps, minimize ceiling brightness and veiling reflections, while providing good directional lighting. However, they do not eliminate direct glare.

The bat-wing reflector, used with fluorescent lamps, spreads light over a wide area and provides good, inexpensive, evenly distributed stack lighting.

White ceilings and white walls will increase light, especially in small rooms.

Visibility in a room is affected by:
1. Room size.
2. Color and contrast within the room.
3. Time. The eye accommodates to low light levels after a time.
4. Brightness of lamps.

Warm white fluorescent lamps (not deluxe) provide better rendition of skin tones than do cool white lamps.

Light colored surfaces minimize contrast.

Elliptical reflectors in a new installation or elliptical lamps in an incandescent lighting situation will increase light output at lower wattage.

Artificial lighting near windows or skylights should be switched so that some lamps can be turned off during the day. For example, four lamp fixtures should have only two lamps on during daylight.

Electrical Costs.

The electric company establishes a peak demand charge for each installation. This is the maximum electrical power required at one time by all electrical consumption devices in the building. New devices can regulate this by shutting off equipment to limit peak demand.

A charge is made for each kilowatt hour of consumption. (A kilowatt hour (kwh) represents 1,000 watts of electricity in use for one hour.) This change varies geographically but in some areas it can be as high as 5¢ per KWH. Here are some approximate costs to operate for a 60-hour week.

A 4-foot long fluorescent lamp= 12¢
A 150 watt bulb= 45¢
A 1,000 watt room heater= $3

Current practice, reflecting concern with energy conservation, suggests that lighting should consume no more than 2 watts of power for every square foot of space. Total energy consumption should not exceed 55,000 Btu per cubic foot per year, or 18 watts per square foot per year.

Energy Conservation

Concern with energy conservation has become a primary consideration in library building design. Listed here are a number of suggestions for conserving energy.

1. Underground or berm buildings: the new libraries at Yale and Harvard are examples of placing libraries underground to preserve the open beauty of college campuses. This system has the added advantage of being very economical to heat and cool. It is peculiarly suited to library design because of the nature of library use—the need for quiet, undisturbed concentration. Central courts or perimeter skylights can be effectively used to bring blue sky and green trees into the view of library users. Protection of materials and users from damage by heavy storms or explosions is a minor advantage of this location. A good capability for darkening areas to be used for projection screens is another advantage.

2. Lighting advances. Lighting requires a relatively small amount of energy consumption. Fluorescent lamps are still the energy saving champions, especially the new 35 watt 4-foot lamps for which reflectors louvers and lenses should be carefully chosen to disperse light evenly and prevent glare. Mercury vapor or other high intensity discharge lamps may be used to conserve energy in high-ceilinged installations, but they must have quiet remote ballasts and protective coverings in case of bulb explosion. Task lighting distributed throughout the building provides users with control over their own illumination and saves money when not in use. Careful planning of switches can provide the capability of reducing lighting without turning it off, especially near windows and other natural light sources.

3. Insulation can produce significant savings. Cavity wall construction and fiberglass or spray foam insulation permanently in place will reduce heat loss.

4. Perimeter heat pump units may save energy in existing buildings as well as new construction. These units can control heat in a room very precisely as well as providing cooling. They have the further advantage of being able to be replaced one at a time so that a failure in one machine will not result in the complete lack of heating or cooling.

5. New economizer air-conditioning control systems with large outside air intakes can dramatically improve the capability of a system to use outside air for cooling in the marginal fall and spring months. These systems permit great flexibility in fine-tuning modulating dampers to mix outside and inside return air

for cooling. Air conditioning is one of the most energy consuming processes.

6. Solar control windows with built-in venetian blinds, or solar control film added to existing windows, will prevent heat build-up from the sun during the summer.

7. Skylights should be insulated by double or triple glass and a system provided to allow hot air to escape through them in the summer.

8. Location of air-conditioning filters can cause great difficulty in preventing efficient cooling. All filters should be located so that they are easily accessible for cleaning and replacement.

9. Duct insulation to prevent noise can come unglued inside ducts and block cooling air flow. Provision should be made both to lessen the likelihood of this happening and to provide access to ducts when it does.

10. Operable windows are increasingly in use in areas where cool ocean breezes are useful for cooling, but they will have to be controlled carefully to prevent hot air build-up on sunny mornings.

11. Solar heat is now practical for hot water heating, but not yet for general building heating nor for air conditioning. One of the difficulties is in storing solar energy in cloudy weather.

12. Building orientation and placement of windows can be very important. Try to avoid too many windows on north walls; face most of the windows toward the south and the entrance also.

13. Peak demand reducers are devices that turn off major pieces of electrical equipment to regulate peak electrical demand and thus limit electrical costs.

14. Maintenance is of prime importance. Change filters, adjust fan belts, and change idler gear wheels. Train all staff to be conscious of energy conservation opportunities.

15. Locating thermostats to prevent them from being affected by drafts can conserve fuel. They should also be locked or concealed so the public and staff cannot tamper with them, or careful instructions on their use should be placed at each thermostat.

16. Burner adjustment and monitoring devices, cleaning of flues and chimneys, and use of special furnace lining material can reduce consumption.

17. Scheduling of cleaning after hours so that lights are turned off as areas are cleaned can save electricity.
18. Time clocks for thermostatic controls can reduce fuel consumption when the building is unoccupied.
19. Switching off of incandescent lamps should be encouraged, but fluorescent lamps require more starting energy and should not be turned off so readily.
20. Entry and exit via a double set of doors with vestibule or other space between them planned so that cold air/heat does not flow directly through both of them into the library as users enter and leave. Baffling for wind, and orientation for minimal heating/cooling loss (on the southwest side of the building if possible) also helps reduce costs and conserve energy.
21. Passive insulation can be achieved by having large masses, such as earth berms, surrounding the building. Compact book stacks supply thermal mass that tends to stabilize indoor temperatures also.
22. Window wells below ground level for ground floor windows prevent cold drafts.
23. Multiple boilers and variable volume pumps will save energy by tailoring boiler use to outside temperature as well as internal load.
24. No more than 25% of the exterior wall should be glass.
25. Insulation should be of U factor .05 and R 20 (This has to do with transmission of heat).

Graphics

Graphics, lighting, furniture, color, space, and shapes are all part of a design concept that can affect human behavior. These design elements should be considered concurrently at an early stage in schematic design of libraries. Behavioral or performance objectives for each functional area in the library should be determined, and then design elements combined to meet these behavioral objectives.

Considerations for the treatment of graphics include:

1. Size and scale of lettering should be determined by
   a. Distance from sign to library user.
   b. Size of other signs in the area.
   c. Importance of sign in relation to other signs.
   d. Size of area and other objects in the area.
2. Need for a sign. Can the users behavior be affected by

other indicators—lighting, furniture arrangement, acoustical isolation, maps, directories, flyers, posters?

3. Type style: simple, bold sans serif type, such as Helvetica, is easier to read, matches a wider variety of designs, and is familiar to the patron.

4. Negative behavior signs (DO NOT . . .) should be avoided if at all possible.

5. A lighted background of bright ceiling light fixtures will make a hanging sign almost invisible. Consider using internally lighted signs or a spotlight on each sign.

6. Vinyl stick-on letters that may be applied directly to glass, plastic, or wood, called "Letterlign," are available from:
Philadelphia
Enameling Works
N.E. Corner 13th and Race Streets,
Philadelphia, PA 19107

A useful new book on
Library graphics is
*Sign Systems for
Libraries:
Solving the Wayfinding
Problem*
edited by Dorothy Pollet and
Peter C. Haskell
Bowker 1979

6 Organizing Books and Other Media for Use

As we have already stated in chapter 4, both professional library standards and systems concepts have changed rapidly since the 1960s. At that time and with the realization that a generally higher education level and rapidly increasing information needs made equal access to good libraries a necessity for all the people, the American Library Association recommended that a population of 150,000 was a minimum base for adequate library and information services. Only a population of this size, it was felt, could support a large enough library to meet successfully the information needs of most citizens. The concept urged that smaller communities try to band together to achieve a viable tax base.

Now, more than 20 years after this concept was promulgated, many small community libraries are still not part of such a system; but our technology may soon link many libraries into communication networks that will have the effect of creating library systems by rapidly supplying books and information from wider sources.

Although population growth has at present slowed considerably, book quantity requirements must take into consideration population projections for a 20-year period since library buildings are costly capital projects that are seldom undertaken more than twice in a century. If the projections are uncertain, careful provision should be made in the structural system—electrical, heating, ventilating, and air conditioning—for flexible growth.

Population projections ideally would be based on estimates made by demographic expert planners familiar with the community. They should be compared with land zoning requirements and with other regional projections, as well as being checked carefully by the library governing body.

Circulation and Shelf Space

Book circulation in libraries varies from 3 to 20 books per capita per year. Libraries in communities with heavy circulation will need a larger book collection to satisfy their needs, but libraries in communities with low circulation should examine their selection methods as related to community wants before making a decision to keep their book stock at a lower figure than three per capita. Libraries with budgets greater than 2 percent of the town budget or greater than $20 per capita will have unusually high circulations and greater bookstack requirements. In libraries with an unusually high circulation per capita, it may be possible to accommodate more books in a smaller bookstack, since a high percentage of them will always be in circulation.

Seasonal circulation patterns must be closely examined. If the community attracts many summer residents, the circulation may be markedly lower in the winter months so that the shelves will be overflowing in the winter. Subject circulation will vary seasonally; for example, the travel book shelves will be empty in summer and full in winter. If shelf space is too tight, the book collection will have to be constantly shifted and costs for shelvers will increase.

A count of empty shelf spaces can be made to determine the actual capacity of the existing bookstacks to hold the books to be purchased within the next year or two. As we mentioned previously, the number of books in circulation will vary according to the time of year, with the end of June being the time when the largest number of books will be in the library. If the empty shelf count is taken at any other time, monthly circulation figures should be checked to determine how many more books will have to be accommodated at slower circulation periods.

If half the books do not circulate each year, an accelerated weeding program may greatly reduce the need for book space. Shelf space for little used books is a costly luxury when other larger libraries may be able to supply the book quickly through interlibrary loan. Determine how many volumes the library acquired over the past several years and how many were discarded. The net growth figure can then be applied over the 20-year planning period to determine how many books the library will own.

A library that discards 90 percent of all books that do not circulate in a year will require much less bookstack space than one that discards 50 percent of the books that do not circulate in a year. Modern computerized circulation control systems automatically provide this kind of monitoring of book activity.

Acquisition Practices.

The traditional ALA standard was 0.2 books per capita per year added to the collection. If this rule were followed and no books were discarded, a library serving 10,000 people would add 2,000 books per year and would require about six 3-feet sections of 90-inch high double-faced shelving each year to accommodate these new books, or about 150 square feet of additional building space each year. In ten years, the library would need 1,500 square feet and in 20 years, 3,000 square feet. Of course, every library does some discarding, so that these figures are exaggerated. However, to determine bookstack requirements it will be essential to establish a rate of *net acquisitions* based on an acquisitions policy and budget and a discard average. This net rate of acquisitions should then be projected over a 20-year period and compared with the figures derived from the population projection for the same period.

Theft Control

If the library does not take inventory and has no theft prevention system, the shelf list statistics as to the size of the collection may be very inaccurate. Theft loss can vary from 3 percent to 25 percent a year. A sampling of the accuracy of the shelf list or actual counting of the books on the shelves on a particular day may be necessary to establish the present size of the collection. Inaccuracy of card catalogs is extreme in libraries that do not inventory and have no theft detection systems. In these libraries one out of every 4 catalog cards may represent a book no longer owned by the library.

Theft detection systems are often negative design elements in a library entrance that attempts to be open and accessible to all users. However, most libraries find them economically essential. Recent efforts have been made to incorporate them into the entrance area design by sizing the entrances and exits to theft detection requirements for narrow entrances and by tying them in with electrical door operators. The design concept should be for the detection system to be completely concealed and to operate only when an actual theft is occurring. An electrical conduit from the circulation desk to entry is needed.

Bookstack Subdivision

As libraries grow in size, it becomes increasingly confusing to break up the bookstacks into irregular configurations. In using both the Dewey and Library of Congress book classification systems, the reader will find it easier to use bookstacks with a continuous sequential numbering system without breaks for seating. For several reasons, it is also most economical to design a building with all the bookstacks in one continuous pattern. Books on 90-inch high bookstacks require a structural strength

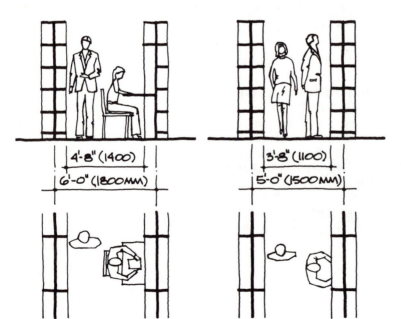

Aisle Space In Busy Stacks.

of 150 pounds per square foot, while reading rooms require only 75 pounds per square foot, so that these two areas have different design requirements. Bookstack aisles vary from zero in compact shelving for little-used book storage to 44 inches in heavily used public areas. For most convenient access, it is essential to design the support columns for the building structure to match the aisle spacing; this can only be done early in the design process if the architect and library consultant coordinate aisle spacing and column locations by placing the bookstacks in a single stack area within the building.

Multilevel Stacks

As libraries grow in size beyond the 30,000 square foot single floor building, there will be pressures to double deck the stack area. There are some arguments in favor of this. A multilevel, self-supporting stack is economical to build and adds architectural interest to a space. However, consider the high cost of heating, cooling and lighting the high ceiling space that may result. Consider that almost everyone that walks into a library building uses materials, but only a small percentage require study space. Consider that weight support requirements make it more economical to put a reading area above a stack than to put a stack above a reading area. Handicapped requirements will make a $30,000 elevator necessary. It will be difficult to control users in a stack area with little or no staff supervision. How will you determine which materials are placed on the less accessible level? This will inconvenience some users more than others. How will the card catalog indicate book locations on varying levels? Will the card catalog be duplicated on all bookstack levels?

Community Analysis

Determining the educational and economic level of the community, and examining the availability and quality of other libraries, may also have an effect on bookstack size and will certainly have an effect on library use and on subdivisions within the book collection. Census tract analysis will determine age group relationships to guide decisions on whether the children's collection should be 10 or 20 percent of the total. Educational and occupational analysis will determine whether the reference collection should be 5 or 10 percent of the total. The

overall size of the book collection will also affect the
percent devoted to reference, since studies have shown
that reference use increases greatly as the book collection grows. Similarly, nonfiction circulation as a percentage of the total circulation also increases with the size of
the library, so that a library growing from a collection of
50,000 books to one of 150,000 should allow for a much
higher percentage of nonfiction at the end of the projected growth period.

Bookstacks are the important first contact with library materials.

A popular design alternative in recent years has been the resource center library with bookstacks and readers' seating grouped in subject areas. The Newport (Rhode Island) Library is an example of this design. At its best, such a design in a small library creates a central staffing information location surrounded by bookstack and seating areas on science, literature, history, art. Some subject juxtapositions in the Dewey Decimal classification system are awkward in this arrangement (such as the integration of art and sports, both in the same general 700 number). The point made above concerning the extra cost of combining seating and books in the same structural system is also a constraint.

Major Subdivisions

The classified adult nonfiction collection should be kept in one single sequential location for ease of access and for public convenience. This section will contain the largest number of books and is the most difficult to find your way around in, so it should be arranged as simply as possible—preferably on one level.

Fiction and biography are often split off from the rest of the book collection since they are lettered rather than numbered in some libraries. In the case of biography, some confusion can result since many biographies are placed in the numbered Dewey subject categories so that others with letter would be far away from those in the numbered subject categories. Biographies arranged alphabetically by subject can most easily be separated.

Oversize materials ideally should be shelved in the same numerical sequence as other books. However, this requires a great many more bookstacks than does segregating oversize books, because in each 3-foot section a shelf will have to be removed to accommodate them. Therefore, the most cost effective solution is to shelve oversize books at the end of each aisle. The problem is to indicate to the public by careful signs in each section and at the end of each aisle just where oversize books are located.

Every library likes to feature *display books*—recent materials are most often segregated from the regular numerical bookstacks, but topical displays are also featured. How can we indicate to people using the card catalog that the book they are searching for may be in the library but not in its proper numerical location? A sign above the catalog or a small locational brochure may accomplish this or grouping these topical and recent displays so that they are apparent to everyone entering the library may be helpful. In some libraries, transparent plastic covers are placed over each catalog card to indicate alternative locations and it may even be possible to purchase duplicate materials to assure that at least one copy is in its correct shelf location.

Paperbacks uniquely available in paper are often catalogued and shelved with hardcover books. Duplicate paperbacks of popular subjects can be handled most cost effectively by minimum processing—merely protecting them against theft, identifying them as library property with a large label, and placing them on special shelving featuring the colorful front covers, but permitting spine titles to be read underneath the front book. Many libraries have found that a substantial quantity of paperbacks must be available to attract browsers before any quantity circulation is possible. A single dilapidated wire rack with a few dog-eared titles will not attract any users at all. Cost savings in paperbacks are not only in the low initial cost of the books but also in the low processing cost and in low ordering cost if a procedure for direct selection, delivery, and handling can be set up with a local jobber. A large area with separate subject signs and good lighting, incorporating angled display shelving revealing front covers and spines, will result in cost-effective high volume circulation. Librarians concerned about theft of paperbacks have often been surprised to find that users not only return library paperbacks but also donate to the library paperbacks they have purchased.

Children's bookstacks should be in a different location and shelved on lower shelves. Oversized and thin picture books, which would be lost in conventional shelving, should be placed in bookbins.

Graphics in stack areas should include end panel signs indicating subject or alphabetical sequence of material at the end of the stack and shelf labels for each section.

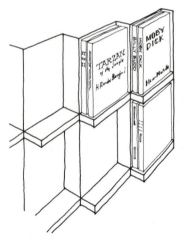

Paperback book rack permitting view of spine *and* front cover.

Protecting and Preserving Books

Paper deteriorates because it is acidic. In the presence of atmospheric moisture, the alum-rosin sizing in the paper generates sulfuric acid, which destroys the paper in conditions of high temperature and high humidity. In addition, unpurified wood fibers (groundwood) in papers such as newsprint are weaker than chemically purified wood pulps and contain lignins that may form acids. Other enemies of book papers are ultraviolet radiation in sunlight and flourescent light and microorganisms such as mold and bacteria that grow under conditions of high temperature and humidity.

Research libraries try to maintain temperatures of 55°. Such a low temperature is helpful both in preserving books and in conserving energy. This is also an argument for separating book and reader spaces in libraries, since the book spaces should be at considerably lower temperatures than will be comfortable for most readers. The relative humidity for books should be 40 to 50 percent. Changes greater than 10° or 15 percent humidity can also deteriorate paper. The growth of mold is prevented by keeping the temperature lower than 75° and the humidity lower than 70 percent and by keeping air moving through the books. For further information, see Preservation Leaflet no. 2, *Environmental Protection of Books and Related Material*, available free from the Assistant Director for Preservation, Administrative Department, Library of Congress, Washington, D.C. 20540.

Types and Sizes of Bookstacks

Structurally, a building must carry 150 pounds of live load per square foot to support the weight of 90-inch high bookstacks. This is much stronger than the requirement for an above-grade automobile parking garage, while school classrooms require about 75 pounds per square foot structural capacity. Six shelves instead of seven reduces capacity by 15 percent.

Bookstacks come in a variety of configurations:

Open base.
Closed base.
Wooden.
"T" base.

Some standard heights are: 42", 66", 90". Welded frame uprights are slightly more expensive than bolted uprights but do not require cross bracing. A good system is to alternate welded and bolted uprights. Top bracing is the only sure way to complete rigidity. Stack ranges are joined by box girders that can also be designed to support lighting or carry electrical wiring. Securing uprights to the floor with serrated-edged nails powered by a Hilti-system gun can be effective depending on the floor material.

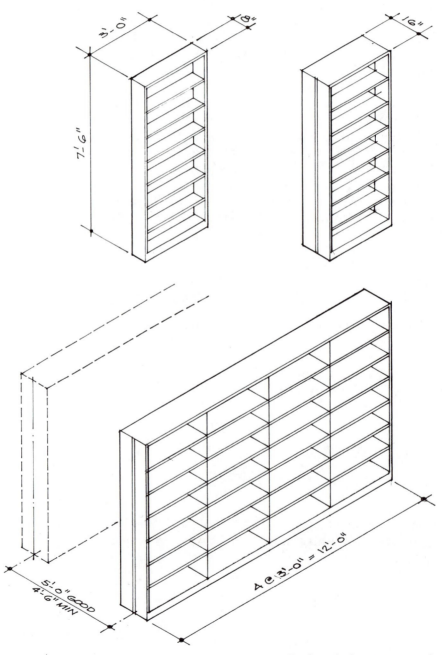

Bookstack dimensions and spacing.

BASIC FORMULA: For average volumes—7 books/linear foot.

90″ High × 36″ Wide Section
Single-faced - 7 Shelves=150 Books
Double-faced - 14 Shelves=300 Books

66″ High × 36″ Wide Section
Single-faced - 5 Shelves=100 Books
Double-faced - 10 Shelves=200 Books

42″ High × 36″ Wide Section
Single-faced - 3 Shelves=50 Books*
Double-faced - 6 Shelves=100 Books*

*Reference books, larger than average, are usually shelved on 42″ high units to permit use of top for consulting books.

NOTE: 46″ high units may be used with one additional shelf to accommodate fiction or children's books. Capacity in this case as follows:
Single-faced - 4 Shelves=85 Books
Double-faced - 8 Shelves=170 Books

Heights and book capacity of library shelving.

Bookstack lighting for the bottom shelf.

Bookstack Lighting

Lighting can be installed as part of the stack system using inverted "U" brackets to lift the fluorescent fixtures above the stack for good light on the top shelf. This installation can be moved easily as part of the stack system. However, care should be taken to obtain a stack light design that angles light down to the bottom shelf while protecting the library user from oppressive direct light on top of the head.

The use of angled parawedge louvers will both direct light and prevent glare. Lighting hung from the ceiling in bookstack areas can be sufficient, but it will lack the drama of a lighting system specifically designed to light the books and not the stack aisles. This system will enhance that all important first contact between the reader and the book. A recently introduced lighting fixture manufactured by the Lightolier Company offers fluorescent lamps mounted in a bat-wing reflector housing that spreads light out to the sides of the fixture. The light distribution properties of this fixture are such that it will distribute relatively glare free light uniformly onto the books. The louver for this fixture is a 2-inch metal parawedge.

None of these lighting systems will deliver as much light to the lower shelves as to the higher shelves. This is a continuing problem with bookstack lighting. Only a system that mounted fluorescent lamps vertically parallel to each stack section could accomplish this, and such a system would have to project into the aisle in order to cast light onto the books in the middle.

Compact Storage

As building costs increase, the interest in compact storage of books has attracted a wide range of manufac-

A less expensive stack light suspended above counter height reference.

turers. The Wilson Company in New England has recently introduced a manually operated compact movable stack with a hand crank. In this configuration, one wall of a room is equipped with continuous shelving that stores the most used materials in the front of the stacks. If a user is searching for a lesser used book, a nine-foot long section is cranked out of the stack and the book is retrieved.

Bookstacks are useful for a quick conference.

Another use of this type of shelving would be to open out all the compact nine-foot sections during normal operations, but in the evening or when the area was needed for a community program, the compact sections could be cranked in, revealing 50 percent more floor program space. In this case, the unit is not mounted on floor tracks, so that when it is cranked in, there are no unsightly floor obstacles.

Mobile stacks mounted on wheels can also be used to create more floor space when it is needed. Both these products cost about 50 percent more than conventional shelving.

Larger and more elaborate compact shelving systems are offered by a number of domestic and foreign companies. This includes stacks with motor-operation and even more sophisticated automatic retrieval systems, such as the Randtriever offered by Library Bureau with a capability of tripling area storage capacities by building very high stacks with minimal aisle width, and storing books and other materials in plastic boxes retrievable by a punched card or keyboard actuated device. Of course, these complex systems are expensive and require careful maintenance in addition to being costly to install. However, they can dramatically reduce building size requirements and are somewhat conserving of energy, since book areas would not be heated for human use but kept at 50–60° temperatures with humidity control only for book preservation. There has been at least one fatality in a motorized compact stack installation, so safety features are important.

Frazier Poole at the Library of Congress is in charge of a project to develop an optimum compact stack storage system, and O'Brien and Justin, architects in New York City, worked with Harold Roth to develop a design for the largest automated storage and retrieval system in the world. This system would have saved 90,000 square feet of floor space in a large reference library installation on Long Island, but the project was dropped for local financial reasons.

These compact storage systems require very strong structural systems and can seldom be accommodated above grade in existing buildings. With the gradual building of library networks, it is doubtful that such systems will be needed by any but the largest reference libraries. The lack of browsing capabilities of such installations make their use of limited value.

Ideally, a library would consist of a series of individual cubicles in which the users would sit in controlled environments and with an interactive communication system call in any kind of media needed, whether book, film, magazine, or specific information item. There are pilots for such complex systems—St. Cloud Community College in Minnesota and Trumbull High School in Connecticut are two. In addition to the initial expense, the maintenance costs are great.

Integrated Shelving

In school media centers an attempt is often made to intershelve media and books. In addition to the wide variation in size, the difficulty of browsing in media without a suitable machine and the problems of material and equipment maintenance should be carefully considered before adopting such a system. (Card catalogs including all media under a particular subject heading and with clear locator information are perhaps a more practical solution.)

In an integrated system, *equipment areas* can be located throughout the library with self-service machines and instructions on how to use them. But this often proves frustrating to the user because machines are broken and inoperable, and the staff may not be aware of the breakdown.

Dial access systems have had an interesting vogue in many libraries. These systems permit a user to sit at a library carrel desk and dial up a wide variety of audio, film, slide, video, filmstrip, and programmed material. Naturally, the technology for this is expensive, complicated, and requires dedicated maintenance staff. At its best, dial access employs sophisticated optical film chains that enable a user to dial into the beginning of a program already in use by one or more additional users. The educational advantages of such a system include incredibly flexible scheduling for students and a learning sequence individually geared to each student's capabilities. In many cases, these systems have been expensive failures because of a failure to understand the maintenance and program support requirements. Cost of equipment and maintenance must be placed in proper perspective against the cost of acquiring software. If $100,000 is spent for hardware, the annual maintenance and software budget should approach this figure to support an adequate program.

Physical planning requirements for dial access include carefully planned wiring throughout the building and a centralized control room with many electrical circuits, wiring panels, spare machines, and a well-equipped electronics repair shop.

A central *dial-access media machine* and distributed stations are a good alternative, at least theoretically. The user sits at a carrel with headphone and screen and a telephone dial and dials up a program from a technically complex central station. Systems have been designed to deliver dozens of different audio and video/film programs to dozens of stations at the same time. The disadvantage is the technical complexity of maintenance, but the advantage is that this complexity is centralized and not subject to user abuse.

Centralized Media

Centralized equipment near staff areas can be controlled and maintained more easily, but it is less convenient to the user of integrated shelving. Hennepin County (Minnesota) Regional Library currently operates a centralized media program with the future option of distributed user stations. A staff area for media includes production facilities for video, slides, audio with a public access workshop, and viewing stations for film, slides, video, and audio. The concept here is for the staff to handle machines and materials.

Video tapes and discs communicate through several senses and can quickly give an understanding of a community problem or a sense of involvement in an experience.

Media Counter

A variation is a centralized area with a large counter and with many machines near a staff area for easy assistance, but with the users permitted to operate the machines. The advantages are the delight in learning to do something new and the reduction in staff time involved; the disadvantage is the potential user's frustration when machines are broken. This may be minimized by careful selection and specification of machines and frequent change for preventive maintenance. It is unwise to wait for a machine to break before replacing it. A rigorous maintenance and replacement schedule should be established. Counters will have to be designed for easy machine changing by placing a hinged, lockable panel on the front of a slide-in slot, so that players can be merely unlocked, slid out, and replaced in minutes. A minimum of automatic devices and controls and a maximum of engraved instructions to operate the machine will result in the least frustration for users. Picture instructions are much easier to follow than written instructions.

As people use libraries more frequently, they learn to use machines more easily. Many teenagers can handle microfilm readers and projectors better than adults. However, the variety of services required of staff members and the need for good maintenance will require that machines be located right at a staff-controlled service area. Here users and staff can work together rapidly and effectively, with all the equipment centralized for convenient access and maintenance. Spare machines are also available for rapid replacement and a nearby repair facility can quickly repair damage.

Video discs offer the potential of media experiences in one format that combines the use of several senses. Discs can store thousands of book pages, a half-hour of film, audio or still pictures on a single compact disc 10-inches in diameter and ⅛-inch thick. Any TV set can be adapted for playback. Low production costs may revolutionize library shelving requirements. Predictions are for a 5–20 year development time.

Films give people an incredible variety of experiences—dance, music, painting, filmic motion, art; lifestyle experiences of differing cultures, experiences of history and tradition, travel experiences. Audiotapes and records are incomparably better than books to experience music, language, dialogue, and drama.

Rear view screens, the use of headsets to control sound, and the installation of counters with electrical outlets can turn existing libraries quickly and inexpensively into multimedia centers.

Production of media by citizens through library lending of equipment and library availability of products can bring an entire new dimension of communication and experience to bear on the solution of community problems.

The planning for media use in libraries is neither complicated nor expensive. Here are some considerations in media planning:

1. Electrical outlets at convenient intervals, or the capability to add outlets by ceiling poles or floor conduits.
2. A maintenance and replacement plan including local repairs, regional repairs, and a regular maintenance schedule. Easy replacement of machines and components.
3. Staff training in operation and simple repair of machines.
4. Back-up units ready for replacing operational units.
5. Sound control by acoustical materials and headsets.
6. Centralized staff-controlled location of all machines.
7. Controlled task lighting so that small areas in the library can be partially darkened or so that direct lighting does not strike a screen.

A number of separate electrical circuits and individual circuit breakers should be available at the information-media center. At least two should be sized for a 30 ampere machine. Electrical circuit breaker panels should be carefully marked and easily available to the staff. Underfloor conduits and separate electrical and telephone conduits must be placed so as to assure future flexibility. A nine-foot electrical floor receptacle grid or more expensive raceways can provide future access at any point should be considered.

Low-voltage wiring, such as is used for speakers, requires inexpensive conduits, and, in some lightly trafficked areas, can run without any conduit protection at all. Hollow floors under information-media centers can be employed to change wiring patterns, especially if they are connected to the outside of the building by large crawl spaces that can be used for ducts for outside wiring of cable TV systems.

Ceilings with revealed spline T-bar construction can be easily lifted out to provide wiring access and lighting flexibility. Ceiling mounted electrical pole systems can provide convenient electrical receptacles wherever needed.

In a medium-sized library designed as a combined information-media center, a counter with built-in electrical receptacles and knee-holes on both sides will provide for a number of machines. The counter should be no more than 28-inches high, slightly lower than most desks.

Lighting controls are important so that overhead light will not white-out a screen in this location. Ideally, each work station will have separate lighting that can be directed to an individual spot, so that a film can be watched and notes taken simultaneously.

Telephone

A centrex telephone system should be installed to provide the capability for the public to dial directly into the library function they need, rather than having to go through a switchboard.

Media Machines

Learning machines do not require any more than the above provisions. *16 mm film projectors* with rear-screen projection and a short throw lens can be mounted on a movie-mover or built into one of the counter stations. Rear screen projection has the advantage of being able to be used in a lighted room. *Audio-cassettes* with headphones can be used anywhere, and the cassettes can be housed in card catalog drawers at the information center or in locked glass display cabinets nearby. In some cases, if the copying rights are owned by the library, copying for the public on a high-speed machine can be a simple procedure right at the information center. *Video players* can also be located here with cassettes or videodiscs in cabinets nearby. Machines do require maintenance; operating a damaged machine can destroy materials and lead to great user frustration, so this centralized system is suited to the present state of machine durability and public machine competence.

Media Production

The production of media requires a somewhat more elaborate installation—darkrooms, large circulating water tanks, equipment and material storage, and technical assistance are needed, so these programs should be carefully analyzed and priorities examined before space is allotted and designed. Production facilities can be installed in the future as long as basic hot and cold water and drain facilities are available in an appropriate location.

Community video facilities are perhaps the simplest media production program. A video portapac is simpler to operate and learn to use than an instant camera. Editing is easily accomplished by a tape recorder that fits any electrical receptacle. Community video, as pioneered by Edward de Sciora and his staff at the Port Washington, New York public library, provides a unique individualized system of communication for a community, and brings medium-sized communities into a communications environment that permits rapid dissemination of information on the nature of community issues and organizations. Dozens of organizations in that community were trained to use video equipment in meetings and in the course of their activities.

Instant feedback capabilities of video portapacs make them extremely easy to learn to use. People enjoy their immediacy and their capability to convey nuances of meaning in expressions and oral interchange. Many basic community issues began to involve library activities as a result of this training, and the library soon became the center of community life in an entirely new, active, and direct way. Since the library budget goes directly to the voters for approval each year, the popularity of this experiment was measured directly in increased library revenues.

An Example of Media Planning

The Southdale Regional Library of the Hennepin County Library System in Minnesota is a fine example of modern media planning. Media services include:

1. Media lab for loaning and processing material produced by the general public, including children. Don Roberts, formerly the media coordinator at Hennepin County, is dedicated to using a wide variety of media for public production of slides, photographs, and video.
2. An indoor and outdoor theater. In addition to an indoor auditorium, the entire open area underneath

the building is wired for lighting and sound so that dramatic performances, concerts, and music can be played outdoors in good weather.

3. A V-shaped media center with a variety of rear-view projection facilities so that 8 and 16 mm films, slides filmstrips, and video can be seen individually projected on many separate screens. In this installation, the machines are bolted on the inside of the rear-view projection screens and the public is not permitted to operate the machines.

4. Six channel wireless broadcast loops permit library patrons to listen with headset radio receivers to programs selected by staff and users.

Don Roberts' concept is that media production services can change libraries and communities and that the library staff can act as consultants to facilitate this change with library users of all ages. He believes in active staff and public participation, and in building flexibility accomplished by wiring the entire building with large conduits for future access to a variety of media. Video will probably be most important because of flexibility. Some specific guidelines for audio-visual materials include:

Phonorecords

Housing and circulating - These should be readily available to the public in bins that make it easy to browse through the colorful front record jackets which should be protected with heavy plastic see-through covers of a non-glare material. Ideally they should be individually inspected upon return to determine if there are any visible scratches. Scratched records should be discarded from the collection to assure a good listening experience. Several cleaning devices are on the market, but most require careful staff training and handling to prevent record damage. Nevertheless, the records should be washed at least once a year to provide good performance. Borrowers should be cautioned not to leave records in a hot place to prevent warping damage. Each record jacket must be inspected to be certain the correct record is inside when it is returned. Record jackets, unlike cassettes can be protected by applying theft detection strips so that they cannot be easily stolen.

A color-coded tape system of identifying broad categories of records can be useful in browsing and reshelving.

Phonorecord players in a library are difficult to maintain because the needles and tone arms are light and delicately balanced to assure light tracking pressure and avoid record damage. It is useful to provide for rapid dismantling of the player so it can be sent out for repair and replaced easily and quickly when damaged. Spare players should be on hand for this purpose. Cartridges or needles should be dated when installed and replaced every six months. An automatic push-button operated player is one approach to avoiding damage; however, most phonoplayer users will want to pick up the tone arm and move it to another band on the record often causing damage to record or tone-arm. Recently introduced cueing levers dampened to result in gentle needle lowering will alleviate this problem if the user is patient enough to use the cueing lever, but many are not.

Phonoplayers may be kept at a staff location and users may then request a particular record which can then be heard at a remote location with headphone plugged into a wall wiring system or wireless headphone used with a broadcast loop. The disadvantage is that users cannot control what they want to hear as precisely as when they operate the player, and staff must be paid to operate the machines. This kind of installation is typically found in big city libraries such as New York or Boston. The broadcast loop has a further disadvantage in that only one program can be played on most simple systems.

An advanced design has recently been introduced which makes it less likely for a tonearm to damage a record. Although expensive, this seemed like a useful solution for New Canaan, Ct. A routine should be set up each morning for a staff member to play a record and briefly listen to all equipment including headphones. Equipment that is inoperable should be unplugged and replaced immediately with spare equipment kept on hand for that purpose.

Audio-Cassettes

are a marvelous almost indestructible form of sound reproduction. The cassettes are enclosed thus less susceptible to damage than a phonorecord. By removing a small plastic tab they cannot be erased. Their disadvantages are that they can be easily concealed and stolen from the library, and they must be run through the machine sequentially. Library storage can be at a service desk in drawers with a typed catalog for public reference or a card catalog. They can be housed in large plastic locked displayers near a service desk with a staff member unlocking the case when the patron has made a selection. They cannot be protected with the usual library theft detection equipment because they are not large enough to accommodate the detection strip and they may be damage by running them through a theft detection desensitizer.

In-library use can most easily be provided by constructing a 2 × 2 foot front-loading formica cube with the player mounted in the cube in a locking-slide device intended for automobile use. An automobile cassette player/amplifier with a small conversion transformer to go from the 12 volt player to the 120 volt AC line can easily drive 2 headsets and can be easily and cheaply replaced when damaged. The playing heads should be cleaned at least once a month, with a cleaning tape sprayed with fluid.

Cassette reproduction with a high-speed copier can be used for voice tapes as long as the library has purchased reproduction rights, but music is more difficult to reproduce requiring a better copier, and reproduction rights are harder to obtain. Many users can play cassettes in their cars and will use learning cassettes available from the library for this purpose.

Art Reproductions

These can be in two general categories. Original prints in which the artist participated in the work required for the reproduction. These cost more initially but tend to appreciate in value and will give the viewer a more honest participatory experience of what the artist had in mind. Other reproductions not involving the artist directly are less expensive, but do not appreciate in value and it is often difficult to judge the accuracy and quality of this kind of reproduction unless you can experience the original simultaneously.

Both kinds of reproductions should be displayed at the library on a wall without vertical or horizontal mullions and with lighting designed to provide accurate color experience, natural sunlight if possible. If artificial light is used consider VERILUX Fluorescent or incandescent, but avoid cool white fluorescent. Each reproduction should be housed in a canvas bag of the correct size printed with the library's logo when it is checkout out. Each reproduction must be examined when it is returned. If there is not enough space to display all the reproductions, then bins can be provided under the display wall, with heavy foam board ¼" thick dividers between each print. Mar Line/Gaylord has them.

The Chicago Art Institute has an elaborate method of judging, handling and selling the work of local artists to provide a constantly changing collection. They appoint a different judging panel of experts each year who accept a limited number of works for loan. Each picture is rented with the rent counting towards eventual purchase. A volunteer committee organizes the annual judging process. This system introduces original art to a broad range of community users and stimulates art work in the entire area.

Children's media

The children's room should afford a variety of spaces and experiences - quiet study areas neatly organized, game playing areas with a wide range of realia - large sturdy educational toys, comfortable floor cushions, and there should be an area near or at the children's desk for the use of audio-visual media.

The Dukane A-V Matic cassette automatic sound filmstrip projector with its large rear screen format is a sturdy, handsome, colorful device for children to experience a variety of cassette/filmstrip programs.

The AVS-10 is a marvelous device for programmed learning with cassettes on reading, mathematics, and story-telling that permit children to operate in an interactive programmed mode with pictures and sound synchronized to the individuals own learning speed.

Sound-slide projectors such as the Singer Caramate can be used with materials made by the staff and the children.

7 The Adult User: Browsing, Studying, Finding and Using Information

We have previously described the physical aspects of library design. The purpose of it all is to make it convenient and pleasant for the user to use the library in all its programs, services, and resources. The independent self-service concept of libraries is a tremendous asset in comparison with the restrictive structure of most other educational institutions. The library environment should encourage an easy-going pattern of access and use. In general, people will respond to planning that attempts to provide alternating quiet and busy areas, with efforts at unobtrusive sound separation between these areas. Recent books on psychological attitudes toward architecture provide useful planning suggestions.

Quiet areas can include widely spaced individual seating with sound absorbing materials in walls, floors, and ceilings; low lamps with shades sized so that light bulbs are not visible; subdued, neutral colors such as grays and browns. Bookstack areas can separate these quiet areas from the noisier environments, but care will have to be taken to keep books grouped in easily definable subject areas, with lighted graphics clearly delineating subject markings.

"Noisy" areas will encourage communication by providing group seating and media that is audibly and visually noisy—magazines, tapes, film, players, and video. Provision of food dispensing machines; high, gen-

eral, illumination; bright colors; hard-edged surfaces and floors; and angular furnishings can contribute to this setting.

Individual user stations can be carrels with low sides or small rooms with individual lighting and ventilation. These should be provided in or near the quiet areas.

Group use areas or rooms should be provided in or near the noisy areas with blackboards, bulletin boards, speaker systems, projection facilities, and media production facilities such as video portapacs and player units.

This alternating of environments between quiet and noisy areas should be accomplished on a relatively small scale with a number of alternating areas in larger libraries.

Control of these areas can be a problem, especially as equipment becomes more sophisticated. There are several possible control approaches:

1. A centralized staff station and an open floor plan with a concentration on low-sided furnishings grouped around the staff station. If stacks are arranged for visibility down the aisles, grouped closely, and brightly lit with nonglare fixtures, the alternating user areas can be isolated and still be supervised from the central location.
2. Closed-circuit television and a guard surveillance system such as that at the Dearborn (Michigan) Library.
3. Multilevel design can separate noise, but can separate functions also, requiring excessive staffing and a building that is often difficult for the user to understand.

Ekornes "stressless" chair with shoulder and back support.

4. Centralized remote-controlled media, such as that used at the Lincoln Center Library in New York City or the Boston Public Library, or an optical film chain operation, can provide wide media flexibility of operation to remote stations distributed throughout the building.

The Browsing Function

A large percentage of library users enter the building to *become* interested in something; they do not have a particular question or book in mind. Others enter for a specific book but may become interested in a different book or another service if it is offered. The browsing area, therefore, should have the ambience of a bookstore or a living room. Books should be displayed with the covers showing, on wide tables carefully lit with incandescent lights. Above these tables should be shelves angled to display colorful paperbacks and hardcover books of current interest; nearby should be record browsing bins and some children's books. A small slide theater with a rear-view projection screen can show continuous slides of recent film and video acquisitions, or stills of library or town art exhibits. Recently returned books can be gathered on book trucks in book truck corrals and the trucks grouped together in this area for easy browsing and a saving in reshelving labor. Besides, books that other people have been reading have allure.

Current magazines displayed with the covers showing, can be in this area; behind the hinged, angled shelving, older issues of the current year can be stored. Magazines can be powerful design features, with their colorful covers and their exciting variety of subjects. They should be brightly lit and visible as an important design element. Functionally, a problem exists in relating current and older reference magazines; proximity of magazine browsing and micro reference areas or graphics relating one function to the other may solve this problem. Newspapers should also be in this area.

Seating here should be comfortable lounge chairs, such as the Charles Eames design lounger. Since the library is a community building used by all the people in town, it should have the best quality seating—comfortable and durable with support for the back and shoulders and comfortable ottomans to rest the legs. As our popu-

lation gets older, it will be even more important to
provide this comfortable seating, but it will be equally
important to find seating that is easy to get up from. This
is difficult in the current furniture market, since most
comfortable lounge chairs are low and hard to get out of.

Reader Seating

Adequate space for each seated reader requires 30
square feet. Total seating should be related to population
and library use, with flexibility among types. Joseph
Wheeler, the dean of public library building consultants,
used a formula of five seats per 1,000 population in towns
of 10,000 or more. International library standards are
less. Libraries and communities will differ in seating
requirements. A method for determining seating requirements in existing libraries is to record times when
all seats or a good percentage are occupied and determine, which kinds of seating are occupied first and how
many users are turned away. Most libraries that provide
a wide range of seating choices find that individual chairs
are always preferred to couches, so few new libraries
provide much group seating. On the other hand, comfortable lounge seating is immensely popular.

Children/adult seating distribution should be a
result of use study in the children's room, an analysis of
future children's population changes in the community,
and the provision of a variety of use formats so children
can choose seating they like. Children's seating will probably not exceed 25 percent of the total.

Adult seating may be distributed among the following areas of choice:

Lounge seating	5%
Individual rooms	Up to 5%
Individual carrels	Up to 75% (including infor- mation center seating)
Group rooms accommo- dating 5 or 10 people	Up to 5%
Group seating at tables for four	No more than 10%

The reason for presenting the percentages in this
fashion is that group seating is the least costly kind so
that there will be a natural tendency to provide more of
this kind of seating than library users really want.

For a library serving 50,000 people, seating break-down might be as follows:

Adult seating
Individual rooms	8
Lounge seating individual	14
Individual carrels	132
Group rooms: 2 seating 8 each	16
Group tables: 5 seating 4 at each	20
Children's seating	60
Total	250

Individual Study

A small percentage of people come to libraries to spend some period of time working intensively on a project, for instance, an author working on a book. Occasionally they use materials from the library or materials from another library through the interloan system, but in many cases they spend their time writing or typing. A few libraries provide individual study carrels completely enclosed to create small offices or studies. Perhaps the most dramatic example of such a library is the Goddard Memorial Library at Clark University in Worcester, Massachusetts, where the study area is broken up into many small spaces of varying size, some with individual lighting and ventilating systems.

Ideally, the elements of a study space would be: lighting adjustable by rheostat; temperature controlled by individual thermostat; chair with upholstered seat and back and adjustable lumbar support, seat height, and back angle; a nonreflective, writing surface, warm to the touch, with a neutral beige color, approximately 18-inches deep and 36 inches wide and adjustable in height from 26–30 inches, with the capability of raising or lowering a portion of it for typewriter use. In addition to the general adjustable illumination, there should be a warm-white 20 watt fluorescent light mounted on the left or right wall about 18 inches above the writing surface and shielded with parabolic wedge egg-crate ¾-inch louvers and/or a diffuser. Adjustable shelves would be placed above the writing surface, 12-inches deep and 36-inches long with book support brackets on each side.

Obviously, this is an expensive user service that

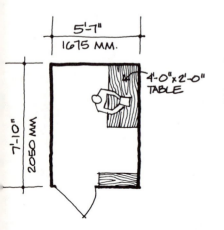

5'-7"
1675 MM.

7'-10"
2050 MM

4'-0"x2'-0"
TABLE

Dimensions for a single-person carrel.

might require a number of small rooms 3-feet wide by 6-feet long with sliding door. Some public libraries provide six such rooms. The "forest-of-legs" appearance of so many reading rooms may be avoided by breaking up study areas with office landscape panels.

Lighting for carrels presents some interesting

HIGH CARREL
IS DIFFICULT TO SUPERVISE
INTERRUPTS STANDING EYE LEVEL
CREATES VISUAL CLUTTER

54" 1360 MM

LOW CARREL
IS EASIER TO SUPERVISE
MAINTAINS SENSE OF OPENNESS AT EYE LEVEL
PROVIDES ADEQUATE PRIVACY AT WORK SURFACE

40" 1000 MM

NOTE: PRIVACY REQUIRES SIDE PANELS TO EDGE OF DESK

Proper height for study carrels.

problems that have been carefully studied by Frank F. LaGiusa and John F. McNelis in the November 1971 issue of *Lighting Design and Appliaction*. Their conclusions were that:

The side walls of carrels reduce the amount of general lighting falling on the work surface.
Supplemental lighting is necessary to restore lost light and reduce shadows.
Supplemental lighting mounted to the side of instead of in front of the user substantially reduces veiling reflections.
Large light sources yield better distribution and reduced shadows.
Adequate shielding of light sources is necessary for visual comfort.

Light finishes greatly improve luminance ratios between
task and surround.
Matte finishes reduce specular reflections.

These conclusions would yield a carrel design with
light writing surfaces and a fluorescent lamp mounted on
the left/right of the carrel and shielded with parawedge
louvers.

Proper carrel lighting to reduce glare.

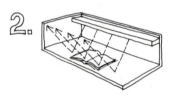

1. Uncontrolled light radiates from a
fluorescent tube.

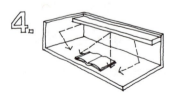

2. When this uncontrolled light
reaches the reading surface, it
reflects up and into the reader's
eyes, producing glare.

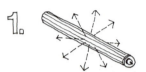

3. A prismatic lens controls the light
radiating from the fluorescent
tube by directing it to either side
of the carrel.

Light is directed back
to reading surface
from side of carrel.

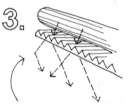

4. When the reading surface is
illuminated from either side, glare
is eliminated.

In many older libraries, the reading room was a huge ceilinged area with masses of heavy oak tables and chairs arranged in symmetrical rows. In modern libraries, architects and planners are beginning to realize that library users have a wide variety of wants and study styles. Probably the majority of users would like to study in small-scale quiet areas, some designed for individual use, and some in carrel areas with defined study areas and a degree of light control. However, some studying and learning is done as a group process with the opportunity for casual conversation or the need for continuous group discussion. Some of this group study should be accommodated in rooms seating 5–10 people and equipped with a long table, upholstered chairs, and a combination blackboard/tackboard. These rooms should also have a white wall for projection and electrical receptacle for projection machines. The remaining group seating will be conventional tables and chairs—round and rectangular tables with durable nonreflecting smooth surfaces and upholstered, ergonomically designed chairs that glide on carpet. In most cases, there should be an effort to provide user controllable task lighting for each work area, with general lighting at a minimal supplemental level.

THE ADULT USER

Minimum size of alcove with six-person reading table.

In selecting library chairs, several characteristics should be considered:

1. *Durability:* Thousands of people will be using the chairs; therefore, it is important to select fabric material and structure that will last a long time. High grades of vinyl, such as number 13 grade, will often last indefinitely, if not abused. Metal frame chairs will also tend to last a long time in the library situation without deteriorating. Wood frame chairs should be carefully examined for their construction before a decision is made as to their durability. Mil-nylo and other breathable artificial fabrics are also durable and more comfortable than vinyl because they allow better air circulation.

2. *Comfort:* People spend a great deal of time in library chairs. Therefore, they should be extremely comfortable and conform to the human body. Ergonomic design is a design concept emphasizing the rounded, shaped contours of the human body rather than the hard-edged architectural shapes of many "designer" furniture styles. Several manufacturers now make ergonomically designed chairs. Both Herman Miller and Harter are examples. These chairs not only conform to the curve of the back but also tend to provide side-to-side support for the lower back.

Comparison of lounge chairs.

William Stumpf, the designer, sitting in his ergonomic chair manufactured by Herman Miller. This completely adjustable chair is designed to fit the human body.

The Charles Eames design chair with ottoman by Herman Miller offers good support for lower back and shoulders and is curved to fit people.

3. *Costs:* It is, of course, very important to get good value for your money. In a library situation this usually means buying an extremely costly chair. Libraries that have purchased cheap copies of good designs have found that they pay more in repairs than the expensive chair would have cost. Library chairs will tend to last 30 to 40 years in regular use; it is very difficult to get an inexpensive chair that will hold up and still be handsome over that span of time. The lounge chair designed by Charles Eames many years ago is now selling for approximately $900 and is an example of the kind of quality furniture that will last for over 20 years without reupholstering. This chair comes upholstered in leather, a breathable fabric. Vinyl, on the other hand, will not permit air circulation and can deteriorate in the upper part of the chair

Swivel-base version of Ekornes chair.

where oil from human hair may react with the vinyl and harden it, causing cracks. Woven nylon fabric covered chairs also tend to be more breathable than vinyl and more comfortable to sit in.

Modular repair is a useful concept. A chair such as the Norwegian Stressless lounger manufactured by the J. B. Ekornes Co. has upholstery that can be quickly unbuttoned and replaced at a fraction of the usual re-upholstery cost.

In order to move chairs easily on carpeting, they should be light and have some sort of runner on the bottom so they can slide on the carpet without having to be picked up. There are several designs of such a chair. The Marcel Breuer "Cesca" design for a side chair is one example. This bent chrome chair will last a long time, is very comfortable to sit in, and comes in a wide variety of fabrics. Although this chair costs over $100, it is a wise investment for long-term library use. The J. B. Ekornes Company of Norway manufactures the Global reclining stressless chair and footstool constructed of tubular steel with a leather upholstered curved foam back. This is an extremely comfortable chair that can be easily adjusted to fit any size person and is relatively easy to get into and out of. It is also completely modular, so that broken parts can be easily replaced. A chair designed by Marc Held has no mechanism, yet it tilts and swivels and rocks. It is a high quality chair designed to last for a long time.

Groton, CT., Library designed by Arnold Gustafson of Lyons, Mather and Lechner.

The most vital function in a library is the information center, where library users and librarians work together on a variety of things: asking and answering questions, using reference books and card files; using computers to tap into remote data banks; recommending good books to read; consulting on independent learning projects; and referring users to a range of community services. The design objective for the information reference area is to link users and librarians in a busy location with convenient access to all resources available.

In libraries that are too small to afford specialist staffing of separate subject resource centers at all times when the library is open, a single information center staffing location promotes user convenience and staffing economy. This information center can have up to 100 running feet of counter space and a wide range of services. In the smallest libraries (populations of 10,000 or less), it will probably combine all public services. In such a small library the counter would include:

1. *Check-in and check-out area:* 39-inch high standing-height counter with 30-inch high work surface on the staff side and provision for electrical charging machines or computer terminal (a double 15 amp.

THE ADULT USER

Everything happens at the information center.

circuit with breaker nearby) and a telephone line for computer connection. Borrower and book card files may still be necessary with older circulation control systems. Behind the counter should be a place for three or four book trucks to hold recently returned materials, as well as storage on adjustable shelves for media equipment to be borrowed from the library— 16 mm films, projectors, microfiche readers, cameras, video portapacs.

2. *Reference and referral counter:* 30-inch high with seating on both sides and storage for 50 ready reference books for answering telephone questions (about 35 percent of information queries are handled by phone), a telephone below the counter, and other media—microfiche and film reader printer, and fiche and film storage with indexes nearby. There should be a computer terminal for computer information services, a computer for interlibrary loan; and a public access computer terminal for catalog and interloan information on a swivel base so that it can be used by patron and/or librarian. There should be provision for two rear-view projection screens or movie-movers and a variety of equipment that can be used with them, and some video cassettes, 16 mm film, filmstrip, slides, with headphone storage for four headphones for listening to media.

3. *Children's counter:* a wide variety of media that can be used at four stations on a 28-inch high counter. In addition, provision for operating a 16 mm projector that can be projected into a glassed-in area supervisable but with sound separated from the information center.

In this small information center library, the area behind this counter provides staff offices where some privacy can be obtained while assuring staff control of public functions. Around the perimeter of the information center are a variety of user spaces:

Children's story hour and group activity: an open carpeted area sound separated from other areas with an activity counter and many cushions on the floor.

Children's book and study area: with carrels and tables and 42-inch high reference shelving and 72-inch high bookstacks.

Adult reading area: carrels, tables, and 42-inch high shelving for the reference collection. The card catalog is in this area.

Adult bookstacks: 90-inch high stacks in one regularly organized area.

Adult browsing: magazines, newspapers, recent books, lounge seating.

These areas require 100 upholstered seats, a projection booth, a small stage, and a sound system. Programs are on another level, but are controlled from the information center.

Larger libraries (20,000–100,000 population) necessitate distributing service counters among several major functions:

1. *Check-in and check-out areas:* A separate counter close to the library entrance. In the largest libraries, this will be further subdivided into a return area on the right of the entrance and a check-out area on the left. These should not be emphasized by lighting and location, since they are monitoring activities and are not direct public service areas. Ideally, the public would rather not go through a check-out process at all. The check-in and -out areas are equipped with electrical circuits and telephone and computer conduits. There will be storage space for many book trucks to hold returns, although these should be wheeled out often so that the public has a chance to borrow materials before they are shelved, thus saving the shelving cost.

2. *Information counter:* several staff stations with storage for several hundred ready reference books and vertical files. Computer terminals for interloans and for information data bank access, several telephones, and several public seats on the other side of the counter.

3. *Media stations:* electrical receptacles and/or remote wired conduits for a wide variety of media—films, filmstrips, audio-and video-cassettes, phonorecords, with headphones available. This area must be convenient for media maintenance, and there should be a service and production area with storage for materials, booking facilities, and equipment for loan nearby.

4. *Micro materials center:* Micro materials are a useful way

of making available large quantities of information in a small space. The micro materials center must include index volumes as a subject guide to the chronologically arranged micro materials. Such a center might contain as a minimum:

A. Equipment:
Microfilm readers
(1) Capable of projecting a full page of the *New York Times* on a 22" × 24" flat screen, dark viewing area.
(2) Lighted note-taking area next to the darkened screen area, 10" × 20".
(3) Motorized switch capable of single and multipage variable scanning speed.
(4) Modular mechanism for easy repair and easy bulb replacement.
(5) External focusing control.
(6) The screen should be evenly illuminated from the corners to the center.
(7) The glass flats that hold the film in place must be separable and easily removed for cleaning. The glass flats should automatically separate when the film knob is rotated, and it should be impossible to advance the film if flats are closed.
(8) Maintenance: Parts should be accessible for cleaning and repair. The projection lamp should be of a type readily available from commercial sources and easy to change. Glass flats, mirror, screen, and lenses should be easy to clean.

B. Microfilm reader-printer,
(1) Capable of printing one-fourth of a page of the *New York Times*.
(2) Motorized single or multipage scanning.
(3) Modular repair, easy bulb replacement.
(4) Engraved, lighted self-service instructions.
(5) Coin box
(6) Dry, no chemicals
(7) Qualities of the hard copy: sharp, clear, legible, noncurling, nonsmearing, nonfading. Capable of being marked with pen, pencil, felt-tip, typewriter. Permanent paper and image. Available in two sizes, 8½ × 11 inch and 11 × 14 inch.

(8) Controls: print buttons should be easily accessible from a seated position. Multiple copy feature. Finished hard copy should be accessible from seated position.

(9) Loading the paper supply should be an easy operation.

(10) The amount of surface area the reader occupies at each machine should be considered since there should be enough space at each machine to accommodate books and the taking of notes. A pull-out shelf can add to available space.

C. Microfiche readers
   (1) Engraved, lighted self-service instructions.
   (2) Modular repair.
   (3) Easy bulb replacement.
   (4) Screen, 8½ × 11 inch or larger.
   (5) Scanning, manual and indexed.
   (6) Easy-changing lenses,

D. Micro materials
   Microfilm: each 3-3¾ 4" reel fits in a 4" box or cartridge. *New York Times:* 1 reel = 10 days approximately; 80 reels fit in 1 drawer = 3 years of the newspaper. 1 drawer holds 5 rows of 16 reels each row; 10 drawer cabinet holds 30 years. Cabinet is 24" W, 28" D, 51" H. Complete run 1851–1975 = 3+ cabinets. *Time* magazine 1923–1975 = 90 reels, which fit in a little more than 1 drawer.
   College catalogs: complete set on microfiche fit in a file drawer 7–14" × 16–12" D, each fiche is 5-3¾ 4" W × 4" H,

E. Indexes: 42" high counters or tables for brief index use. *New York Times Index;* 1851–1975 = 110 vols. 24 running feet of shelf space = 1+ section of steel single faced shelving 36" W × 10" D × 90" H. *Readers Guide to Periodical Literature,* 1910–1975 = 52 vols. 15 running feet = 1 square foot section 60" H.

Readers materials and indexes should be visually and functionally integrated with large graphics tying these interrelated materials together and the entire space strongly related to the library information center. Other materials that should be located nearby include:

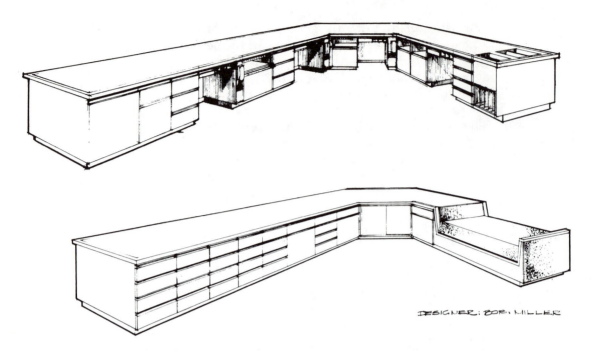

DESIGNER: BOB. MILLER

A carefully designed information-reference counter at the Groton Connecticut Library with projector return area, staff stations, microfilm drawers, form slots, telephone slots, film return and pickup.

Union lists of periodicals.
Interlibrary loan indexes.
Computer terminals.
Teletypes.

Albert James Druz in his *Microforms in Libraries* gives more detailed information.

The most recent indexes and materials will be used most frequently. Therefore, the most convenient accessibility would include the latest five years of indexes and materials closest to the equipment. Reference periodicals in loose format should be kept in clear plastic boxes with titles arranged alphabetically and each title boxed chronologically. Loose and bound periodicals can then be intershelved. However, the public should be asked to place loose copies in a central return location rather than back in the boxes, so that a staff member can keep the magazines chronological in the boxes. Graphics or proximity should relate reference periodicals to newer magazines located in the browsing area.

5. *Adult learning consultation:* Providing adult learners with advice on how the library can be used to achieve their career or lifestyle objectives can be accomplished in a nearby private office with staff trained in interviewing and counseling, and familiar with community learning resources. Both formal courses and informal human and material resources should be used.

6. *Information offices:* 2 offices, one for the head reference librarian consisting of a double pedestal desk, swivel chair on carpet casters, and side chair and 4 drawer side file plus 12 feet of shelving (1 square foot section 60″ high). This office will be 100 square feet. The second office will include work stations for 4–6 staff members, including a 30″ high work surface, lockable drawers large enough for purses, shelving at each station, 4 chairs, and a typewriter and typing table. This office will be 300 square feet.

7. *Reference books* housed in 42″ or 46″ high shelving of a different color and in a different location than circulating books. Shelving tops can have open dividers to house books, but it the tops overhang the lower shelves, some kind of lighting should be provided, such as cove fluorescent lamps attached underneath the shelf tops.

If full 90-inch height shelving is used in the reference area, sliding reference shelves should be installed in every other section to provide a place to rest heavy reference books for quick use in answering questions. These sliding reference shelves will require permanent installation of bracket shelves on both sides of the stack, thereby making these stacks somewhat less flexible than regular shelving.

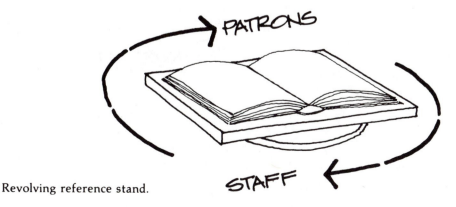

Revolving reference stand.

Card catalogs are used by surprisingly few library users, but they are essential tools for the staff and those users coming to the library for a particular book or subject. They will obviously be used by many people at the same time, so the drawers should be spread out rather than concentrated. The face of the catalog should be constructed of Densiwood to absorb constant banging, but the drawers may be hardwood (preferably northern grown) or Cycolac plastic. Rods should have a locking device. Height should not be greater than 48-inches, reference tables should be nearby, and sliding reference drawers should be provided in the catalog itself. Drawers should be numbered as well as lettered so they can be accurately replaced. A single 18-inch deep tray will hold enough cards for 250 books, five trays for 1,250 books, including cards for author, title, and subjects.

The on-line touch terminal for public use has been recently introduced and may eventually replace the card catalog. It is easier for the public to use. It can be placed in many convenient locations throughout the library and can be quickly and economically changed so as to represent book status and subject information much more accurately than a card catalog. It saves both user and staff time.

Recommended drawer heights for Card Catalog.

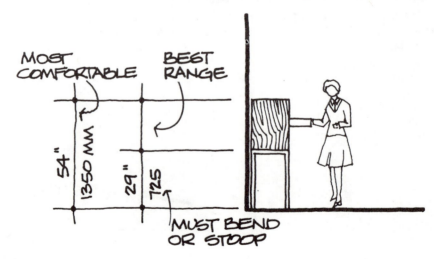

The card catalog must be spread out so many people can use it.

Card catalog spread out and at a convenient working height (*Groton Connecticut Library*).

8　Children's Services

Concepts in Planning for the Design of Children's Rooms

The introduction of children to the public library is of demonstrable importance in determining their life pattern of library use.

The child is expected to use libraries as he matures to reinforce his school experiences. Most school libraries instruct students in the use of their facilities as support for the curriculum. The question of whether he will also choose to use the public library will be substantially decided by his initial experiences. This, in turn, will affect whether he will use the library as a parent with his own children.

When the pre-school child comes to the library, it is often his first experience with books and materials. The story hour may be his first group experience. Sometimes, especially in urban areas, regular use of the children's room is substituted for nursery school.

If the child comes to the library for the first time with his school class, he is likely to assume that the children's room is another version of the school media center. This does not encourage the child to use the public library on an individual basis. It is important when defining the public library for the child that studying and curriculum support are not emphasized. The learning experience is possible at the library and is available, but it is not required. The child who wishes to learn will be encouraged, but should not feel that he must have a reason to go to the library; his purpose should never be asked.

What the children's room looks like makes the initial impact. The space should be inviting and friendly, colorful and approachable.

The bulk of the child's reaction is made up of what it feels like: Is it welcoming (are the staff friendly, helpful—but not too pushy); Is it comfortable; Is it fun; and so on. Essentially, the child should feel that the room is for him.

In order to achieve this, planners for children's rooms should try to understand the ways in which children react to environments and create specific requirements to insure positive, functioning design.

It must be recognized that children make noise (and it's okay) and need supervision and protection (but not control). The children's room should be a maximum distance from adult reference and minimum distance from the circulation/information point. Ideally, the children should pass this circulation area when entering and leaving the building.

Circulation should not be done from the Children's Room if at all possible. While it is true the children's librarians identify the process of circulating children's materials with getting to know the children and their needs, the results are often the opposite of service. A child hesitates to ask a question (or to ask for help) of someone who looks "busy"; he feels he is interrupting. Real professional work lies in assisting/advising children in the library. Circulation is a comforting routine, but not an essential relationship between librarian and child.

The children's space should be designed to lend itself to change/adaptation by the user. The child can then decide whether he wishes to be active or passive in the environment. Arrangements should be flexible, using easily movable furniture with stacks and tables and chairs in a variety of sizes to differentiate areas rather than labeling (which inhibits individual choice). The child must be able to choose how much he wants to experience. Sometimes a child goes to the library to be alone; quiet places should be available.

The following are some additional specifics to be considered by the planner:

Children should be able to reach toilets without crossing adult service areas;

A variety of possible spaces and styles of furnishings should be available for programs. For example, children should be able to draw pictures or make puppets as follow-through for story hour, not be restricted to verbal communication with the librarian;

A centralized area for media might be necessary for control of behavior as well as machinery; but the design of the area should be as informal as possible.

Many items need to be provided in shorter sizes such as coat racks and water fountains.

It is also essential that the requirements of the handicapped child be considered. Exceptional children must be served; those who are gifted as well as those who need special encouragement from staff.

When planning the area for pre-schoolers, seating for parents should be included so that they can comfortably join their children. Appropriate materials for parents and other child-oriented adults should be available.

For children to enjoy libraries and to be active in libraries, they must feel that they can affect the space allocated to them and its contents. They should be able to create their own study area, select their own materials, and operate their own machines. Essentially, we want to create a space and objects in that space so that children will make it their own.

How can we help children do this?

1. *Entrance:* make the main library entrance easy to enter by having doors that children can open. A recent prize-winning library design in suburban Connecticut literally has doors that cannot be opened by children.
2. *Size and scale:* think of children as special people. Walk around on your knees to begin to understand how a library looks and operates for people that size. To a four-year old, a 5-foot bookstack can be a barrier and a 30-inch high table is more like a ceiling than a working surface.
3. *Private places:* a children's library should contain small alcoves surrounded by low shelves, controllable by the staff but accessible to children, so they can pick out a book or game and settle individually or in small groups to enjoy it. Opportunities for children to share experiences with one another as well as to

Make the library doors easy to open.

work comfortably alone should alternate in the children's area.

4. *Friendly objects:* orderly, tightly shelved, and neatly arranged bookstacks may be an inhibiting experience to children. A long counter—26-inches high—with a variety of books, games, toys and machines available to teach, feel, handle, and take out would be a much more inviting initial experience, especially if combined with glare-free task lighting on the objects.

First Impressions

Just as the initial visit of an adult to a new library is of crucial importance, so the first visit of a child to a library will form impressions that may never be changed. This first impression should be of a magical, colorful world of variety and activity, offering creative freedom to each child's individuality. The area should be open and light, full of colorful shapes, spaces, and places with a variety of activities. Ideally, this first visit will take place before the child can read, so the room should feature strong visual experiences, some familiar and some totally new and exotic. It should include:

Picture books arranged in low browsing bins like phonograph records, with their colorful covers available for easy inspection, and nearby a slide show featuring picture books.

Filmstrip/cassette players with headphones so that children can share the experience of a story.

Video/cassette or disc players on which children can view films or see story hours videotaped at the library.

Audio-cassette players to hear stories.

Movie-movers, 16 mm rear-projection carts on which a group of children can view films without the need to darken a room.

Play/Learning Areas

Part of the children's room should be available for open play. A community service such as a library is, in a sense, a buying cooperative. Toys and games that could not be afforded by an individual can be purchased for the community from the pooling of tax funds. The librarian can serve as the expert in guiding the selection of these materials so that they are durable, safe, and educational. But it is equally important that they be enjoyable experi-

ences for children, because one of the virtues of a public
library is that children do not have to go to it—they must
want to go because it is useful and pleasurable. Large,
sturdy wooden toys, and other Realia, are attractive, and
they help in the learning of motor skills and in the
knowledge of how things work. They should be large
enough to sit on and move around. Some libraries lend
toys to children. Large shapes, plastic or wooden, that
children can pile together or pull apart are often interesting. Immense Tinker Toys or doll houses are also delight-
ful and unique experiences for many children.

Activity Areas

The concept that a library can engage the individual in an activity experience, as well as in a book or in

Children love media
(Greenwich Connecticut
Public Library)

viewing a film is consonant with our multifaceted educational philosophy. This concept can be a structured program such as in Middletown, Connecticut, which operates craft, art, and educational activities for groups of preschoolers each day. Even the smallest library, however, will provide story hours once a week, if it is serious about developing good library use habits in young children.

In addition to art and craft activities, some libraries encourage poetry and short-story writing by posting poems and stories on display walls, or publishing them in an annual.

Activity areas for crafts require several 28-inch high counters made of sturdy butcher-block wood or formica anchored to the floor; a sink and, if possible, a floor with a drain in it for easy cleaning; several lockable cabinets with adjustable shelves inside; walls with burlap-covered homosote for a tackboard and adjustable shelf standards spaced every 30-inches for display of craft work. Avoid carpeting in this area.

Lighting should be fluorescent with sunlight-spectrum lamps and ¾-inch egg-crate parawedge louvers over the work counters, and light track or cove lighting for the walls. The lamps should be as invisible as possible to emphasize materials and activities.

Picture book bins are just right for pre schoolers (Greenwich Connecticut Public Library).

The transition from children's to adult libraries should be considered carefully in the design of children's areas. Older children requiring study assistance after school and on weekends should have an easily identified quiet area, where the learning and activity noise and bustle will not disturb them. This area should closely resemble the adult library and might even be located near the adult reading room. Children should be freely encouraged to use both adult and children's reference resources.

Forty-six-inch high children's bookstacks have good book capacity and can be arranged in an alcove system to provide many private areas. Full 90-inch high adult bookstacks in the children's room have the disadvantage of creating huge, forbidding canyons that children may be reluctant to enter. However, directional stack lighting using angled egg-crate parawedge louvers will help to create a fascinating pathway between brightly lit books, and step stools at intervals will make the higher shelves easily accessible. The two top shelves can be converted to useful locked storage space. The cost for this stack will be almost identical to a 5-foot stack, which would have the disadvantage of reduced storage and a less effective lighting system.

Reference books should be stored on lower 30 or 42-inch shelving, with the top available for resting books and looking up answers. Children seem to prefer group tables to study carrels. Work surfaces and chairs should be sized for children.

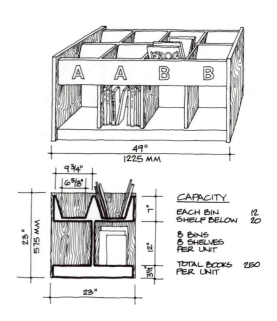

Children's picture book bins.

Combining children's and adult check-in- and -out facilities in a small library has many advantages. Staff can be available for both clientele groups at a single location near the entrance, providing user convenience, reduction of waiting time, and making most effective use of staff. The same check-out machine can be used for both groups. Files and materials can be uniform and take up less space in the building. There are problems, however, that careful design can avoid. Smaller children will need a lower counter than adults and a separate part of the counter set aside and visibly marked by large graphics. Color, lighting, and location will prevent adults from dominating the line of children waiting for service.

When library activity at the children's check-out approaches 50,000 circulations per year, a separate check-out area can be considered. At this level, separate staffing is reasonable; the separation of the two areas will reduce congestion and result in better service without increasing staff costs. Many libraries are designed with adult and childrens' check-out areas in a V-or L-shape configuration that makes it possible to share staff office facilities, but to separate the public side.

Communications with Children

Children should be encouraged to communicate their wants to librarians and designers. This can be done through a bulletin board displaying children's comments on services, along with the librarians' responses. Occasionally, books can be circulated with sheets asking for comments about them, and these comments can be pasted into the front of the book for the benefit of other potential readers. Small group meeting rooms can be used for a monthly meeting after story hour to let children and parents voice their opinions and desires. New children's books, magazines, and catalogs of films, equipment, and educational toys can be displayed with a poster encouraging requests. Staff field trips to other libraries with a video portapac along can produce a record of the visit to be played back to children, parents, library administration, and board members to test reactions to different service patterns and program ideas.

The vast flood of new media into libraries predicted in the late 1960s by media enthusiasts has not occurred, partly because of high costs but also partly because most public libraries do not feel equipped to handle nonbook materials. However, it would be unthinkable for new libraries or library improvement programs in the 1970s not to include ample provision for media experiences for children. Much excellent material exists, and many librarians have found that a generation of children brought up on a diet of TV (and parents who don't remember a TV-less world) respond quickly to a multimedia approach.

Area for Children

The number of children as a percentage of the total population may provide a general guide to the area of the children's room as related to the overall area of the library. However, in actuality there is a wide variation in the ages that are attracted to children's services. In each individual the desire to use more advanced materials will differ depending upon the topic. A sports-minded child

A childrens learning activity center at the Groton Public Library. A learning machine counter and stools are in the foreground. Work tables and a sink are in the background, in an area with a vinyl floor. The staff workroom is to the left.

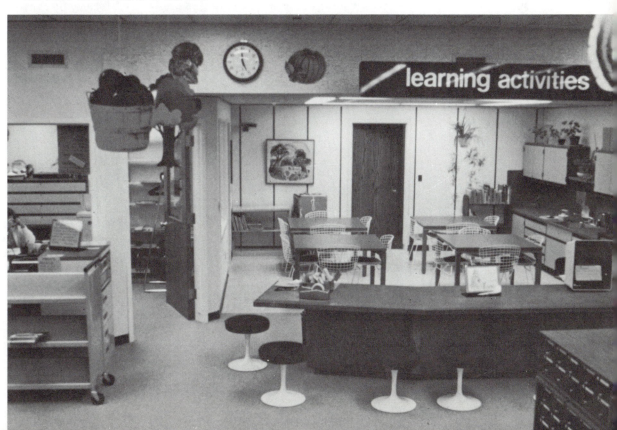

who is not a very fast reader may nevertheless have read through all the children's books on baseball before he is nine years old. Although children's books on other subjects may be satisfactory, he should be reading adult materials on baseball.

In smaller communities, the relatively small adult collection may not attract a very large percentage of adults—many of whom may find it necessary to use a much larger library in a nearby community, but all children will use the local community children's area. Therefore, in smaller communities, the children's area may require a larger percentage of the total space than the proportion of the children's population.

In urban centers, it may be difficult for children to come to the large central library, which may be far away from any residential area and have insufficient parking or mass transit access. In this case, the children's section may be smaller than the proportion of children to the total population.

Development of good school libraries usually results in greater use of public library facilities. Even if the school library is open in the evening, students will enjoy a nonschool environment. Duplication of materials, where it exists, can serve to reinforce in-school learning combined with recreational informational searching. Few school libraries are available on the weekend or during the summertime or during vacation periods. It is more cost effective, if a choice must be made, to operate a single large children's library as part of an already operating adult library than it would be to open, staff, heat or cool a dozen smaller, widely scattered school libraries during nonschool hours or weeks. In general, however, the more access points available, the more users.

The children's program and its objectives will have a major effect on the area required. A varied program of learning and craft activities combined with group films, creative drama, and puppets, story hours, and other media experience or individual study will require a much larger area than a circulating children's library of books. The area of children's services might thus vary from 10 to 35 percent of the total building area in addition to sharing adult program facilities for larger children's programs.

The book collection will generally be a somewhat small percentage of total library books—20 percent or less—since children require less subject depth and variety than do adults.

Seating will also be less, since children's activities do not always require individual seating and many children enjoy using floor cushions or foam shapes. Children's study time in the library may be less than adults' because of shorter assignments and briefer projects, but libraries, especially in poor communities, may have a core of regular homework doers who have no place to study at home.

Flexible Usage

With the birthrate declining and overall population age growing, it may be necessary to design children's facilities so they can be converted to adult use. This is another reason for full-height children's bookstacks and a single central check-out desk. Furniture and partitions can be easily moved and electrical receptacles are always needed. Column modules should be the same as for adult areas, and sound barriers should be removable. Staff control of children's areas and children's staff facilities should be closely related to adult staff areas so that they can be recovered for adult use. Children's learning/activity areas and group meeting areas should also be located near similar adult facilities for possible future conversion.

Integrating Children's and Adult Materials

Several libraries have tried an integrated system. In Wilmington, Delaware, the library intershelved children's and adult nonfiction, with no separate children's nonfiction section. Children's books in the adult nonfiction stack were identified by spine labels. Children's librarians and adult librarians worked in the same stack area, but with different clientele groups. There were separate children's study and activity areas with the appropriate sized furnishings, and children's fiction and

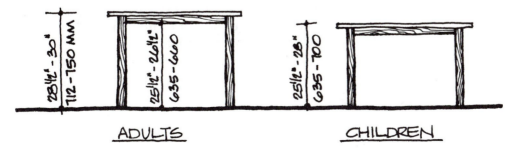

ADULTS   CHILDREN

Reading table heights.

picture books were shelved in a separate areas designed for children, but accessible from the central staff area.

The rationale for this is that children's books are often useful to adults beginning to learn about a new subject (the "First Book" series is an example), while many children often develop a depth of interest in a subject that cannot be satisfied by the few books or other media available in the children's room.

This system makes it possible for children with a strong knowledge of particular areas to easily obtain the advanced adult materials in these areas that are essential to their interests and capabilities. It also makes immediately available to adults with limited capabilities materials necessary for a basic, simplified understanding of these subjects. High shelving is seldom a problem because of the provision of gliding steps, and professional assistants with special skills in children's work are available.

Staffing under this integrated system would include staff members who are specially trained in children's services working along with other staff in the central information center. This might result in improved knowledge of children's services by the adult services staff, but could also result in children being intimidated by too many adults and being deprived of the colorful and varied activities and unique design features that might be developed in areas designed especially for children.

Children's programs and activities are carried out in an adjacent but separate location. The disadvantages may be in the loss of children's area identity and the potential noise in adult areas. Most children's librarians object strenuously to this concept because it does not provide the completely unique ambience and the careful attention of an area and staff designed for children's needs.

Staff Facilities

Although book selection and reference work may not be quantitatively as great as for adult services, the children's staff will have an even greater need for individual consultation space to work with children. These offices should be located so as to control the entry to the children's area and provide visual control over all parts of the room. Two 10 x 10 offices with desks, adjustable shelving, and chairs would be a minimum if circulation control and processing of children's materials are handled elsewhere. Lockers should also be provided, with a few also available for public use. Equipment and materials storage in a 75 square foot closet will also be necessary

Public Services to Children

The library can provide many services for children, including:

Reader's advisory services to children and to adults concerned with children.

Reference services to children and to adults concerned with children. (May involve circulating collection, vertical file, as well as the reference collection.)

Catalog use assistance and instructions, with goal of independence for children.

Quiet browsing.

Studying.

Examining displays and assisting with creating displays.

Checking the community calendar.

Sharing ideas, reactions, spontaneously, about books, records, films, and games through talking together—librarian with children, or children with children, librarian with adult concerned with children.

Looking at filmstrips independently.

Listening to records or cassettes alone.

Quiet reading.

Requesting materials to be reserved or sent for on interlibrary loan.

Children assisting other children with reading or using library materials or equipment.

Programming activities:

Preschool story-telling.

Parent support program series.

Traditional story-telling.

Reading aloud.

Book talking.

Creative dramatics (skits, puppetry, choral reading,

Playing musical instruments/making instruments.

Creative writing.

Book discussion club.
Science fiction/science club.
Filmmaking (animation.)
Craft-making.
Paper murals.
Origami.
Group visits to the library and librarians visiting groups
of children and adults.

Checklist of Equipment and Furnishings

Shelving

>*Book bins:* for picture books, beginning to read, early reading.
>>Low for use by preschool children.
>>Deep enough to accommodate oversized books 11″ deep.
>>Sloped both ways for easy browsing.
>>Wide enough—13″.
>>Shelving below bins.
>>On wheels for flexibility.

>*Fiction and nonfiction*
>>Low enough for use by primary as well as intermediate grades.
>>Ability to interfile oversized books (width as well as height).
>>Shelf units 60″ high.
>>Shelves 12″ deep.
>>Adjustable.
>>Interspersed slope shelving for face-out display.

>*Paperbacks*
>>Accommodate all sizes of paperbacks (trade, mass market, and picture books).
>>Face-out display of some covers.
>>Visibility of all spines.
>>No more than 60″ high.
>>Circular rotating racks.
>>Pegboard racks to accommodate variety of picture book sized paperbacks.

>*Phonorecords/cassettes*
>>Accommodate cassettes as well as LP's.

Ability to examine all covers.
Face-out display of some covers.
Low enough for use by preschool children.
LP's: raised bins no more than 36″ high.
Cassettes: circular rotating cassette racks no more than 60″ high.
Cassettes will fit in 3 × 5 card catalog drawers.
Possibility of integrating recordings with book collection.

Realia
Accommodate a variety of sizes.
Display some realia.
Ability to examine realia.
Storage for circulating and noncirculating.
Movable storage units that attach to wall with plexiglas fronts.

Filmstrip storage
Display of all titles.
Accommodate any accompanying cassettes and paperbacks and guides.

Picture/pamphlet file (and maps)
Low enough for use by primary children.
Accommodate commercial study prints.

Poster collection
Easy access to all posters.
Display of some posters.

Art print
Accommodate standard sizes as well as miniature prints.
Access to all prints.
Display of some prints.

Films
Accommodate 8 mm as well as 16 mm.
Easy access to all cans.
Integrate films with adult film collection or locate films in programming room.
Two storage areas for programming collection and circulating collection.

Periodicals

Face-out display of at least one issue of each title.
Low enough for primary grade access.
Storage of back issues behind hinged display shelf.
Shelf unit no more than 60″ high.

Furniture

Preschool/primary area

Place for adult and child to share books together.
Lounge seating.
Tables and chairs.
Colorful furniture.
Able to withstand adult weight.
Washable table tops.
Some imaginative pieces of furniture for visual surprise.
Modular units to be manipulated by children.
Easels.
Puppet theater.
Doll house.

Primary/intermediate area

Small group study.
Individual study.
Comfortable seating.
Furniture that is comfortable for a wide age range—primary to adult.
Colorful furniture.
Washable table tops.
Tables and chairs.
Study carrels.
Lounge seating (sofas, foam or bean bag chairs).
Cubbies: area to accommodate individual boxes for children to store work in progress (writing, crafts, etc.).

Display areas

Safely display hobbies, art objects, etc., shared by children and community.
Publicize community information.
Display booklists, brochures, program flyers for distribution.
Space for involvement-type bulletin board display.

Enclosed display case, either free standing or
built in.
Community bulletin board.
Pegboard racks for handouts.
Large tackboard area for involvement displays.

Reference area
　　Card catalog:
　　　　Low enough for child visibility and use.
　　　　High enough for adult comfort.
　　　　Spread out so that many children can use it at
　　　　the same time.
Professional materials file:
　　Near reference desk for easy use by staff.
　　Low enough so it doesn't obstruct vision or
　　create barrier.
　　Atlas-dictionary stand.
　　Slide-out shelves for storage.
　　Slant top for use.
　　Low enough for children.
Reference counter:
　　Drawer to hold work materials, small enough so
　　it doesn't create a psychological barrier.
　　Chairs for patrons consulting librarian.
　　Electrical receptacles for media and data termi-
　　nal.

Graphics for
childrens
catalog.

Circulation (if not centralized)
    Counter at child height.
    Storage for library cards kept at library.
    Storage for registration files.
    Storage for circulation materials (extra cards, pamphlet envelopes, realia bags, etc.).
    Book trucks for returned materials.
    Storage for circulating AV equipment.
    Storage for any headphones or room toys kept at desk.

Coat racks
    Hooks at child height.
    Low shelf to sit on while putting on boots.
    Storage under shelf for boots.
    Shelf for gloves, lunch boxes, etc., overhead.

Restrooms
    Mirror and wash basin and towel dispenser at child height.
    Child-protected lock (door always opens for person inside even though it has been locked, plus access from outside in emergency).

Drinking fountain
    Low level.
    Easily operated by very young children.
    Step stool for very small children.

Staff work area
    Work station for each staff person.
    Desk with typing platform.
    Individual bulletin board.
    Files.
    Shelving.
    Storage.
    Tables and chairs for staff meetings, conferences, etc.
    Staff bulletin board to post schedules, announcements, etc.
    Work counters for assembling book lists, realia, etc.
    Files to store catalogs, library files.
    Storage for:
        Craft materials.
        Duplicating materials.
        Office supplies.
        Display materials.

AV supplies.
Materials being processed.
Materials awaiting repair.
Picture mounting materials.
Coat storage.
Security for handbags and personal belongings.

Program room
Chalkboard.
Bulletin board.
Sink.
Storage for craft supplies.
Stackable chairs.
Book display.
Collapsible tables.
Storage for chairs and tables.

Bookstacks
Book trucks.
Sorting shelves.
Bins for records, periodicals, comics, pictures,

A library is a family place.

pamphlets.
Bins for materials in need of repair.

Audiovisual equipment
   Circulating
     Sound filmstrip projector.
     Filmstrip viewer.
     Cassette players.

   Noncirculating
     16 mm projector, movie-mover.
     Slide projector.
     Sound filmstrip projector.
     Sound filmstrip viewer.
     Record players with earphones.
     Television, video cassette.
     Typewriter for public use.

Selected Suppliers of Children's Equipment
   Realia storage
     Herman Miller movable wall storage units
     (from their hospital line).

   Tables and chairs
     Artek tables and chairs from IFC (birch with
     linoleum or formica).
     Juhani Manner tables and chairs from Stendig
     (birch with plastic laminate).

   Imaginative furniture
     Pony by Eero Aarnio from Stendig

Fathers need a place in the childrens room also.

Elephant and hippo by Juhani Manner from
Stendig (foam covered by vinyl).
Terraza by Stendig (leather lounge area, tiered).
Joe from Stendig (leather baseball glove sofa).
Tractor seat from IFC.

Study carrels
Carrola by Risom.

Lounge seating
Alvar Jr. chair from Stendig (foam and poly-
urethane).
Hexagons from Stendig (foam seating block).
Bean bag chairs from Carter.

Staff work area
Herman Miller office components designed by
Propst.
Paperback shelving
Rotating lucite racks from Gaylord.
Cassette racks from Gaylord.
Skandi-Land, a division of Rudd International
1066 31st St. NW
Washington D.C. 2007,
makes attractive natural wood children's furni-
ture in 4 sizes table heights are: $12\frac{1}{4}$, $14\frac{1}{4}$, $17\frac{1}{4}$ and
$20\frac{1}{4}$

Young Adults

In the 1950s, libraries were designed with special
areas for teenagers featuring books written for teenagers, informal lounge furnishings, a few paperbacks.
These areas were small, inadequate in terms of program
space, and close to quiet study facilities. If teenagers used
such areas, their behavior patterns were forced into
unnatural quiet that was uncomfortable for this age
level. In the 1960s, many libraries did not provide any
special young adult areas but assumed that existing adult
functions would also be used by young adults with behavior patterns appropriate to the area. But recently,
fashions in library facilities designed for young adults
have changed. For example, at Great Neck, Long Island, a
large library room has become a community teenage
center open until midnight for rock music, paperback
books, conversation, and social communication.

Teenagers are confusing to many people because
they fluctuate between acting like children and adults.

Perhaps libraries need to provide noisy areas or activity areas, sound-separated from other parts of the building, where the natural desire of young people to meet and talk can take place. In English libraries, there are seldom any areas set aside for teenagers, but there is often a coffee bar where young people can obtain refreshment, talk casually and meet socially in a respectable environment with a pleasant educational ambience.

Teenagers use libraries to experience music—yet few record collections exhibit any real knowledge of popular music on the part of librarians. A typical library record collection will not have any Beatles records, but will have pale "Boston Pops Beatle" music arrangements. A teenage center in a library should have these elements:

1. *Music center:* cassette players with headphones and a selection of several hundred cassettes.
2. *Video center:* several video-cassette players with cassettes featuring films on sports, rock music, fantasy.
3. *Paperback racks:* filled with books selected by teenagers.
4. *Magazines: Playboy,* conservative and religious magazines.
5. Coffee bar: with soda, candy, natural foods.
6. Group meeting room: for ten people, committee of librarians and teenagers meeting weekly to program this area and other library facilities for the needs of teenagers.

It is exceedingly difficult for librarians to keep pace with the changing sophisticated tastes of young people and almost impossible to provide satisfactory services to them without their continual input.

9 Designing Facilities for School Library Media Centers

Media Programs

In designing a school library media center, the director must work closely with the architect in order that the philosophy of the center be translated into physical terms. If school administrators or architects are left alone, the resultant design may well be something that does not fit the requirements of the community it is to serve.

The Role of the School Library Media Center

Essentially, a school library media center has four basic jobs that must be done. These are to:

1. Provide all media support service.
2. Provide production service.
3. Provide library and reference support for the local school community.
4. Provide a storage and duplication area for all original materials, both print and nonprint.

The business of achieving these tasks successfully is directly dependent on the physical arrangement of the media center. Listed below is a series of space requirements. In following paragraphs, the functions of these areas will be discussed in terms of their particular requirements.

1. Reception and display area.
2. Office and administrative area.
3. Materials storage space.
4. Equipment storage space.
5. Technical services area.
6. Circulation
7. Conference rooms.
8. Reading/listening area
9 Graphic production center.
10. Film and video production area.
11. Audio recording area.
12. Print duplication area.
13. Materials inspection and repair area.
14. Equipment inspection and repair area.
15. Restrooms.
16. Blind storage space.

Reception and Display Area (175–250 sq. ft.)

As the opening to the center, the reception and display area should have a lighted bulletin board and display case. The coloring and appointments should be harmonious and cheerful in order to display creative talent and to invite people into the center for further individual investigation.

Office and Administrative Area (250 sq. ft.)

The office area should be within easy distance of other areas so that the routine of the center is smooth and efficient. Administrative offices need to be reached by a variety of people. The administrative area must afford a good degree of privacy but at the same time not close off the director from the staff or the clientele. In a building where space is at a premium, the office space may be included with part of the professional study area. If an office space is being redesigned for inclusion into one area where there will be many activities, then the director's area must be confined to a minimum and no partitioning should be used.

Assuming that there is enough space for a degree of separation, then the secretarial space should provide for displays of brochures, handouts, current material on media and teaching, as well as items of general educational interest. Anyone who enters the administrative area should be met with an air of order, calm, friendship, and helpfulness. The appointments should reflect the feeling and atmosphere of the center. There should be nothing ostentatious, but the area should be one that provides working comfort.

Materials Storage Space (1,000 users; 1,500 sq. ft.)

Of all the areas involved in a media center, materials storage space can cause the greatest problem. Materials storage involves *all* materials storage—print and nonprint—and is, of course, a function of budget. The director must choose whether or not the materials storage will be along traditional lines or whether the materials will be divided into centers that house each discipline. Centralization lends itself to better inventory and tighter control. Decentralization into centers provides the user with access to the material almost immediately, and a browsing patron can be invited to explore in a quiet, easy manner. In this space the director can allot 30–35 square feet per reader, or 15 percent of the school enrollment.

The flexibility of the area is dependent on student enrollment. The director who designs with 30–35 square feet in mind should have sufficient space on the floor to handle three-fourths of the book collection and shelving units and sufficient space for the circulation desk, card catalog, vertical files, and free-standing or mobile equipment away from the walls.

Equipment Storage Space (150–300 sq. ft.)

Depending on the kind of center that is established, equipment storage may be needed for supplying classrooms with equipment. In this case, there must be provision for housing equipment when it is not in classroom use. If the equipment is to be housed only within the media center, then storage in the normal sense is not critical in terms of floor space, because equipment will be out on the floor in a use station that will also be its storage station. Fifteen "wet" (fitted with electrical outlets) carrels will call for 15 small rear-screen projection units, 15 cassette synchronizers, and 15 automatic slide projectors. These are not items to be stored in normal use. Their category involves what would properly be called use-space and was accounted for in the preceding section. The storage facility should be secure. Locking cabinets are the ideal solution and can provide easy access with good security.

Technical Services Area (360–720 sq. ft.)

Processing and classifying newly acquired material, both print and nonprint, is done in the technical services area. There must be a minimum of 160 square feet of floor space for each clerk and a minimum of 200 square feet of storage and operations service for each clerk.

Circulation (40–60 square feet)

Pick-up points are those areas in which patrons will pick up materials packages as well as text materials. These areas are designated for use where the center is willing to move entire packets of material out for either classroom or individual use. Drop points are those areas where the same material or equipment is returned without disturbing the routine of the center. Clearly, they are part of checking materials in and out, but since they are part of an inspection service and may involve some degree of storage, the space must be allocated.

Conference Rooms (150 sq. ft. each)

The number of conference rooms will be dependent upon the number of students in the school and the philosophy of the media center. In any case, the room should provide for:

Large conference table.
Seating for up to 15.
Electric outlets on all four walls or floor.
Storage facility for material not stricly part of media center—easels, tripods, decorations, etc.
Projection screen located on main axis of the room.
Intercom telephone.
Small chalkboard and bulletin board space.

If movable partitions become the walls, then the

possibility of expanding the area for large group accommodation is quite possible. Soundproofing in this case is difficult and can lead to problems when adjacent meetings are being held.

Conference rooms are difficult to justify unless they are going to be well used. The floor space could have gone to stack space, general reading and browsing, a sound studio, or such. A basic guide would be to establish how many groups will be needing such an area. Instruction will be taken care of in either the formal library classroom or in the specific areas of the media center. Certainly one such area is needed in a school of a thousand pupils but only specific need can determine if more are needed.

Carrel Space (12 sq. ft. each)

Carrel space is going to be space within the main reading/listening area. Sixty percent of the total space will be given to carrels, which should be electrified. A single carrel equipped for 8 mm cartridge, small TV receiver, and a 2 × 2 slide projector will draw 9 amps. The designer should make this requirement known to the architect or to whomever will be responsible for supplying power.

Graphic Production Center (800 sq. ft.)

No media center can properly exist and properly call itself a library media center unless it has provision for graphic production. Graphic production is defined for this purpose as all material designed and produced in-house that is nonprint in nature.

A well-staffed and equipped media center can become the equivalent of a small ad agency if everything and everyone is properly employed. Graphics production is a free exchange area. The faculty meets easily with students who may be pursuing equal information but on different paths. In addition to providing an area for idea exchange and sharing, this area provides the school with direct support of the individualized program that the school or center used. In the contemporary media center, learning models or packages can be turned out according to the needs and dictates of the various disciplines and departments.

Functions of the Graphic Production Center

The output of this area involves:

1. Preparing mounted and laminated study prints.
2. Preparing overhead transparencies.
3. Preparing 35 mm transparencies.
4. Producing slide programs, both single and multi image.
5. Preparing visuals for motion pictures and in-house television.
6. Producing videotape.
7. Producing super 8 film loops.
8. Producing individualized instructional packages.
9. Producing audio material.
10. Reproducing charts and graphs.
11. Designing brochures, pamphlets, and handouts.
12. Preparing posters.

The list is in an approximate priority order; however, it should be remembered that priorities are individual concerns. Certainly audio production is not a low rank priority, nor is the ability to inform a community via pamphlets. In actuality, the first ten items have equal value and should be so considered.

Here are some details of Space requirements:

2 × 2 Slide Production.

An always-ready camera and copy stand require 15 square feet. Working space requires approximately another 15 square feet for a total of 30 square feet. Access space is a consideration but not vital if the copy unit is in a general service area.

Overhead Transparencies (84 sq. ft.).

Overhead production should be in two formats; however, three sets of equipment will be necessary. These are: a dry-process photocopier unit to make transparencies directly from single sheet source materials; one similar unit for the production of transparencies from sources appearing in books or booklets; and one set of equipment components for exposing and developing diazo-coated sheets for multicolor static or overlay transparencies. Clearly, three kinds of equipment can serve three users. Bench space for equipment and working room would amount to 12 square feet for each of the first two components and 18 square feet for the third. An operating room would require an additional minimum of 42 square feet, which totals to 84 square feet.

Posters are continually used in schools either for school activities or because people close to the school system—PTA, Father's Club, Touchdown Club, and such—request some to be made to announce a fund-raising affair or a meeting (or whatever the need may be). What generally occurs is that an art or printing teacher gets delegated. He or she in turn hands the project to a class. This is a travesty, because the teacher is paid to teach art or printing and the students are there to learn art or printing, not to serve as cogs in a poster assembly line. It is also clear that once the precedent is set, such a favor easily becomes obligatory. The school does not desire to make enemies, and the people who need announcement posters don't understand why a teacher is hesitant "to knock out a few signs." The media center provides the place for conciliation. A simple sign press machine or even an easily duplicated poster can be responsible for great happiness on both sides.

Multipurpose Work Area

Such an area is used for a variety of tasks; the simplest way to approach the floor space requirement is to detail the specifics of the area:

1. A workbench with space for three drawing boards and operational area.   36 sq. ft.
2. One slide-selecting sorting and programming bench and operations area.   25 sq ft
3. Multipurpose workbench with a two-sided work area.   64 sq ft
4. One bending and mounting workbench plus work and access area with over and under storage space.
   66 sq ft
5. One working and access area for refrigerator and bench space for printing and duplicator processes over and under shelving.   35 sq ft

6. Space for locating spirit duplicator and mimeo machines plus sign press machine for poster work, plus work access area. 45 sq ft
7. Lazy Susan type storage rack 5-feet tall with access area for choosing supplies for prescribed processes. 15 sq ft
8. Two desk and chair units for technicians. 45 sq ft
9. One stockroom with floor to ceiling shelving and bins for bulk supplies and film stock. 44 sq ft
10. Space for one 2 × 2 inch slide duplicating and modifying unit and access area. 30 sq ft

Total 395 sq ft

A small photographic darkroom should be part of the multipurpose work area and the space selected need not be more than a 9 × 12 feet, with an adjoining workroom of the same size. The adjoining space should be used for storage of materials and picture trimming and mounting.

Graphics and photographic facilities have certain needs, including:

Electric outlets near workbenches, approximately 36 inches high if wall mounted.
Exhaust fans with light traps.
Regular lights and safe lights for the darkroom.
Running hot and cold water with high quality mixing valves to assure good temperature control.

Film and Video Production Area (934 sq. ft.)

For indoor shooting space that can double as either a film or a video production area, the following footage is used as a guide:

1. Indoor filming or taping under lights. 400 sq ft
2. General service and work area for storage, mounting of special graphics, storage of supplies and cameras, and accessories and lighting equipment. 400 sq ft
3. Space for the preparation of animation sequences, isolated from other operations to permit maximum exposure control. 40 sq ft
4. Viewing of editing footage or videotape. 40 sq ft
5. Editing, splicing, and conforming footage. 54 sq ft

Total 934 sq ft

If the audio recording area is to be located within the major production area, then it must be self-contained within a soundproof area. Provisions must be made for:

1. Audio copying from desk and/or tape to tape.
2. Straight copying for multiple copies.
3. Microphone recording.
4. Editing.

An audio recording room should also contain one or two carrel type installations for copy work or editing. The amount of floor space to be allocated is directly dependent on the amount of use that will be forecast. The guideline purposes let each workroom measure approximately 7 × 10 feet. The duplicating stations would require approximately 15 square feet each. Therefore, a total figure of 70 square feet plus at least 15 square feet would yield the total of 85 square feet for a very modest installation.

Print Duplication Area (150 sq ft)

The print duplication area will be used for in-house production of study guides, bibliographies, programmed instruction material, tests, brochures, newsletters, and other informational material. Copy and reproduction equipment will be in the following format:

Thermal process multiple copy machine for reproducing photos and printed material.	12 sq ft
Equipment to produce spirit masters from printed material.	9 sq ft
Spirit duplicator capable of making up to 200 copies from a single spirit master.	9 sq ft
Mimeo machine capable of making up to 2,000 copies from a mimeo master.	10 sq ft
Sign press machine for making multiple copies of posters and announcements.	15 sq ft

Storage and work space for this equipment can be computed by doubling all the space requirements given by the machine; for example, the spirit master duplicator will require 18 square feet including storage and access. This area can be located within the graphics area if necessary, but because of noise factors, it is better located in a separate area. The floor space indicates that 100 square feet will accommodate all the apparatus, however, another 50 square feet will provide better storage and access.

The Media Specialists as Leader

Harry Truman, who was noted for concise honesty, had on his desk a sign that said "The buck stops here." The library media specialist today who is running a contemporary library media center has to have that same degree of responsible leadership. Today's media center calls for an administrator who seeks responsibility and follows through with actions. The media center is an area that cuts across the whole of the school curriculum touching every student and teacher and, indirectly, even the wider community. Because of the potential that such a center offers, it is necessary that the person who will be running it be creative and able to help users utilize the capabilities of the center to their maximum.

The media center director is not alone in decision-making. He or she is responsible to a superior and at the same time must try to provide a maximum of service to the faculty and students. Budget restraints, the problems of involving faculty in new ways of using information, and keeping abreast of the technological changes are more than a full-time task. The role of director can be analyzed as falling into four critical areas. These are:

1. Administrator.
2. Coordinator of teacher and student activites.
3. Media specialist.
4. Technician.

Although these general areas include many specific duties, the four areas are closely related.

Administrator

As the chief administrator of the center and the one who gives the program life, scope, and energy, the director must lead in policy formulation. This requires planning for both long- and short-range goals and the implementation of policy. The director must take care to see that the media center staff is trained and employed in such a way that they are comfortable in their jobs and able to perform their special tasks.

In addition to policy making and properly deploying staff, the media center director must be an effective communicator. This will provide the basis for rapport and will build mutual feelings of trust and confidence. Such feeling is vital at budget preparation time as well as those times when new ideas are being introduced. People oftentimes will not support the ideas of a person they do not know, nor will they support unexplained concepts. When the director explains why he believes in his actions in clearly stated terms, superiors, colleagues, and subordinates are likely to work and support the proposals and daily operations of the center.

Coordinator.

Because the media center is a resource for learning and because its inventory is made up of instructional materials, the director must be able to coordinate the activities of the professional staff and help them make optimal use of the center. The director must know all the ways people learn and the best way to select media for use. As a coordinator, the director will instruct the faculty and students in a gentle, warm fashion until they are able to operate independently. Anyone within the sphere of the media center who has either a teaching or learning problem or a combination should feel that the logical place to go for help is to the director. The effective media center director establishes the fact that he or she is in a position to help and does help.

Media Specialist

In the role of media specialist, the director must be able to prescribe and advise with authority based on knowledge and experience in matters relating to a wide range of instructional materials. The specialist has the ability to appraise both print and nonprint materials in terms of value to both students and faculty. In this role, the director must keep in mind that he or she is searching for fresh material and the most effective ways to employ it.

Regular patterns of preview and selection of nonprint materials must be established. In his role as media specialist, the director is an agent who promotes change based on the needs and problems that are presented to him or her by administrators, faculty, and students. The director must employ surveys, observations, and reports to discover those needs, and he or she must employ research, technical knowledge, and teaching skill to focus on evaluation, need, and scope of change. Again, the open communications employed by the director are what enable the director to function as a media specialist.

Technician

The role of technician is quite like that of the media specialist and calls for nearly the same kind of action. For this role the director must be knowledgable with the information display equipment in the media center. He or she must be able to specify equipment, to make accurate forecasts about the kinds and types of equipment that will be located in the media center. The director should know for example what computer terminals will permit display on video monitors in his area. The director should know the basic equipment requirements for multi-image use; the director should know what microform will afford patrons the best use, what photocopier will have the greatest versatility, what 35 mm camera is simplest to use but provides maximum image sharpness. Again, knowledge of the equipment is like the knowledge of the materials. All the knowledge is dedicated to providing service to users in in the most efficient manner possible. The director must know the specifics, but the specifics must be used to carry forth the service concept of the media center, and it is the director who makes skillful use of all the information to provide users with a complete information service.

Other Considerations

Although it is desirable to have a well designed and amply staffed library media center it is important to remember that these things *in themselves* do not insure a successful program. What *will* lead to an effective program is a strong philosophy of service. The staff must anticipate needs and satisfy patrons and potential patrons whether the desired information is to be found within the resources of the center itself or outside of it.

In light of the new understanding that the school library media center constitutes one of the major links in the total information resources network of the community, it is crucial that the director of the center, its staff, the school personnel and school administration realize this role and that they see the center's function as providing a connective information experience for both students and staff.

In concluding, it is important to recognize that school programs vary and the services and programs offered will depend upon the needs of the community which is being served. In turn it is the obligation of the school library media center to support, enhance, and become a significant, integral part of both the school and the community.

10 The Architect's Work and the Planning Alternatives

The architect is a trained and experienced professional who can translate the library program from a written expression of needs and intentions into a real building that will express the spirit of the library on a particular site.

An architect has creative talent, technical ability, and judgment that come with construction experience. The men and women in the architectural profession serve both society and the art of architecture. They work with abstract ideas and with concrete reality. In the process of creating a building from a written statement of needs, they will be subject to all the conflicting tensions that one might expect. However, at its most basic, architecture is a social art. It must meet human needs—physical, emotional, and intellectual.

A library building must work well. The various functions must relate to one another and to the site and to the surroundings so that the public, the staff, and the materials that they use can move freely and efficiently among one another. As a public building, the library must be safe and accessible to the young and the old, the healthy and the handicapped. It must function year round, day and night. The arrangement of spaces is generally expressed in the graphic form of a plan.

But human needs are not only physical but emotional and intellectual as well. A library building must be visually appropriate to its setting or context. It should reflect a sense of place. The library should look and feel pleasant to enter, and it should have spaces in which one feels comfortable to browse, to study, to meet, to exchange ideas, to check a reference, and to work. The furnishings and equipment; the spaces and the walls that bound them; the materials, colors, and textures; and the lighting—both natural and artificial, all affect the visual character of the spaces.

Technical requirements in a library involving the structure, the materials and methods of construction, and the mechanical and electrical services must be integrated with the spatial and visual needs. The requirements particular to a library include: the weight of the materials to be stored and the spans over which they are to be supported; the choice of materials, colors, and textures that will contribute to the visual and acoustic character of the space as well as the maintenance and durability of the building; the various elements of library equipment to be mechanically or electrically serviced; and the varying requirements for heating, cooling, ventilating, and illuminating appropriate to the varying library uses. The extent and intensity of library use affects library design. The architect is concerned not only with what is seen both inside and outside the building but also with what underlies the structure and what supports and services the library. These unseen elements are as important as those than can be seen. There are also legal requirements related to land use, occupancy, code compliance, and safety that concern the architect.

Finally, as a public building the library must be created within limitations concerning both time and cost. In an inflationary economy the two are interrelated. Public buildings are publicly financed, and the library's construction cost and occupancy schedule must be acceptable to the taxpayer. Decisions in the planning phase affect both the initial construction cost and the long-term staffing and operating cost of the library. A good architect can analyze the relative costs and benefits associated with these decisions. Planning should be timely to be economical, but creation is a patient search. The gestation time for a library building to emerge from the beginning of architectural planning to final occupancy is two to three years.

These four considerations—the spatial, the visual, the technical, and the economic—must be kept in mind throughout the design and construction process. They will be contradictory and complex, but the architect is trained and experienced in resolving contradictory complexities. Solutions will be reached through creative compromise and through emphatic constrasts. Decisions will be based on analysis and design. Architects must have the ability to preexperience or visualize the final reality of a building long before it is built. They must be able to predict the visual and psychological implications of design decisions. How well the architect communicates all this to the librarian is a measure of his talent. How well the librarian responds—with what understanding and constructive criticism—will determine the effectiveness of the design process.

It requires patience, trust, and mutual understanding to produce a good building. Both the architect and the librarian are professionals with special abilities that should complement one another. The librarian is the leader in defining the user's needs and the library's purpose in its largest sense; the architect is the leader in developing a building that satisfies those needs and the many facets of the purpose. The architect must understand the reasoning behind the library's program, just as the librarian must understand what the architect is trying to do.

Good architecture does not just happen, nor is it the triumph of reason over chaos. It is the result of a good client and a good architect working together with respect and cooperation.

Selection of the Architect

The design of a library is an important commission in a community; most architects in the area will want to be considered. The selection of an architect is an important decision, so the committee responsible for this decision should take its job seriously. Each member of the selection committee should be prepared to attend every interview. No member should have a conflict of interest that might affect his or her choice. There should be some selection criteria on which the selection committee should agree before interviews or screening begin. These might involve: the degree of previous library design experience; whether the firm is a local one and therefore readily available during design and construction; and reliability in meeting time schedule and budget limitations. The committee decision might be to consider those with no library design experience but experience on buildings of similar scope and complexity; a more imaginative or more experienced firm whose office is further from the site; one that is less reliable in meeting deadlines or budgets but produces a more satisfactory building in the end. It may be necessary to screen the number of architect applicants and reduce the number of firms to be interviewed to a manageable number. Among the many selection criteria, the most important are:

Design ability.
Construction experience.
Ability to work with people, flexibility and willingness to
    listen and understand library realities rather than
    to cling to pre-conceived notions.

Design ability is the most difficult criteria to measure. However, intelligence and creative talent are generally evident in an architect's work. Look at the photographs or drawings that an architect brings to the interview. Listen to his description of the architectural problems he faced on previous projects and evaluate his solutions. Best of all, visit his completed buildings and talk to those who use them. Library design is not always so complicated that previous library experience is necessarily essential. On a small project, lack of experience can be offset through the services of a library consultant. On a large library project, previous library design experience is more critical. Solicit the opinions of respected authorities in the architectural profession. Design ability is available, but it is certainly a variable among architects.

Construction experience is more subject to quantitative evaluation. The number of building projects successfully completed is one measure. The scope of the projects completed and their complexity relative to the proposed library is another. The age and years of experience of the architect, the number of licensed professionals within the firm, and the stability of the firm's staff in terms of turnover of personnel are other indicators. A comparison of final budget estimates versus the actual contract bids can be made, and the number and cost of change orders or "extras" encountered during construction are measureable. Finally, the frequency of construction problems associated with an architect's work can be determined. Solicit the opinions of respected general contractors in the area. They have probably worked with most of the area architects and can attest to the completeness of the drawings and the degree of coordination between plans and specifications. The engineering consultants that the architect proposes to engage to complete the structural, mechanical, electrical, and site design should be subject to similar evaluation. Again, visits to completed projects are worth more than elaborate photographs or presentations.

Ability to work with people is important in any professional relationship. A library planning and construction project will take several years to complete. Patience, cooperation and the willingness to consider design alternatives are desirable qualities. Personal references are the backbone of a successful practice. An architect or architectural firm generally welcomes the library board's discussing the architect's qualifications with past clients. The architect is often called upon to explain his proposed design to various approval authorities in public meetings. Articulate presentation and clarity of expression are important. Above all, the architect must have honesty and integrity. Both the owner and the builder will look for these qualities in him. The architect may be asked to make decisions during construction that can favor the library or the builder. Although he is the agent of the owner, he may have to judge impartially whether a portion of the work is called for under the contract documents or whether it is beyond the scope of the contract and therefore an "extra."

In planning the interview, the library board or its designated selection committee should allow between 45 minutes and an hour for each architect to show examples of his work, present his qualifications, and discuss the particular project with the committee. It is unfair to schedule too many interviews for one evening or to allow such a limited time for each architect to present his qualifications that the committee is left confused or exhausted. It is helpful to tell the architects to be interviewed, in advance, the number of people to whom they will make their presentations. It is also helpful to provide a projection screen or an easel in the room where the interview is to be held so that each architect does not have to bring his own props or spend time setting up or dismantling these pieces of equipment.

The architect's fee is subject to negotiation. It should not be the basis of selection. The adequacy of the fee will ultimately affect the level of service. Shopping around for the lowest fee is a short-sighted economy. Suggested fee schedules developed by local AIA chapters have been discontinued but still provide a measure of what is appropriate. Most library projects are designed under a *percentage fee* agreement, with the fee based on the total construction cost. The fee varies with the size and complexity of the project. A small project involving a great deal of alteration work within an existing building will require a higher percentage fee than a large project involving all new construction. Libraries are more complicated to design than rental office buildings or warehouses, so the design fee for a library will be higher than the fee for the design of a simpler building type of equal cost. The design and selection of furniture and equipment should be reimbursed on a separate basis as these involve additional work. Other methods of payment for basic architectural services are *a lump sum fee* or a *time basis billing* in which the architect is paid a nominal fee plus a multiple of his payroll costs.

As libraries are public buildings, political patronage may seem to be a factor. But architect selection based on competitive fee bargaining or on political donation does not lead to excellence in professional service. These techniques are improper if not illegal.

The following is an excerpt from the standard AIA form of agreement between owner and architect. These portions of AIA Document B141 Standard Form of Agreement Between Owner and Architect, 1977 edition, have been reproduced with the permission of The American Institute of Architects under application no. 79018. Further reproduction, in part or in whole, is not authorized. Because AIA documents are revised from time to time, users should ascertain from AIA the current edition of the document of which portions are reproduced below.

ARTICLE 1
ARCHITECT'S SERVICES
AND RESPONSIBILITIES

BASIC SERVICES
    The Architect's Basic Services consist of the five phases described in Paragraphs 1.1 through 1.5 and include normal structural, mechanical and electrical engineering services and any other services included in Article 15 as part of Basic Services.

AIA Document B141 ©1977 by the American Institute of Architects.

1.1 SCHEMATIC DESIGN PHASE

1.1.1 The Architect shall review the program furnished by the Owner to ascertain the requirements of the Project and shall review the understanding of such requirements with the Owner.

1.1.2 The Architect shall provide a preliminary evaluation of the program and the Project budget requirements, each in terms of the other, subject to the limitations set forth in Subparagraph 3.2.1.

1.1.3 The Architect shall review with the Owner alternative approaches to design and construction of the Project.

1.1.4 Based on the mutually agreed upon program and Project budget requirements, the Architect shall prepare, for approval by the Owner, Schematic Design Documents consisting of drawings and other documents illustrating the scale and relationship of Project components.

1.1.5 The Architect shall submit to the Owner a Statement of Probable Construction Cost based on current area, volume or other unit costs.

1.2 DESIGN DEVELOPMENT PHASE

1.2.1 Based on the approved Schematic Design Documents and any adjustments authorized by the Owner in the program or Project budget, the Architect shall prepare, for approval by the Owner, Design Development Documents consisting of drawings and other documents to fix and describe the size and character of the entire Project as to architectural, structural, mechanical and electrical systems, materials and such other elements as may be appropriate.

1.2.2 The Architect shall submit to the Owner a further Statement of Probable Construction Cost.

1.3 CONSTRUCTION DOCUMENTS PHASE

1.3.1 Based on the approved Design Development Documents and any further adjustments in the scope or quality of the Project or in the Project budget authorized by the Owner, the Architect shall prepare, for approval by the Owner, Construction Documents consisting of Drawings and Specifications setting forth in detail the requirements for the construction of the Project.

1.3.2 The Architect shall assist the Owner in the preparation of the necessary bidding information, bidding forms, the Conditions of the Contract, and the form of Agreement between the Owner and the Contractor.

1.3.3 The Architect shall advise the Owner of any adjustments to previous Statements of Probable Construction Cost indicated by changes in requirements or general market conditions.

1.3.4 The Architect shall assist the Owner in connection with the Owner's responsibility for filing documents required for the approval of governmental authorities having jurisdiction over the Project.

1.4 BIDDING OR NEGOTIATION PHASE

1.4.1 The Architect, following the Owner's approval of the Construction Documents and of the latest Statement of Probable Construction Cost, shall assist the Owner in obtaining bids or negotiated proposals, and assist in awarding and preparing contracts for construction.

1.5 CONSTRUCTION PHASE— ADMINISTRATION OF THE CONSTRUCTION CONTRACT

1.5.1 The Construction Phase will commence with the award of the Contract for Construction and, together with the Architect's obligation to provide Basic Services under this Agreement, will terminate when final payment to the Contractor is due, or in the absence of a final Certificate for Payment or of such due date, sixty days after the Date of Substantial Completion of the Work, whichever occurs first.

1.5.2 Unless otherwise provided in this Agreement and incorporated in the Contract Documents, the Architect shall provide administration of the Contract for Construction as set forth below and in the edition of AIA Document A201, General Conditions of the Contract for Construction, current as of the date of this Agreement.

1.5.3 The Architect shall be a representative of the Owner during the Construction Phase, and shall advise and consult with the Owner. Instructions to the Contractor shall be forwarded through the Architect. The Architect shall have authority to act on

AIA Document B141 ©1977 by the American Institute of Architects.

behalf of the Owner only to the extent provided in the Contract Documents unless otherwise modified by written instrument in accordance with Subparagraph 1.5.16.

1.5.4 The Architect shall visit the site at intervals appropriate to the stage of construction or as otherwise agreed by the Architect in writing to become generally familiar with the progress and quality of the Work and to determine in general if the Work is proceeding in accordance with the Contract Documents. However, the Architect shall not be required to make exhaustive or continuous on-site inspections to check the quality or quantity of the Work. On the basis of such on-site observations as an architect, the Architect shall keep the Owner informed of the progress and quality of the Work, and shall endeavor to guard the Owner against defects and deficiencies in the Work of the Contractor.

1.5.5 The Architect shall not have control or charge of and shall not be responsible for construction means, methods, techniques, sequences or procedures, or for safety precautions and programs in connection with the Work, for the acts or omissions of the Contractor, Subcontractors or any other persons performing any of the Work, or for the failure of any of them to carry out the Work in accordance with the Contract Documents.

1.5.6 The Architect shall at all times have access to the Work wherever it is in preparation or progress.

1.5.7 The Architect shall determine the amounts owing to the Contractor based on observations at the site and on evaluations of the Contractor's Applications for Payment, and shall issue Certificates for Payment in such amounts, as provided in the Contract Documents.

1.5.8 The issuance of a Certificate for Payment shall constitute a representation by the Architect to the Owner, based on the Architect's observations at the site as provided in Subparagraph 1.5.4 and on the data comprising the Contractor's Application for Payment, that the Work has progressed to the point indicated; that, to the best of the Architect's knowledge, information and belief, the quality of the Work is in accordance with the Contract Documents (subject to an evaluation of the Work for conformance

AIA Document B141 ©1977 by the American Institute of Architects.

with the Contract Documents upon Substantial Completion, to the results of any subsequent tests required by or performed under the Contract Documents, to minor deviations from the Contract Documents correctable prior to completion, and to any specific qualifications stated in the Certificate for Payment); and that the Contractor is entitled to payment in the amount certified. However, the issuance of a Certificate for Payment shall not be a representation that the Architect has made any examination to ascertain how and for what purpose the Contractor has used the moneys paid on account of the Contract Sum.

1.5.9 The Architect shall be the interpreter of the requirements of the Contract Documents and the judge of the performance thereunder by both the Owner and Contractor. The Architect shall render interpretations necessary for the proper execution or progress of the Work with reasonable promptness on written request of either the Owner or the Contractor, and shall render written decisions, within a reasonable time, on all claims, disputes and other matters in question between the Owner and the Contractor relating to the execution or progress of the Work or the interpretation of the Contract Documents.

1.5.10 Interpretations and decisions of the Architect shall be consistent with the intent of and reasonably inferable from the Contract Documents and shall be in written or graphic form. In the capacity of interpreter and judge, the Architect shall endeavor to secure faithful performance by both the Owner and the Contractor, shall not show partiality to either, and shall not be liable for the result of any interpretation or decision rendered in good faith in such capacity.

1.5.11 The Architect's decisions in matters relating to artistic effect shall be final if consistent with the intent of the Contract Documents. The Architect's decisions on any other claims, disputes or other matters, including those in question between the Owner and the Contractor, shall be subject to arbitration as provided in this Agreement and in the Contract Documents.

1.5.12 The Architect shall have authority to reject Work which does not conform to the Contract Documents. Whenever, in the Architect's reasonable opinion, it is necessary or advisable for the implementation of the intent of the Contract Documents, the Architect will have authority to require special inspection or testing of the Work in accordance with the provisions of the Contract Documents, whether or not such Work be then fabricated, installed or completed.

1.5.13 The Architect shall review and approve or take other appropriate action upon the Contractor's submittals such as Shop Drawings, Product Data and Samples, but only for conformance with the design concept of the Work and with the information given in the Contract Documents. Such action shall be taken with reasonable promptness so as to cause no delay. The Architect's approval of a specific item shall not indicate approval of an assembly of which the item is a component.

1.5.14 The Architect shall prepare Change Orders for the Owner's approval and execution in accordance with the Contract Documents, and shall have authority to order minor changes in the Work not involving an adjustment in the Contract Sum or an extension of the Contract Time which are not inconsistent with the intent of the Contract Documents.

1.5.15 The Architect shall conduct inspections to determine the Dates of Substantial Completion and final completion, shall receive and forward to the Owner for the Owner's review written warranties and related documents required by the Contract Documents and assembled by the Contractor, and shall issue a final Certificate for Payment.

1.5.16 The extent of the duties, responsibilities and limitations of authority of the Architect as the Owner's representative during construction shall not be modified or extended without written consent of the Owner, the Contractor and the Architect.

1.6 PROJECT REPRESENTATION BEYOND BASIC SERVICES

1.6.1 If the Owner and Architect agree that more extensive representation at the site than is described in Paragraph 1.5 shall be provided, the Architect shall provide one or more Project Representatives to assist the Architect in carrying out such responsibilities at the site.

AIA Document B141 ©1977 by the American Institute of Architects.

1.6.2 Such Project Representatives shall be selected, employed and directed by the Architect, and the Architect shall be compensated therefore as mutually agreed between the Owner and the Architect as set forth in an exhibit appended to this Agreement, which shall describe the duties, responsibilities and limitations of authority of such Project Representatives.

1.6.3 Through the observations by such Project Representatives, the Architect shall endeavor to provide further protection for the Owner against defects and deficiencies in the Work, but the furnishing of such project representation shall not modify the rights, responsibilities or obligations of the Architect as described in Paragraph 1.5.

1.7 ADDITIONAL SERVICES

The following Services are not included in Basic Services unless so identified in Article 15. They shall be provided if authorized or confirmed in writing by the Owner, and they shall be paid for by the Owner as provided in this Agreement, in addition to the compensation for Basic Services.

1.7.1 Providing analyses of the Owner's needs, and programming the requirements of the Project.

1.7.2 Providing financial feasibility or other special studies.

1.7.3 Providing planning surveys, site evaluations, environmental studies or comparative studies of prospective sites, and preparing special surveys, studies and submissions required for approvals of governmental authorities or others having jurisdiction over the Project.

1.7.4 Providing services relative to future facilities, systems and equipment which are not intended to be constructed during the Construction Phase.

1.7.5 Providing services to investigate existing conditions or facilities or to make measured drawings thereof, or to verify the accuracy of drawings or other information furnished by the Owner.

1.7.6 Preparing documents of alternate, separate or sequential bids or providing extra services in connection with bidding, negotiation or construction prior to the completion of the Construction Documents Phase, when requested by the Owner.

1.7.7 Providing coordination of Work performed by separate contractors or by the Owner's own forces.

1.7.8 Providing services in connection with the work of a construction manager or separate consultants retained by the Owner.

1.7.9 Providing Detailed Estimates of Construction Cost, analyses of owning and operating costs, or detailed quantity surveys or inventories of material, equipment and labor.

1.7.10 Providing interior design and other similar services required for or in connection with the selection, procurement or installation of furniture, furnishings and related equipment.

1.7.11 Providing services for planning tenant or rental spaces.

1.7.12 Making revisions in Drawings, Specifications or other documents when such revisions are inconsistent with written approvals or instructions previously given, are required by the enactment or revision of codes, laws or regulations subsequent to the preparation of such documents or are due to other causes not solely within the control of the Architect.

1.7.13 Preparing Drawings, Specifications and supporting data and providing other services in connection with Change Orders to the extent that the adjustment in the Basic Compensation resulting from the adjusted Construction Cost is not commensurate with the services required of the Architect, provided such Change Orders are required by causes not solely within the control of the Architect.

1.7.14 Making investigations, surveys, valuations, inventories or detailed appraisals of existing facilities, and services required in connection with construction performed by the Owner.

1.7.15 Providing consultation concerning replacement of any Work damaged by fire or other cause during construction, and furnishing services as may be required in connection with the replacement of such Work.

1.7.16 Providing services made necessary by the default of the Contractor, or by major defects or deficiencies in the Work of the Contractor, or by failure of performance of either the Owner or Contractor under the Contract for Construction.

1.7.17 Preparing a set of reproducible record drawings showing significant changes in the Work made during construction based on marked-up prints, drawings and other data furnished by the Contractor to the Architect.

1.7.18 Providing extensive assistance in the utilization of any equipment or system such as initial start-up or testing, adjusting and balancing, preparation of operation and maintenance manuals, training personnel for operation and maintenance, and consultation during operation.

1.7.19 Providing services after issuance to the Owner of the final Certificate for Payment, or in the absence of a final Certificate for Payment, more than sixty days after the Date of Substantial Completion of the Work.

1.7.20 Preparing to serve or serving as an expert witness in connection with any public hearing, arbitration proceeding or legal proceeding.

1.7.21 Providing services of consultants for other than the normal architectural, structural, mechanical and electrical engineering services for the Project.

1.7.22 Providing any other services not otherwise included in this Agreement or not customarily furnished in accordance with generally accepted architectural practice.

1.8 TIME

1.8.1 The Architect shall perform Basic and Additional Services as expeditiously as is consistent with professional skill and care and the orderly progress of the Work. Upon request of the Owner, the Architect shall submit for the Owner's approval, a schedule for the performance of the Architect's services which shall be adjusted as required as the Project proceeds, and shall include allowances for periods of time required for the Owner's review and approval of submissions and for approvals of authorities having jurisdiction over the Project. This schedule, when approved by the Owner, shall not, except for reasonable cause, be exceeded by the Architect.

AIA Document B141 ©1977 by the American Institute of Architects.

Architects work from the general to the specific. The first drawings that the librarian sees will describe the site, functional relationships, or flow diagrams. Invariably, the librarian will want to discuss "details" while the architect will want to discuss "concepts."

Both architect and librarian must understand the other's background and approach. The librarian has pragmatic experience with what works. The librarian has been defining the user's needs and preparing the program for months before the architect has even been interviewed. He is impatient to get to the specifics. On the other hand, the architect has just begun to assimilate the particulars of the program and the site. He has his own experience with the institution of "Library." The architect is ruminating about his own understanding of the essence of Library with a capital "L." Each party brings his own special talent to the task. Each must spend the necessary time to explain his respective specialty to the other. Librarians do not always visualize the size and shape of spaces from sketch plans or sections. The architect must patiently explain these sketches to be sure that the librarian understands them. The librarian, in turn, must explain today's concept of "Library" and the reasoning behind some of the relationships suggested in the program. A searching question may uncover the basis of a new understanding.

The library improvement program was described in chapters 3 and 4. It is a written document describing the philosophy and objectives of the library and what its physical needs include. It is not architecture. It is impossible to make architecture out of words and a good program does not attempt to do so. Architects have an intuitive understanding of the scale of a space of a given area. Many librarians have difficulty visualizing how big such a space is. Bringing the librarian to an understanding of size and scale is important.

One way to help both the architect and the librarian better understand the program is to draw the elements of the program in diagrammatic form at a common scale, say 1" = 20'. If the scale of the graphic analysis of the program is the same scale as the site survey, or site analysis, this is ideal. Users will quickly understand how big is big; the program and the site can be compared; and the architect can begin to study the functional relationships suggested in the program without becoming committed to a building shape or concept too early in the project's development.

The site is particular to each library project. Assuming that the site has been selected before the architect is retained, the architect will begin any planning study with an analysis of the site. This graphic study is

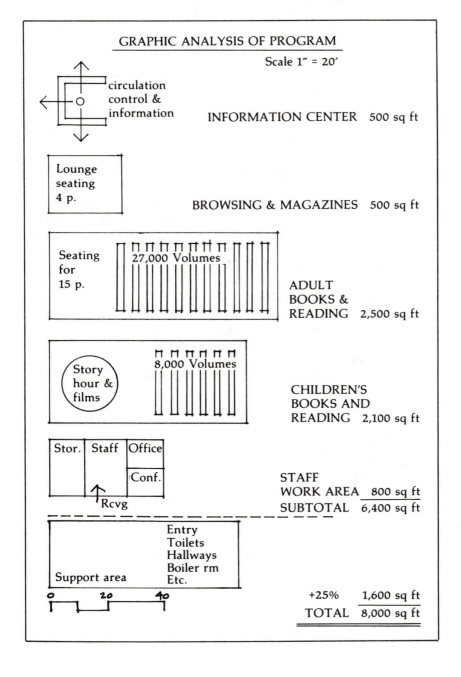

GRAPHIC ANALYSIS OF PROGRAM

Scale 1" = 20'

circulation control & information

INFORMATION CENTER   500 sq ft

Lounge seating 4 p.

BROWSING & MAGAZINES   500 sq ft

Seating for 15 p.   27,000 Volumes

ADULT BOOKS & READING   2,500 sq ft

Story hour & films   8,000 Volumes

CHILDREN'S BOOKS AND READING   2,100 sq ft

Stor. | Staff | Office | Conf.
Rcvg

STAFF WORK AREA   800 sq ft
SUBTOTAL   6,400 sq ft

Entry
Toilets
Hallways
Boiler rm
Etc.

Support area

+25%   1,600 sq ft
TOTAL   8,000 sq ft

0   20   40

based on a survey prepared at the user's expense. The survey should be prepared by a qualified land surveyor and include:

1. Property lines and names of adjoining property owners.
2. Zoning or land use classification.
3. Topography at 2'–0" vertical contours, spot elevations at curb, gutters, and at crown of street.
4. Utilities
   a. Electric power lines, poles, transformer locations, telephone lines.
   b. Water service, location, depth, size; fire hydrants, pressure.
   c. Sanitary sewer, location, depth, size, direction of flow and gradient, manhole locations, inverts and elevations.
   d. Storm sewer, location, depth, size, direction of flow and gradient, manhole and catch basin locations, inverts and elevations.
   e. Gas or steam lines, location, depth, size, pressure.
5. Restrictions: rights-of-way, easements, deed restrictions if any. Taking lines for proposed street widening, etc.
6. Trees—diameter of trunk (caliper), location, species, of all trees over a given diameter (usually 6" to 8"), plantings, shrubbery, etc.
7. Existing structures on the site, size, location, and description of walls, exterior stairs, walks, etc.
8. Rock outcroppings, streams, wetlands.
9. Scale and north arrow.
10. Total acreage or square footage of the property

An analysis of the site, which is based on the survey, will include consideration of the following elements:

1. *Access*
   Pedestrian and vehicular.
   Where will people come from?
   How will they enter the site?
   Where will they park?
   What about service and delivery vehicles?
2. *Setbacks and Zoning Criteria*
   Front yard, side yard, rear yard setbacks.
   Parking setbacks if different from building setbacks.
   Coverage permitted by zoning for:
   a. Building.

b. Building and paved areas combined.
Number of stories or height restrictions.
Amount of parking required.
3. *Site Features to be Preserved*
Major trees, existing structures, stone walls.
Views to and from the site.
4. *Site Features to be Screened or Deemphasized*
Bad views.
Neighboring structures or uses.
Noise.
5. *Orientation*
Sunlight: north—good for reading, working.
    east—next best exposure.
    south—receives most sunlight.
    west—hot in summer.
These will vary depending on latitude and climate.
Prevailing wind: cold winter winds.
welcome summer breeze.
6. *Site Limitations*
Steep slopes difficult to develop.
Rock areas expensive to excavate.
Low areas subject to flooding or high water table.
Locations of utilities to serve building.

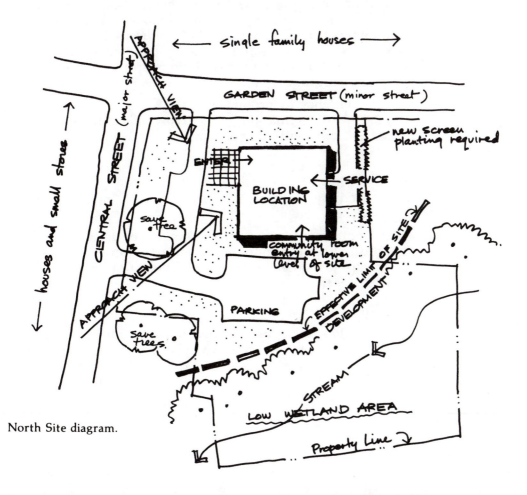

North Site diagram.

7. *Provision for Future Expansion*
   Building expansion.
   Parking expansion.

Functional Relationships

Michael Brawne has defined four basic functions or activities within a library:

1. Locate information.
2. Retrieve and store information.
3. Communicate information.
4. Return information to storage.

Each element in the program is devoted to one of these basic activities: the information center and card catalog to *locating* the information and helping the user; the stack to *storing* the information; the reader seats or program room to *communicating* information; and the circulation control desk to *returning* information to storage. These activities are often closely related or combined in a single space. They are listed separately so they may be analyzed, but they are not exclusionary. Inductive analysis precedes deductive integration.

The program differentiates the various elements with specific criteria for the number of volumes or seats. It will also suggest the critical adjacencies based on the number of contacts between staff or users. Finally, it will describe the activity in terms of "quiet," "noisy," etc. The diagrams that express the relationship among elements of the program should indicate:

1. Adjacency by proximity.
2. Flow of circulation by an arrow indicating direction and differentiating among:
   a. Flow of public.
   b. Flow of staff.
   c. Flow of materials.
3. Activity in terms of "quiet," "noisy," "private," "enclosed," etc.

It is not necessary that these elements be drawn to scale, at least at the beginning, because the proper relationships among elements is more important than their size or shape.

Design Considerations

The following considerations are hardly all-inclusive but should be of concern to librarians and architects.

A library should be accessible and convenient. This begins with the site selection and extends through building design into the selection of furnishings and equipment. A library should be easy to find, easy to enter, and easy to use. Compare the planning of and access to the library with the planning of and access to a market or department store. Modern merchandising practice invites, entices, and draws the customer into the store. An underused public building is a poor investment.

There are no obstacles to entering a commercial building. We expect treadle operated doors on supermarkets, why not on libraries? The shopper carries parcels; the library user carries books, films, or other circulating material. The path from parking or sidewalk to entrance should be as direct as possible. Merchants who plan supermarkets claim that the public must see the entrance from the parking area. Similarly, the library patron should see the entrance rather than be faced with a twisting walk around a series of corners. Directional

THE ARCHITECT'S WORK

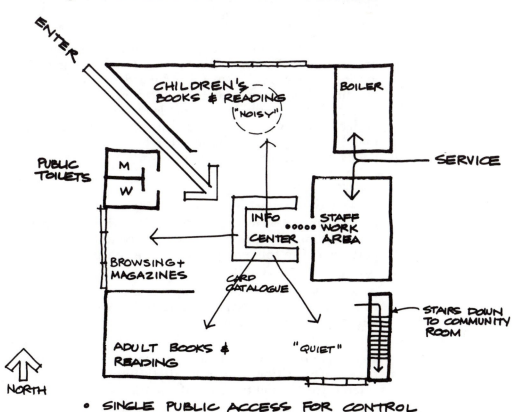

Relationship among elements of the program.

signs to the entrance of a public building are Band-aids on the wounds of poor planning.

Libraries should have a minimum number of entrances to simplify control. A single point of access at the center is the ideal control situation. Often portions of the building, such as the program room, will need to be open when the rest of the library is closed. A single lobby serving the program room and the main library entrance can satisfy this requirement. However, as the program room becomes more remote to satisfy the after hours use, it becomes more difficult to supervise.

Many libraries are installing theft detection systems at the entrance-exit. These require space and equipment that are difficult to integrate into the entrance sequence. These detection units may seem contradictory to the spirit of human dignity the library exists to foster, but the reality of society's breakdown of moral values in regard to theft and respect for property requires them in many communities. As a necessary evil, the detection devices should be designed to be as inconspicuous as possible.

Budget.

A good library program requires an adequate library budget. A building that is easy to use will generate greater public use than an awkward or inconvenient building. Public use leads to public demand for more or better programs; public support leads to a better library budget. The cycle of increased use leads to higher demand for service; the budget for increased service depends on justification based on use.

Staffing

Staff salaries represent the largest item in a library's annual operating budget. Does the simplicity of the building design contribute to economical staffing patterns? The following common design problems cost future staffing dollars:

Spaces that are difficult to supervise.
Multilevel libraries with staff at each level.
Division of departments or functions.

A library is open to the public almost 70 hours a week. There are at least two staff salaries for every full time staff position. Centralized staffing should be considered for flexibility. The information center provides centralized staff with the collections and/or reader seats at the perimeter. Traditional library design divides the collection into departments with a staff position assigned to each section. Some staff are idle while others are overworked. It is better to provide staff at a central area where they can assist each other during peak periods of activity. The public has one place to go to seek help or advice rather than being shunted from one staff area to another in search of information. This planning approach requires an open area near the entrance with the various elements around it. As a minimum the information center would be adjacent to:

The card catalog.
The noncirculating reference collection.
The reader indexes.
The business collection.
The reference collection.
The circulation desk.
Microfilm readers and materials.

Small, one room branch libraries up to 10,000 square feet in size have been planned around this concept with *all* activities radiating from the information center circulation desk.

The circulation work area should be adjacent to and overlook the circulation desk. A common solution is a window behind the desk through which the circulation clerical staff can keep an eye on the desk. During peak periods, the backup staff can come forward and assist at the desk. This solution follows the principle of centralized staffing for flexibility.

Number of Levels

An early basic decision to be faced is the number of floor levels in the building. The architect and librarian should analyze this question carefully because it is of critical importance to the ease of public access, to future staffing patterns, and to the cost of library service. Consider the user's point of view. Generally, a small library can be planned on a single floor level, or at least the public areas can be limited to a single floor level. This is ideal in simplifying public access, decreasing the problems of supervision with resulting lower staffing costs, and easing the movement of materials. Each of the three types of circulation or movement of public, staff, and materials has its own requirement. The size and slope of the site will influence the decision as to the number of levels. Multilevel libraries offer spatial variety but require expensive elevators or space consuming ramps to make all levels and all elements of library service accessible to the handicapped, the young, and the infirm.

One of the first elements to be considered for a multilevel solution is the stack area. Many libraries have a two level stack with reading at the lower or main floor level. This is in contradiction to the way a library is used. If a choice must be made, it is more convenient to locate materials on a single level and provide reader seats on an upper mezzanine or on a lower level.

Maintenance

Materials should be chosen for ease of maintenance. The portion of the library budget that is devoted to maintenance is subject to intensive scrutiny. Materials and equipment should be easy to clean and forgiving of wear and tear. For example, carpet has become a normal floor covering in public libraries. Choose a color and texture that will camouflage dirt and stains rather than a clear, fragile color that will emphasize them. In furniture selection, beware of crisply brittle corners or edges that will crack, chip, or delaminate. Seek slightly rounded or "eased" edges in wood or a vinyl that will absorb routine dents rather than be permanently scarred by them. Acoustic tile ceilings that are within reach of rambunctious young people will soon show finger marks and wear. If ceilings are low and acoustically absorbent, they are also likely to be fragile and vulnerable. Light fixtures should be chosen with relamping in mind. Where fixtures are inaccessible or difficult to relamp, it is sensible to select a higher cost but longer life lamp. These are a few examples of a maintenance-conscious design approach. The librarian is well aware of the problems associated with maintenance and should look critically at the details and choice of finishes as plans develop.

Future Needs

Libraries should be designed for future growth and change. This raises the problem of flexibility. Future expansion can be made simpler by an open-ended design approach that is essentially asymmetrical and consciously incomplete rather than classically balanced and complete. If the architect knows that an addition will be planned or that a future upper floor may be added, this will be a major design determinant. It will also affect the size of the mechanical core facilities, such as the boiler and electrical service.

Libraries do change in their layout and organization. The increase in the use of periodicals, microfilm, film circulation, and data processing are all recent developments that have been absorbed into library service in buildings designed before these elements were considered a normal library activity. It is impractical to design for total flexibility. To assume that any activity can occur anywhere in a public library is asking too much: structural flexibility that permits stack loads anywhere; unlimited potential partition rearrangement; varying air-conditioning and heating zones; and unlimited electrical capability are very expensive. When a librarian asks for "flexibility" it is prudent to question the degree of flexibility that is really essential. Often flexibility has become an excuse for delaying decisions on what is really needed.

The computer looms on the horizon as the next major library activity. It is generally agreed that books and other printed matter will be the primary source of information for at least the next ten years. Computerized circulation control and processing are becoming a normal activity. The floor loading for these activities is no different from normal library design loads. The pieces of equipment are becoming smaller and lighter. The major requirement is for more electrical power and conduit rather than for heavier structural floor loads or increased air-conditioning capacity.

Certainly the libraries designed today will be operating in the year 2000, although they will have been modified in some way to accommodate the changes that will certainly occur. No one on the design team can claim to be a prophet, but both the architect and the librarian can approach the question of future change with an open-minded attitude and a good measure of common sense. Robert Probst has said that "planning that does not recognize error is unrealistic planning."

11 Building on What You Have: Renovations and Additions

The public library movement in the United States from 1880 to the 1920s was characterized by some of the most expensive monumental architecture ever accomplished on a national scale. Architects gloried in assignments that would leave such permanent and lasting impressions on so many minds. These libraries, whether financed by private or public funding, achieved a high level of use and stimulated a strong sense of emotional attachment in their users. Many of them have lasted more than 40 years with ample room for books and readers.

Many of these libraries were carefully and thoughtfully designed. Bookstacks requiring very strong structural systems capable of supporting live loads of 150 pounds per square foot (twice as strong as schools) were located to provide well-organized book collections easy to use and capable of expansion. Natural and artificial lighting was planned to take advantage of the latest technical developments, such as long flourescent lamps ideally suited to bookstacks. Card catalogs were carefully located where they could be used by many people and where they were close to the books. Community meeting rooms were almost always included, with seats and lighting suited to a multipurpose use.

Many of these buildings have been useful in communities over an incredibly long span of time, considering the explosion of population and the many changes in library use over this period. In determining whether or not they should continue to be used as libraries, it is useful to proceed carefully through the process of identifying needs and capabilities.

Community and Library History

When was the building constructed and what was the population and nature of the community at that time? How has the community changed during that time? Describe this in 20-year phases. How has the library met these changes in the community? How has the building changed to accommodate new library service requirements? When were additions built; how were they added to existing functional areas? How have new library functions been handled?

Present Library Situation

Describe the library services delivered to the community at the present time. Compare these with the services delivered 20 and 40 years ago. How many people enter the building each day? How do they come to the library—by car, on foot, or public transportation? How do they use the library: Book circulation, reading, asking questions, looking at films, listening to records? What are the use relationships? How many children use the library compared to adults? How does this relate to the population percentages? How does this relate to the facilities—seating book collection? How do library users relate to population distribution? On a map of the town, locate the library and draw a two mile circle around the library location. Now locate library users on the map. Do most library users come from the immediate area? How does this two mile circle relate to town population clusters, transportation, and shopping centers?

Future Library Needs

Estimate the population in 20 years. Determine the net books added to the library each year, multiply this by 20. Estimate the number of empty book spaces on each shelf and the total number of empty book spaces in the entire library. (About 5–10 percent of the book spaces must remain empty in order for books to be efficiently shelved without having to shift large parts of the collection to shelve just a few books.) This basic calculation will tell you how many new book spaces will be needed in 20 years at the current rate of growth and discard. Sample the collection for frequency of use by randomly selecting 400 books from the shelves to see when they last circulated, and to indicate whether or not the rate of discards can be accelerated, thus postponing the need for more book space. Determine how often most of the seats in the library are in use. Estimate the number of seats required in 20 years by dividing the population by 1,000 and multiplying the result by 5. A town of 20,000 should have 100 seats for children and adults, exclusive of program seats.

By visiting other libraries, reading library literature and consulting with other librarians, determine what new services and facilities should be considered for library expansion. These might include:

Cassette players and duplicators.
Films—16 mm and 8 mm with projectors and screening
    areas.
Video—tape, cassette, disc—and players.
Video and photo reproduction equipment and facilities.
Micro films, fiche—readers, reproducers, and storage.
Computer data bank terminals.
Additional program facilities and art exhibit areas.

After preparing information on facilities to consider, assess community resources already available for any of these functions—other program rooms in the community, art facilities, technical and school libraries—and their accessibility to the general public.

Community Capabilities and Attitudes

Identify community leaders interested in library expansion. Create an expansions committee with the objective of determining community capabilities to support various options in library expansion. Inform these leaders of the expansion information developed above. Work with them to develop a library program that is realistic for the town, remembering that it will take several years to build community support and that this must be done by carefully informing the community about its information needs that could be met by an expanded library.

Examine the capability of the existing building to support expanded services:

Are there empty spaces or little used areas?
Can little used services be eliminated or consolidated?
Can compact storage be used for little used books?
Can technical services be purchased, such as commercially processed books?
Can materials be stored in microform?
Can administrative areas be reduced?
Can the building accommodate handicapped users and staff?
Can the electrical services be expanded and new wiring installed in public areas?
Can the building structure support the weight of additional books?

Evaluating Alternatives

The information collected should now be organized in a factual report indicating present and future needs, community capabilities, and the adequacy of existing physical facilities. This report should clarify a number of basic issues that may never be faced if they are clouded by early discussion of particular plans for an addition or renovation or discussion of the suitability of a particular building for library pruposes. With these issues resolved, it now becomes possible to examine a number of service alternatives in connection with their suitability for accomplishing the program:

Site Evaluations

Transportation, shopping patterns, and neighborhoods may change considerably over the 40-year life of a library building. So the site of the existing building should be carefully reexamined before determining its suitability for an addition:

1. Is it in a location where people will go for a variety of reasons?
2. Is it large enough for the present contemplated addition, and can a further addition be accommodated 20 years from now? Is it large enough for parking? (100 parking spaces require roughly an acre of land.)

3. Is it convenient to public transportation?
4. Will site work require rock excavation?
5. Does the site permit a variety of solutions to the addition, or does the site restrict an addition to only one possible location?
6. Is the area changing?
7. Do most library users live nearby?
8. Do town residents live closer to this area than to other possible sites?
9. Would other sites be more convenient for library users because of roads or mass transportation routes?
10. Is the configuration of the site convenient for library users? A sharply sloping lot will be laborious to climb to get into the building.

One-story Addition

Functional relationships will determine whether or not the shape of the enlarged building is convenient for the public to use and economical to staff. A square building with a multistaff area in the center will yield the shortest distances to various services and materials within the building, while permitting staff members to help the public most easily and to control and supervise all activities within the area. If the building is oblong, parts of it will be less accessible and more difficult to control. If an addition is added to a square building on only one side (the most economical solution), then the building becomes oblong and parts of it become less accessible. The question immediately arises: What services and materials will be in the least accessible area?

Multistory Addition

A single-story building of 10,000 square feet will be more accessible than a two-story building of 10,000 square feet that requires library patrons to climb stairs or wait for an elevator to reach some services. In addition, these services will be less apparent to people using only the main floor and will be used less than similar services available on the main floor. Supervision of staff members working remotely from their supervisors will also be less effective.

Materials will have to be transported vertically,

requiring more staff and public time for this transportation. Cataloguing materials will be more complex in a two-level building, since decisions will have to be made about locating each item and this decision communicated in the card catalog.

Public self-service in a library building is much more difficult to structure in a two-level building, since the location of materials is not immediately apparent but must be communicated by signs. Operating costs of elevators and maintenance is very costly. Decisions regarding location of services on the upper floor of a building addition are complex. Here are some basic services that can be located on an upper floor:

Program Services. If program services are to be located on an upper floor, a separate elevator entrance must be designed that can be opened when the rest of the building is closed, so that library materials can be secured while program facilities are open. However, when program facilities are used during the times that the library is open, the regular staff should be able to control access to these facilities. These conflicting requirements make successful design difficult. Many program facilities are multipurpose rooms that could be used for art exhibits and even for library study rooms at busy times of the year. If these facilities are located on an upper floor, they cannot be supervised by regular staff, nor can they be functionally related to other library activities, such as reference book collections or media viewing areas. Program services should be closely related to such activities as childrens story hours or adult education programs. Libraries can seldom predict how many people will attend their functions. It is difficult for staff and public to make quick decisions to use program areas if they are located on another level.

Children's Services. Often, children's services are put on a different level from adult services because the clientele is easily differentiated from adults and behavior is often noisier and different from adult behavior. However, many children can use adult materials at an early age, but they will be less likely to do so if they cannot gain easy access to those materials. In our present type of use, children coming to the library are usually accompanied by parents. If the children's area is not near the adult area, adults will not be able to use their materials while the children are using children's materials. In even the smallest libraries, children's and adult staffs are quite separate. In some cases, this does not result in the best service because there is not sufficient understanding of materials and service patterns that would be mutually useful. For example, many simplified explanations for adults may be found in childrens books, and many children's reference questions require adult materials to answer. Nearby physical locations would enhance both types of services. Staff economies in circulation and processing routines can result from close coordination of children's and adult services—coordinated sending of overdue notices and registrations, for example.

Media Services. Comparatively new media services are often located on another level. Hours are often curtailed because there are insufficient staff to operate both levels of the library. Referrals from one medium to another seldom occur when they are physically separated. The basic concept of the full service library is one that envisions the library user being given a wide range of opportunities every time the user comes to the library. If an artificial vertical barrier is placed separating library services, the user may never learn to think of media as an integrated physical concept.

Scale and Size

Libraries serving 50,000 people or more will require buildings with more than 25,000 square feet of space. At this scale, a single-story building begins to defeat its basic purpose of integrating library self-service concepts. Someday we may come to realize that no library should be that large and that the optimum library size is 20,000 square feet on one level. Libraries of that size fit the human scale and can be understood and used effectively by most human beings.

The only argument for larger libraries is better service and materials—more specialized staff and a wider range of choice—but perhaps the occasions when most of us need that wide range of choice are comparatively rare, and perhaps we would obtain better service on those occasions by contacting a network through the smaller service outlet that is more familiar with our needs.

Networking and electronic access are, however, probably at least ten years away, so regional libraries and major city libraries will continue to expand and to serve large segments of the population. These large, multistory service agencies with specialized services require buildings designed in modular formats with extremely flexible electrical and partition systems, and an alternating of service areas so that staff and public can use a wide range of materials and store these materials nearby. Most large library additions have not related usefully to their original building design, yet they still have been able to achieve this flexibility.

Incorporating Old and New

Buildings designed as monumental structures tended to be built around large rooms with a great deal of cubic area, with high ceilings and great distance between support columns. The basic nature of libraries envisioned by these designers was that library buildings had three important basic functions:

1. *Storage of books* requiring modular column design to support the great weight of stacks. Stack areas were set aside from reading areas because of this difference in their support system requirements and were often not intended to be available to the public. Since they were not used intensively, the aisles were narrow, light was dim, and they were noisy and uncomfortable. Today, stack areas need to be accessible to the public with wider aisles, better lighting, better ventilation, and with convenient seating nearby.

2. *Reading rooms* were wide open, high-ceilinged areas, which were not strong enough to support the weight of books in any quantity. They were lit by natural light. Now these reading rooms should be closer to the books, well-lighted because they are used mostly at night, and with comfortable seating because they are used for long periods of time.

3. *Check-out and staff areas* to control the flow of books were near the entrance, not near the reading or book areas, and were very large to accommodate the book cards, book storage, and slipping areas necessary for circulation control systems of that time. Now much smaller areas are needed because of automated circulation systems.

Building an addition to these large buildings big enough for 20 years of new materials requires an entirely new design concept that recognizes the changing nature of libraries and information. This new concept is the information center library, designed to place the librarian at the center of services. How can this information center, with its requirements for computer terminals, film projectors, and a wide range of reference services and books, be fitted into a large library building designed to break library functions down into separate areas for books, readers and staff? This will, of course, depend on the actual building in question and on the money and technical skills available to design and build the addition.

Bookstack access must be controlled but convenient for the user and the staff. Recently introduced theft detection devices and television monitoring systems make this much easier than it was ten years ago. New computerized circulation control and inventory and cataloguing systems make it possible to have instant staff and public access to book information in a widely scattered bookstack area. Computerized catalogs make it possible to gain access to cataloguing information at many different areas in a multilevel building.

Summary of Addition Considerations

Relationship to existing structure:

1. What are the site limitations to adding to the building?
2. Can there be a single, convenient entrance for users arriving by automobile and on foot?
3. If there are two entrances, can they be controlled from one internal location? Added control stations mean added operating cost.
4. Can the existing bookstack area be added onto in an addition, or will the bookstacks be in several locations? How do these locations relate to the size requirements for various parts of the book collection in 20 years? For example, if the existing bookstack will hold all the new fiction books for 20 years in addition to the present fiction collection, it will be more convenient for the public to use than if there has to be a split in the adult fiction collection.
5. Will the existing building fit in reasonably with the functional area requirements for any of the new service areas? Often, old buildings are used as staff support areas with the addition designed for public service. This may be a useful solution if these areas provide good staff supervision in the public areas and

are related in size to the program needs for staff support areas.

6. If both old and new buildings are used for public service, will they be easily accessible from one another?
7. Can similar functions be accommodated on one floor or will functions be split onto several levels? Will the existing building plus the addition be large enough to accommodate all adult services on one level?
8. If single functions must be split, how can they be controlled? Can the staff see other levels (mezzanine, closed-circuit TV)?

Mechanical systems considerations:

1. Is the existing electrical service adequate for the existing building? For an addition?
2. Do the existing boilers have surplus capacity?
3. Will the old library be more expensive to heat and cool with an addition than a new building?
4. How expensive will it be to improve the lighting system in the old building?
5. How will the old building be cooled? Can this be controlled well?
6. How will the old building be protected against fire and smoke? Can an alarm system be installed inexpensively?

12 Case Studies and Plan Critiques

After a library improvement program has been completed and approved by the library board and administration, it should be discussed fully and carefully with the architect. For the purposes of this discussion, it may be useful to prepare an area relationship scaled plan. This plan can be made by cutting out rectangular boxes of various color of cardboard scaled to the area required for each function. In this way, each function can be related to others in the same scale and a series of alternative relationships can be discussed with the architect.

Schematic Plans and Critique

The detail presented in schematic plans will vary considerably with the architectural firm. Since libraries require careful coordination of furniture, lighting, heating, and graphics, the architect should be required to include equipment and furnishings on schematic plans. These schematic plans developed from the area relationships should show the widest variation between alternatives.

Each plan should be critically evaluated according to the library improvement program. Consider the advantages and disadvantages of the plan:

1. From the point of view of *user convenience*. Walk through the plan as if you were the library user experiencing the building sequentially:

a. Drive into the parking lot.
b. Find the building entrance.
c. Enter the building.
d. Find staff assistance.
e. Find the card catalog and books.
f. Find magazines and films.
g. Look at a film in the library.
h. Find children's services.
i. Read quietly for a long time.
j. Conveniently use indexes, periodicals, and micro-forms.
k. Find an individual carrel.
l. Talk with other library users.
m. Experience a concert or film.
n. Can children play, read, be active?

2. From the point of view of *the staff*, which controls the various public functions and operates a variety of services:
a. Can you see people entering the building and needing assistance?
b. Is there only one clearly marked entrance?
c. Can you see down the stack aisles from the central staff station.?
d. Can you see all reading chairs and tables?
e. Are the card catalog and reference books near the central staff station?
f. In libraries serving 10,000 people or less, can the staff perform both reference and check-out functions at a single library entrance?
g. Is there sufficient counter and storage space at the staff location?
h. Can the staff assist with public use of machines? projectors? cassette players? microform readers?
i. Can the staff work quietly while supervising the public?
j. Can the staff talk with the public and other staff privately?

Preliminary Plans and Critique

When a satisfactory schematic plan has been developed, it should be presented to the library board and funding authorities by the architect and building committee. This will assure that money is not spent on working drawings for a building that cannot be funded. This is the time to make whatever changes are necessary for funding purposes. At each succeeding phase, changes will become more costly.

When all authorities are in agreement, the architect can be authorized to proceed with design development. This phase should result in coordination of the lighting, graphics, and heating/air-conditioning plans. Windows, doors, ductwork, and electrical outlets will be positioned in this phase. Some architects may want to postpone some of these details. This should be avoided, since postponement will make plan changes more difficult.

Plans will again show furniture placement, but electrical outlets, ductwork, and lighting may not be together on a single plan so it now becomes important to match several separate plans to assure coordination. Some questions to consider are:

1. Are doors wide enough for the easy passage of large equipment?
2. Are handicapped requirements met?
3. How do windows work in relation to morning sun and evening cool?
4. Do window locations interfere with wall bookstacks?
5. How is seating related to thermostat location and ducts?
6. How are graphics related to general and specific lighting?
7. Are electrical receptacles conveniently located?
8. What light fixtures are planned?
9. Where will a theft detection system be located?

Detailed drawings of all equipment should be prepared with elevations as well as plan views. Furnishings should be selected now so that they can be coordinated with lighting and graphics. Heating and air-conditioning controls; lighting and electrical controls; and displays and lighting all should be discussed at this stage.

Working Drawings and Critique

The final documents used by the various building trades to construct the building are the working drawings. They take a great deal of time to prepare and include every last building detail. Great care should be taken to avoid making changes in working drawings, but this will not be possible unless the architect supplies considerable detail in design development. Again, it will be much more

costly to make changes after these working drawings are
sent to the bidders. During construction, changes require change orders to the construction company with a
dollar amount assigned to each change. Therefore, all
staff members and the consultant should go over each
drawing.

Look for each electrical outlet, light fixture, and
item of furniture and equipment. Locate window dimensions. Require photos of all fixtures and equipment.

Case Study: Woodville

(These case studies are actual jobs not idealized examples)

In 1950, Woodville had been a sleepy rural town of
3,000 about 15 miles from a small urban center of 75,000.
A wealthy citizen had left a fine Victorian mansion for
use by the town as a library. Split up into several rooms,
it had served as a pleasant place for citizens to visit for a
book and chat with the librarian.

By 1970, the library shelves were bulging with
books, and the community had become an upwardly
mobile town of 10,000 intelligent, well-educated subur-
banites with a modern school system and a wide variety
of library needs. The library board interviewed and hired
a consultant after the librarian had prepared an analysis
of the use of the library and the potential growth of the
community. This community analysis revealed the projected 20-year population size to be 15,000 and the maximum zoning population to be 17,000. It confirmed the
librarian's opinion about the educational quality and the
population age mix, which showed an increasing number
of elderly people.

Book circulation had been growing modestly, but
information use had grown faster. The library was used
by a wide variety of age groups and for purposes that
included meetings, film shows, story hours, and art
exhibits as well as for books and information.

The board and librarian visited nearby new library
buildings and wrote a statement of purpose indicating
their desire for the library to be an information and
cultural media center located in an accessible place with
parking facilities sufficient for the 90 percent of users
who came by car. The library consultant was retained to
prepare a brief building program based on the community information already collected by the staff. Discussion among the staff, consultant, and building committee

revealed the requirements that the building be staffed by the existing staff of five and that it provide the opportunity for a wide variety of services emanating from a central location for the staff.

A preliminary program was prepared and altered after discussion with the staff and building committee. The consultant advised on architect selection criteria and an architect was chosen. Early schematics showed the reference area too close to the noisy entrance and browsing area; after that was changed, design development proceeded with a monthly meeting among architect, consultant, and building committee.

During the design development phase some of the topics discussed were:

1. Perimeter versus centralized air conditioning.
2. Varied lighting requirements: light at the information center and reference and in the bookstacks, but less light in the passage areas. A general agreement was reached to keep the lighting very directional, controlling spread by an assortment of louvers and aiming for variety.
3. Seating mix among carrels, tables, and lounge chairs; mostly single seating with comfort and durability emphasized—good quality, minimum quantity.
4. Parking spaces were developed in front of as well as at the side of the building.
5. Entry display ports for a variety of media and display and viewing purposes were devised.
6. Childrens seating and story hour areas were changed and a flexible partition system introduced into the children's area.

The Improvement of Library Services in Woodville

Since 1950, when the old house was presented to the library to be used as a branch, the people of Woodville have enjoyed library service at minimal cost to the town. As early as 1959, a professional library survey had characterized this building as inadequate for library use. Today anywhere from 50 to 165 people a day crowd into this gracious old Victorian building in an attempt to extract a book from the crowded shelves. The size of the library community is estimated at over 10,000 people; the tiny public service area of approximately 1,000 square feet is considerably below the minimum library standard even if it had been designed for library purposes. As it is, the house is broken up into many small rooms making supervision difficult and the book arrangement confusing to follow. Expansion is not possible within the existing building because the second floor is not strong enough to hold books in any quantity and would require additional staff to operate.

The use of library facilities provides a solid basis for planning improved library services. Annual book circulation is over 44,000. A goodly number of people in addition come to the branch to consult the minimal reference materials located there. The library staff is energetic and active in the community despite such handicaps as heating failures, minimal parking facilities, and the lack of a sign that can be read from an automobile. No more books can be squeezed into this library; some are already stored in the basement in a valiant attempt to increase the small book collection.

The past few years have witnessed a revolutionary new trend in school library services. Educators have rediscovered the school library. They have renamed it a media center or learning center. They have begun to stock it with cassette tapes, filmstrips, movies, and loop-films as well as books, but more importantly, they have begun to realize the power of individualized instruction in which the student takes a more active part in the choice of materials for the learning process. This new trend will mean that public libraries will need to be stronger than ever in providing a wide variety and great depth of resources in all kinds of media.

In Woodville, the elementary and junior high school library facilities are very limited. There are no new schools planned for the area for at least five years. If branch library facilities are to be of any help to young students, it is imperative that they be improved immediately. It will also be necessary to plan for improving school library facilities, but the branch library can serve all ten schools in the area and will continue to serve these students in the evenings (the branch is open until 8 P.M.), in the summer, during winter vacation, and when they graduate from school.

In planning for improved library services, in an area where the town has never had to make a capital investment, it is most prudent to plan for a 20-year growth in services. People's needs for information have rapidly accelerated as our society has grown better educated and more complex. These needs, added to the traditional educational demands satisfied by book circulation, and the future requirements for film, tape, and other media, point to a building plan that is open, flexible, and designed both for built-in and added on growth capabilities. Increasing labor costs require that buildings be designed for minimum maintainence and maximum self-service use. The following building program is an attempt to incorporate these requirements into a set of clear, simple specifications. Their implementation will require careful communication among architect, building committee, librarian, and library consultant.

The Regional Planning Agency estimates the population at 10,612; the projected 20-year population is 15,000. On this basis, Woodville desperately needs now an adequate new community library of its own designed to satisfy the educational needs of its burgeoning population.

	Existing Branch	*New Facilities*
Books	8,000	35,000
Area in square feet	1,400	8,000
Seating	18	50
Hours	48	60
Staff	2	5
Budget	$26,500	$60,000

Building Areas

Information-Media		500
Browsing-Magazines		500
Books-Reading		3,100
Children-Community		1,500
Staff-Work		800
Miscellaneous		1,600
	Total	8,000 sq ft

Woodville Library Building Program

An open plan with provision for future expansion beyond the initial program area of 8,000 square feet will be essential because Woodville is a growing area and library services are constantly changing. The building should be built around a central service area near the entrance and immediately apparent upon entering the building. This *information* center is the nerve center of the community library. It should be carefully designed so that staff can give maximum service as quickly and conveniently as possible.

A four-sided counter, 30 inches high and 20 feet on a side, with two-way gate openings on two sides. Double-faced with chairs and knee openings on both sides:

Side 1: facing Entrance; provision for electrical microfilm charger, provision for book returns; telephone and cash drawer under counter.

Side 2: facing Browsing 4 chairs; reference books under counter.

Side 3: facing Books-Reading 4 chairs; microfilm periodicals under counter; microfilm readers, copying machine on counter.

Side 4: facing Children-Community, 4 chairs; media storage under counter; media hardware on counter.

Inside area: shelving for 200 reserve books above space for 4 book trucks for returns. Storage for 3,000 returned T-cards (3'×5'). Glassed-in office with telephone (10" × 10"). 4 desks and 4 chairs (lockers for bags).

Browsing-Magazines (500 sq ft)

Near entrance: 4 comfortable chairs (future + 4); 2 small low tables (future + 2).

Newspaper rack for 5 papers.

Magazine shelving for 50 magazines, with swinging doors to hold back issues behind. 6 double-faced sections, 84" high, 30" wide, 18' long.

Display wall: vinyl-covered homosote shelving standards every 3 feet (Garcey); 4 flat shelves and brackets (—Garcey); 1 sloping shelf (—Garcey brackets).

Light track to illuminate display wall.

quence. 20 ranges, each range 6 sections double-faced here.

Coat Racks for 10 coats and hats.

Paperback book racks to display 200 titles, cover out.

Mens room and ladies room, near the entrance and visible from Information: 120 foot candle illumination; unbreakable steel mirror, center drains in floor, built-in stainless fixtures, cantilevered sinks and toilet bowls, dark-colored booths, rough-textured walls.

Book return corral for 4 book trucks.

Entry: treadle-operated doors with hot/cold weather barrier in lobby. No center mullion.

Lockable book retrun slot (Mosler Dropository)
with area for 500 returns and CO2 extinguisher
Public telephone, *not* a phone booth.
Drinking Fountain.

Books-Reading (3,100 sq ft)

Shelving for 35,000 books in one standard sequence. 20 ranges, each range 6 sections double-faced 90" high; 2 ranges in each row, 10 rows. Area = **50'** × 50' = 2,500 sq ft. This dimension should determine the width of the building (including walls).

Lighting for the stacks should be fluorescent fixtures hung directly from the stack frames. Parawedge louvers should be included to reduce glare.

Children's nonfiction should be shelved with adult nonfiction in the same numerical sequence. Fiction for children and picture book browsing bins for children should be in the open community area. Adult fiction should be shelved in the books area adjacent to the browsing area.

Reading: Individual carrels and upright upholstered chairs without arms for 10 people 4 tables for 4 each (future + 10).

Card Catalog: 100 drawers (future + 40) to be spread out rather than concentrated.

Children-Community (1,500 sq ft)

5 picture book bin units for children (future +5).

5 phonorecord browser boxes (future +5).

1 cushion dispenser with 20 cushions for children to sit on the floor (future + 20).

4 individual carrels and 4 upholstered chairs (14" seats) for children near outside walls to minimize moving (future + 4). 2 tables for 4 each.

Storage for 20 comfortable upholstered stack chairs (future + 20).

A pull-down movie screen built into the ceiling near the far wall. Two built-in speakers, one on each side of the screen. Wires should lead back through conduit (placed in the floor before pouring) to 2 jacks at the information area.

Librarian's office: 12′ × 12′, typewriter and stand, desk, swivel chair, 4 drawer file.

Lounge: 15′ × 15′, coke machine, trash barrel, table and 4 chairs, sofa, refrigerator, sink, stove, coffee maker, 4 lockers (future + 2), 6 coat hooks.

Storage area and delivery entrance.

Trash pick-up area: 4 cans.

Custodial storage for vacuum, cleaning and paper supplies.

Miscellaneous (1,600 sq ft)

Entry, utilities, halls, and passageways.

Environment: Heating and air conditioning by individual units (Singer-Remington K-15) rather than centralized system, to provide for varying temperature requirements in each area. Special attention should be given to information area and office. Lighting in this area should include parawedge louvers to reduce glare.

Carpeting throughout the library should be light-brown flecked undyed natural wool with Brunsmet grounding wires woven into the fibers. Entry carpet should be easily removable for cleaning and there should be a spare carpet.

Entrance drive should be located near entrance marquee to provide covered delivery and pickup and should include a large trash holder.

Lighting should be recessed, glare-free lighting, with 70 foot candles in all reading areas and parawedge louvers. Entire room must be capable of being darkened.

Mens and ladies rooms: brightly lit with cantilevered fixtures, unbreakable mirrors, center drains.

Graphics: near street, perpendicular to traffic, a large lighted sign with hours.

Drinking fountain, with stool for children to stand on.

Typing stand on carpet casters.

Wood: natural, unstained, minimal hardware, no veneers.

Plastic laminates: nonglare surfaces.

Chairs on glides to move easily on carpet.

Coat hooks distributed throughout building.

Outdoor equipment shed: grass cutter, snow-blower.

Curtains or Twi-Night blinds to darken room for films.

Steel bicycle rack for 10 bicycles.

Copy machine and microfilm reader.

First Schematic Critique

1. Rework staff, office, lounge, and work area to include seminar room and
2. Separate office and lounge areas.
3. Office to have glass view into reference.
4. Change reading name to reference.
5. Interior stair to unfinished lower level at rear of reference.
6. Staff parking near delivery at rear.
7. Bookstack nearest reference to be only 42" high.
8. Photocopier to have separate 30 amp. circuit.
9. Change machine near photocopier.
10. Photocopier moved to near enclosed work area.
11. Alternate additional projection area in one of the children's wings for use when rest of library is in use.
12. Children's card catalog 30 drawers.
13. Alternate additional separate 30 amp. electrical outlet for second copier in browsing area.
14. Community bulletin board.
15. Graphics: interior and exterior.
16. Curb cuts for wheelchairs and bicycles.

Second Schematic Critique

1. Additional storage door for children's chair access.
2. Curb cut in front for bikes and wheelchairs.
3. Trash containers—front and rear; four large cans in rear.
4. Information desk 42" in front, lower reserve and sort shelf behind. 30" high on sides.
5. Paperback and recent book racks lighted and more visible from entrance.
6. Change direction of reference bookstacks.
7. Place reference carrel area between fiction and non-fiction stack.
8. Children's stacks vary in height from 42" to 60" to 90" at rear.
9. Stack chairs to have upholstered seats.
10. Marquee at entrance.

11. Lower level designed for more flexibility, with a movable platform.
12. Lower level: flat floor, movable seating, film screen, divided partitions, speaker at stage, fixed screen with curtains, projection room—sound controls outside. Divider.
13. Two microphone outlets. Speaker wires to go in hung ceiling.
14. Lights above auditorium entrance, high up on building to light parking lot also.
15. Finished auditorium to be bid as an alternate.
16. Lower level: 2,700 sq ft; 150 seats.
17. Check entrance sightlines for relationships among doors, mullions, lighting, information desk, materials. What do people see on entering building?
18. Ways of cutting costs:
    Low cost exterior.
    Lower cost landscaping.
    Excavate *only* for lower level.
    Fewer furnishings.

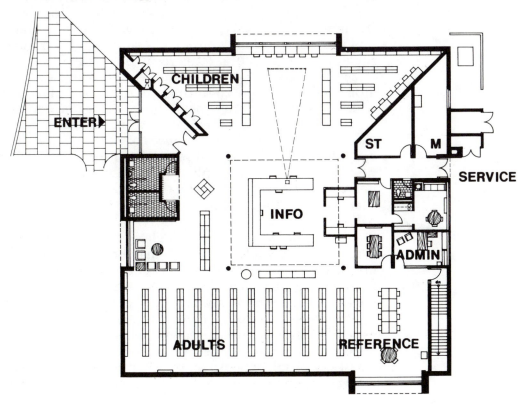

MAIN FLOOR

Woodville Library plan.

Reduce module from 30′ to 28′.
Lower site costs.

Case Study: Crane

Crane is a distinguished small community consisting of about 4,900 people living in carefully zoned neighborhoods with the community focusing on a small historic district of colonial-type retail stores. There are many retired people and a traditional New England town meeting type of government. Population projections are for a town of 7,300 by 1996, with present zoning retained. With the current trend for conservative growth, this population may never be reached, so that this program is predicated on conservative growth possibilities with modest provision for a future addition.

The library building on the edge of the historic district is a small, Tudor-type building constructed in the 1890s. It contains about 1,600 square feet, including a small addition constructed in 1942. 13,000 books are crammed into every available space with about 17 seats squeezed into various nooks and crannies. The annual circulation of 22,000 is 60 percent fiction and has increased by over 50 percent in the last ten years, a much more rapid increase than the growth in population, which was less than 10 percent during the same period.

Although the budget has also increased to keep pace with the population, the needs of citizens for books and information is not well served by the present facilities. The library is open only 26 hours a week. This is an improvement over the 22 hours a week schedule ten years ago, and the 26 hours do include two evenings and half day Saturday.

Lack of any newspaper or phonorecord collections is rather remarkable even in a small library. However, use of the State Library service center for books is an encouraging trend. The library purchases more than 600 books per year and many more are contributed. Withdrawals are over 300 per year, so that the collection generally reflects current town needs. This is highly important to the library user who is often discouraged by masses of obsolete books on the shelves. A fresh, interesting collection is the best way to encourage reader interest, especially since books in lesser demand are now so readily available from the State Library.

The Site

In a compact town (11.7 square miles) with a good road net, a single principal library will offer the best service, concentrating a good book collection within easy reach of all citizens. The site purchased for the new library is about a quarter mile from the old building on a ¾ acre level lot, just outside the historic district and across from the Town Hall. It affords on-site dedicated library parking as well as access to the Town Hall parking lot. Since it is close to the old library, the 40 percent of library patrons who now walk or bicycle should have no trouble gaining access to the new location.

Building Program

The objective of this program is to suggest ways in which the library can be designed for user satisfaction and convenience, staff effectiveness, and future flexibility.

Design Suggestions

The people are proud of their New England background; therefore, a new library in this town should reflect the strength of this pride by being firmly rooted in this heritage. Traditional wood and brick materials would be acceptable in the community. A pitched roof and a symmetrically proportioned window/door design with an overall size in keeping with building lot setbacks found elsewhere in town would assist greatly in the effort that will have to be made to raise funds for the construction of the new library.

Although a wide variety of architectural styles exists in town, the library is uniquely a building for all the citizens and should be integrated into the particular part of the town where it will be built and into the aspirations of the citizens for a traditional community. The landscaping of this new building, both inside and out, can be a very important contributing factor to this image. Selection of shrubs, careful preservation of existing trees, and a design fitted into this natural environment can result in a library that will be a center of the town's cultural life for many years to come.

Interior Design Considerations

The interior of the building should be integrated with traditional exterior design, yet major functions should be strongly stated in the design, selection and arrangement of furnishings. Libraries will offer an increasingly wider variety of materials. Children and adults require different kinds of spaces for their activities. It is easy for library interiors to look like junk shops or marble book vaults. The new library should invite library users to enjoy a variety of environments:

1. A neat, orderly bookstack with integrated graphics and lighting leading readers from the card catalog to the appropriate book and to the check-out desk.
2. A quiet, comfortable reading area with carrels, tables, and lounge chairs, each with lighting individually controlled and consistent comfortable temperature with no drafts.
3. A well-organized check-in area with a community bulletin board, art and book display, book browsing, and magazines.
4. A quiet reference area with orderly arranged books and indexes and a staff counter.
5. A children's activity and story hour area with work table, cushions on the floor, and learning materials.
6. A children's reading and reference area with carrels and tables and reference books.

Colorful material display and task lighting of activities should be considered as design elements in each of these areas. With the exception of the major adult stack area, furnishings should be low and light in appearance so that the library has an open look. Breathable fabrics and body-shaped chairs signify that the building is for people. There should be wall space for up to ten paintings with lighting.

Mechancial Design Considerations

Heating and air-conditioning library buildings can create major problems in design. People tend to spend a good deal of time in libraries. They sit still and their metabolisms tend to slow down and their bodily heating requirements vary markedly. Rooms that occasionally house 100 people may also operate for long periods with only ten people in them. Natural light admitted through windows changes from hour to hour and season to season, and windows can be too hot on a sunny day and too cold when the sun goes down. In buildings smaller than 8,000 square feet, individually thermostated perimeter through wall heating and air-conditioning units are economical to install and operate and offer a distinct maintenance advantage since if one is out of operation, the remaining units are still effective. (Singer manufactures a unit that can use centrally produced hot water to heat and electricity to cool, combining the advantages of cheap oil heat and controlled electrical air-conditioning.) Such a system also provides better local control of temperature.

The need for natural light, and the aesthetic satisfaction that is derived from being able to enjoy green trees and blue skies while being sheltered from the elements, is an important consideration in designing a library. However, in the summer the heat of the sun coming into a building through windows or skylights presents a challenge to any air-conditioning system. This problem can be alleviated by making windows and skylights operable so that hot air rising can escape from the building and by providing light control by means of tinted glass to reduce excessive heat in summer. The location of glass can also be carefully oriented to prevent cold in the winter and to avoid drafts on readers seated for long periods and building overhangs can be used to prevent direct sunlight from striking windows. The location of thermostats can also conserve energy and ensure appropriate consistent temperatures in long-term use locations. Carefully worded instructions to operate the heating and air-conditioning systems is a vital part of this program. The specifying of Economiser type controls, which afford the maximum use of outside air for heating and cooling, is another important consideration, if linked with large outside air ducts and modulating damper controls.

Acoustical and insulation treatment of the building is important for functional and economic considerations. Homosote, both underneath the carpeting and on the walls, is a cheap and effective material as long as its instability is understood in the design of bookstack supports and display walls. A high grade acoustical ceiling and the use of acoustical material in and around ceiling light fixtures can also be helpful. Parawedge louvers to control the brightness of ceiling luminaires will impart a quiet look to the library interior.

Staff Effectiveness

A new library that will provide a greater choice of materials than at present and offer new services, such as adult programs, while keeping staff costs relatively stable, must be designed to emphasize self-service, convenience of the public, and staff operational effectiveness.

Public library services on a single level at grade will result in:

1. 30 percent saving in staff costs compared to a multi-level building.
2. Rapid, convenient service.
3. Ease of control and supervision.
4. Lowest building cost (books require 150-pound load structure). The basic structural cost of the building will increase if books are placed in a structure above grade.
5. Elimination of elevators.
6. Ease of library use by the handicapped and elderly.

Nonpublic services such as maintenance and utilities may be located on a separate level.

Change and Expansion

A library should be designed with the first phase of expansion an integral part of the initial design. In programming this building, we have considered these factors:

1. 7,000 population in 1995.
2. State and national library standards modestly interpreted.
3. Minimum operating cost for staff and utilities.
4. Flexible growth capabilities.

Parking

Some of the people who use the library walk or come on bicycles, but parking is essential for the others.

Space for 12 cars and a covered area to protect people and books while waiting for cars should be provided. Parking should be carefully landscaped to soften the metallic shapes and hard asphalt surfaces. Future additional parking for 10 cars should be included in the plans.

Entrance

There should be a curb cut ramp for wheelchairs so that handicapped people may climb the curb. This curb cut will also be useful for bicycles.

Trash barrels should be provided.

A bookdrop (Mosler Dropository) for the return of books when the library is closed should be built into the entrance to the library. It should be lockable so that it cannot be used when the library is open. On the inside of the bookdrop there should be a large padded area to accommodate returned books. Above the bookdrop on the inside a fire extinguisher with a low-melting point fusible link should be mounted so as to extinguish fires caused by burning materials being dropped in the bookdrop.

A "hair dryer" type temperature curtain at doors and wind baffle should be considered for energy conservation, comfort, and lower cost.

Bicycle racks should be provided so that there is full support for the front wheels and locking capabilities.

A telephone should be available with a coin operated phone outside.

The delivery entrance should be clearly marked and separate from the public parking entrance. The delivery entrance and storage room should include blower space heaters and an outside signal.

Doors should open easily to accommodate people with armloads of books and the handicapped. Signs indicating hours should be on *both* sides of doors.

Near the entrance, there should be paperback books on racks displaying covers and spines; recent books (purchases within six months); notable books, carefully selected from the library collection; and topical books on a topic of current interest.

Wall display areas should intersperse books and art. A lighted bulletin board should be provided for news about books and library and community events with a shelf for flyers below.

Current magazines and back issues for one year should be shelved together with current issues displayed and back issues stored behind hinged sloping shelves. Newspaper racks for 5–10 newspapers should be provided, with one week of older newspapers stored underneath.

Circulation

The circulation area is divided into:

1. *Public:* Counter where library users check-out books and separate return counter, nonglare. Located for one person staffing. Check-out station with electrical outlets for charging machine, and telephone, 30″ high on staff side, 39″ on public side. Reserve control system for setting aside returns (30) that have been reserved by other borrowers.
Lockable cash drawer.
Accessible storage for book trucks to receive returns.
Coat and umbrella racks.
2. *Staff:* Work area for overdue retrieval, addressing, mailing, mending. This area should have counter space and a sink; Wall shelving; and a 30″ high counter with lockable purse drawer, swivel chair, and typewriter with electrical outlets. The office for the librarian should have a closet for supplies with a lock and adjustable shelves.

Bookstacks

Easy access to books requires compact, orderly shelving in a well-lighted, unified area. Lights should be hung from the stacks and brightness shielded with para-wedge louvers. Graphics on end-panels and shelves must be flexible, well-lighted, and easily visible. Temperature is not too critical in this area. A 5° variation is acceptable. Acoustical treatment is not critical, but carpeting and acoustical ceilings would control noise usefully.

In order to simplify public access to books, it is useful for this space to be a single unit with stacks running in the same direction and graphic signs on both shelves and end-panels. This is the largest public service area in the library, and it will be essential to design the building around this area.

Stack aisles should be visible from the centrally-located circulation desk. Stacks for the entire future size of the book collection should be purchased and installed at economical large-volume prices when the building is built. The top shelves should be stored, but a few books should be placed on each of the other shelves so that new books can be placed on their appropriate shelves with no major shifting necessary.

To ensure reader convenience and staff control, the book collection should be placed in a *single continuous one-pattern* arrangement. Books are consecutively numbered; any break in the shelving pattern will be confusing to the reader.

Bookstack design should include these considerations:

1. Each section of books is 3-feet long and 90 inches high.
2. A double-faced section holds 300 volumes if seven shelves on each side are utilized.
3. Stacks must be braced across the top and secured to the walls.
4. A range of shelving should be a maximum of six sections long to make it possible for readers to move easily from one aisle to the next. Ranges should be spaced 5 feet on centers. This will leave an aisle 44" wide if 8" shelving is utilized, or 40" wide if 10" shelving is installed. Each range will hold 1,800 books.
5. Studies have shown that fluorescent lighting (mounted about 3" above the top of the stacks), shielded by angled egg-crate parawedge louvers, will provide optimum lighting with minimum glare.
6. Seating should not be combined with stacks because this would require a wider aisle and a larger area.

Paperbacks are an excellent way of extending the library budget for ephemeral materials (popular fiction and nonfiction). They should not be catalogued, but should be displayed in the browsing area near the library entrance on racks that show both covers and spines simultaneously (such as Gaylord-Mar-Line).

Reading Area

The reading area, which should be near the multi-purpose room, will set the style of the library. It should have an inviting but quiet atmosphere with:

Acoustical ceilings and wall treatment.
Carpeting with thick, sound absorbent underlayment.
Wood with nonglare surfaces.
Coat hooks and trash baskets for public convenience.
Careful heat control, 2° variation and 20–30% relative
    humidity minimum.
A variety of seating and table arrangements in small
    groups.
Carrels with full sides but low backs and no shelves.
Tables for four.
Comfortable lounge seating in chairs for long-time use
    that are easy to get into and out of and economical
    to maintain, with support for lower back and
    shoulders.
Chairs with a sled base that glide on carpets and breatha-
    ble upholstery.
A high level of uniform lighting, 75 fc, but parawedge
    louvers to prevent glare.
Shelves large enough to hold oversize 14″ books.
Visual staff supervision, but not close proximity.
Large print books and magnifying reading device.

Reference Area

    The reference area should be located and designed
for future expansion. It should include:

Seating for librarians and the public on opposite sides of a
    counter and adjustable storage on the staff side
    underneath.
High-intensity 100 fc lighting with glare-free louvers
    because of the need for continuous concentrated
    staff and public use.
Local acoustical separation for several adjacent conversa-
    tions to take place.
Design should concentrate staff services and develop
    small reader groupings while maintaining good
    supervision.

    The reference area should be emphasized by light-
ing and graphics, while the circulation area is less prominent. Materials requiring staff assistance, such as
reference books and indexes, must be grouped close to
the information center.
    The mass public is interested primarily in the
current issue of magazines. For reference purposes,
however, a magazine collection, together with appropri-

ate indexes, will be useful to a smaller number of people over a considerably longer period of time. Older magazines may be available on microfilm. This microfilm center should consist of such indexes as *The Readers Guide* and *New York Times Index*, a table-top microfilm reader, a dry reader-printer, and cabinets. These should be located in the reference area, but close to the current magazines.

Card Catalog

The card catalog should be visible upon entering the library. It should be spread apart rather than squeezed together so that the maximum number of people can use it at a given time. It should be no more than five drawers high, with the top drawer 50 inches from the floor. The top surface and sliding reference drawers at the base of the catalog must be especially durable. It should be constructed in modular form, but the maximum number of drawers should be installed so that expansion is possible with a minimum of card shifting.

Children's Services

Included in children's services are: Reading services, a children's story-telling area, puppet shows, and films in an open area with cushions and movie screen. Acoustical and lighting solutions should aim at the separate treatment of each of these areas in one open space.

Staff Area

The staff office should be carpeted and well-lighted and the future occupants consulted concerning desks, chairs, and files necessary to properly furnish it. It should be near the circulation/reference area and visible to and from that area.

Multipurpose Room

The multipurpose room should be furnished with upholstered stack chairs and projection facilities, with conduits for microphone; slide controls and drape controls; and speakers. The walls should have picture molding and vinyl or burlap covered homosote. There should be fluorescent lighting in the center and light tracks on the perimeter to light display walls. Low shelving is needed for large books.

The multipurpose room should be located and designed so that during busy times of the day, week, month, or year it can accommodate additional reader's seating. For this reason, the design of the multipurpose room should include these considerations:

Lighting should be free of glare and have an intensity of 50 footcandles at a height of 30 inches above the floor.

Storage for chairs and tables to seat a total of 40 people should be provided.

Acoustical materials should be used for floor, ceiling, and walls with some consideration for adjusting acoustics to accommodate musical performance.

The multipurpose and reading areas should be adjacent and there should be some consideration given to acoustical separation and staff supervision of both areas. The possibility of alternate expansion of both areas should be explored.

Provisions for the Handicapped

1. Safe parking close to the library building reserved for the handicapped.
2. Level walks with ramped curbs at crossways. Avoid coarse aggregate cement, bricked walks, or cobblestones.
3. Paved walks in parking lot.
4. Ground level building entrance at least 32-inches wide.
5. Gently sloping ramps (ratio 1 × 12).
6. Nonskid floors.
7. Lower drinking fountains and public telephones for wheelchair users.
8. Restrooms with one wide stall, grab bars, and easily operable faucets.

Lighting. In most cases, fixtures should be recessed into a 2 × 4 foot t-bar acoustical tile ceiling with easy access so that fixture locations can be changed as library functions change. The source of light should be as invisible as possible while providing efficient utilization of electricity. Flourescent lighting with warm white lamps and parawedge louvers will provide a quiet atmosphere and a good lighting level. Flourescent ballasts should be a or b rated for quiet. 35 watt, *not* 40 watt lamps. In outdoor application, quartz or mercury vapor lighting may be considered because of economy of operation and long bulb life.

Display lighting should be mounted on recessed tracks for great flexibility. Lightolier lytespan recessed track with number 7522 fixtures and number 7587 shields will provide an inexpensive and very flexible display lighting system.

In bookstacks, lighting should be mounted directly to the stack frames, with parawedge louvers slanted to deliver maximum light to bottom shelves. Stack lighting is so close to readers that it is essential to use parawedge louvers to reduce glare. Stack lighting fixtures may be obtained from Duxbury Lighting, Great Neck, Long Island.

Miscellaneous

Bicycle racks; steel brackets providing full support for the front wheels.

Coat racks; distributed throughout the building, simple pegs on boards.

Garbage; covered, accessible.

Trash cans; in parking lot, entrance, and throughout building.

Drinking fountain near toilets at entry.

Public telephone; open shelf with acoustical privacy screens, not a booth.

Toilets; cantilevered bowls for easy cleaning, no legs to touch the floor; rails and doors for the handicapped. 120 footcandles of light; stainless, unbreakable mirrors; rough-textured walls; built-in fixtures—soap, towels, trash; tiles and built-in drain for easy cleaning; dark booth walls.

Copying machine; coin-operated, 15 amp. Circuit, near entrance to library.

Curtains

Movable steps for reaching top shelf in bookstack.

All movable equipment to include carpet-type casters, *hard* rubber, large diameter.

A cable television drop and access conduit into the information center and multipurpose room should be provided.

Graphics

Outdoor lighted sign; perpendicular to traffic, lettering on both sides.

Crane Library
Tues. 1:00 - 5:00 & 6:00 - 8:00
Wed. 1:00 - 5:00
Thurs. 1:00 - 5:00 & 6:00 - 8:00
Fri. 9:00 - 12:00 & 1:00 - 5:00
Sat. 9:00 - 12:00

Stack end signs: color-coded to distinguish fiction, nonfiction, and reference books.

lighted, suspended area signs:

Reference		Fiction
Nonfiction		Children

Helvetica type style or similar simple sans serif type should be considered.

Super-graphic signs in children's area.

Furnishings and equipment selection to be approved in detail by the library consultant, building committee, and librarian. Existing furnishings and equipment should be carefully considered for possible use in the new building.

Chairs: comfortable, light-weight, upholstered in breathable durable mil-nylo fabric, to glide on carpet.

Office chairs: adjustable seat and back, no arms. large back.

Carrels: low full sides and back, no shelf, easy control and supervision.

Benches should be provided outside the library for patrons waiting for cars.

Electrical floor outlets should be installed on a 9' grid.

Closets or cabinets for supplies should be provided in staff work areas.

Carpeting:

Dupont Antron III 34 ounce direct glue-down bigelow regent row woven, not tufted. Permanent anti-static; flame retardant. Floor coverings should be a variety of materials—wood, and carpet with a large recessed Pedi-mat area at the entrance so that shoes are cleared of mud before carpet. Book carts may be a problem. All floor levels should be the same therefore carpet areas will have to be recessed so that after carpet is installed, it will be level with wooden floors. Tile floors should also be considered.

Building Program Summary

	Area (sq ft)	Books	Public Seats
Entry/Display	300	1,300	
Reading	280		9
Reference	600	1,500	6
Young Adult	150	600	6
Bookstacks	1,200	18,000	
Children	400	5,250	8
Staff	250		
Multipurpose	700		
Nonassignable	300		
Totals	4,180	26,650	29

Expansion

Further provision should be made for a future expansion of the bookstack area in the 10–15 year period. The reading area should also be expandable as noted. Nonassignable space in this program is minimal. It is doubtful that the building can be constructed with such little non-assignable space. Also, there is no provision for storage space. Storage and nonassignable space together will probably amount to an additional 500 square feet of space that should be included in the minimum building.

Reduction

The bookstack area is full-size. If it is decided to cut the building down below the minimum, the ranges could be cut to only 4 sections. This would reduce the building by 300 square feet and the book capacity by 6,000 volumes. This building would be 3,880 square feet and would hold 20,650 books. The library now holds about 13,000 books and adds 300 net per year. Therefore, this minimum building would be filled in 20 years even if the population does not grow and the library does not accelerate its book additions.

AREA DESIGNATION Entry-Display

Activities: Enter Library, drop off returned books, see how various activities in the library work. Card catalog, bookstacks, and reference, reading and children's areas should be visible.

Occupancy - Public 3 (at one time)	Staff (at one time) 1

Furniture and Equipment Description Quantity Dimensions Area

Book return counter 9' long, 24" wide, 30" high, with book trucks behind.

Book/magazine display with materials on sloping shelves, well lit, 12'.

Display cabinet - Existing.

Paperback rack displaying spines and covers of books (2 future).

Community bulletin board 12' long with lighting.

Book check-out and registration counter, 9' long near exit door.

Under this counter will be stored book cards, registration files, etc. This counter should have sufficient electrical circuits, 2 - 15 amp. for charging machines, theft detection devices and terminals.

Telephone should be mounted behind or in counter.

Newspaper rack as part of the magazine display.

2 toilets.

Close Proximity Desired	Close Proximity NOT Desired
Entrance, children's area	Reference area
Area required (Total) 300 square feet	Proportions - Dimensions 20' × 15'
Book Capacity 100 display books, 600 paperbooks, 20 magazines	Seating Capacity 1 staff stool

Other materials

Current magazines (20), 2 newspapers, several flyer dispensers under bulletin board.

Architectural Features - Ambience - Environment

This area should be organized clearly for the library user to show all library functions. Magazines and interesting new books should be well displayed and carefully lighted. This is not an area of long-time use, so people will come and go rapidly to other library areas. However, library staff may answer questions and town events will cause some conversation in the bulletin board area. Sound control is important here since the sound generated in this area should not escape to the reading area or the reference area. Sound can be absorbed by the magazine/book display wall that separates this area from the reading area, but there should be some supervision. Back issue magazines should be stored behind the hinged magazine display shelves. Doors should operate easily, and careful consideration should be given to prevent cold drafts on staff members working near the entrance. Separate entry and exit doors with a staff station between them would simplify control. A variety of floor materials to absorb mud and sound and simplify maintenance while maintaining an even floor level should be carefully considered.

AREA DESIGNATION Reading

Activities: read quietly and comfortably for some period of time without interruption. Privacy is important in this area, but staff should have some visual control to prevent disturbances.

Occupancy - Public 9-20 (at one time)	Staff (at one time) None

Furniture and Equipment Description Quantity Dimensions Area

5-10 comfortable lounge chairs, easy to get in and out of, with good support for the lower back, and shoulders. Covered in a breathable upholstery that will be durable. These should be sturdy, high quality chairs that will be in daily use for 20 years or more.

1-2 tables, 30" high - wood.

4-8 side chairs with upholstered seats and backs and good support for the lower back for sitting at tables.

4 low tables for books and other materials.

10 visible and accessible hooks for hanging coats.

Trash basket.

Close Proximity Desired	Close Proximity NOT Desired
Bookstack	Children's area
Area required (Total) 280-360 square feet (expandable)	Proportions - Dimensions square
Book Capacity None	Seating Capacity 9-18
Other materials None	

Architectural Features - Ambience - Environment
A quiet place with the illusion of privacy. Very careful temperature controls. Lighting that can be controlled by the user. Absolutely no lighting glare in this area. Light sources should be invisible. Carpet with thick underlayment, sound absorbent walls and ceilings. Decorations should be subtle, neutral shades of earth colors. A book/magazine display wall separates this area from the entrance. Several tables in the room will display good reading books. The ambience should be that of a comfortable, quiet living room inviting library users to spend time enjoying fine books. This can be accomplished with nonglare lighting and chairs that support the lower back and shoulders and are easy to get out of. Chairs should be selected for durability, with spare parts ordered and stored for easy replacement in case of damage.

AREA DESIGNATION Reference

Activities: Consult card catalog, ask questions of the librarian, Use reference books and bibliographic indexes.

Occupancy - Public (at one time) 12	Staff (at one time) 1

Furniture and Equipment Description Quantity Dimensions Area
Information counter: two sided, 30" high, 12" long, 24" wide, with knee holes on both sides.

On staff side, adjustable shelving drawers for pencils, letter size vertical files, forms, materials.

4 chairs for counter, upholstered seat and back, easy glide on carpet.

4 low, full-sided carrels.

4 chairs for carrels (as above).

3 ranges steel bracket shelving 42" high, double-faced with spacers in between for 30" wide tops with spine and dividers for indexes. Tops to be made of non-glare formica with overhangs and flourescent lighting. Each range will be 5 sections or 15' long, and aisles will be 50" wide.

5 card catalog cabinets with 20 drawers each and reference shelves underneath. Top of catalog to be 48" high.

1 table.

4 side chairs.

Close Proximity Desired	Close Proximity NOT Desired
Bookstacks	Childrens area
Area required (Total) 600 square feet	Proportions - Dimensions
Book Capacity 1,500	Seating Capacity 12

Other materials In the future, microfilm and microfiche readers, casette players, computer terminals, video disc players, and others may be used

Architectural Features - Ambience - Environment

A quiet, orderly area for careful, concentrated work by individuals with some assistance from members of the library staff. Sound control materials and task lighting at each work station should be integrated into this design with considerable electrical flexibility and local controls. Floor electrical receptacles on a 9-ft. grid, and built into all counters, carrels, and the 42" bookshelf ranges. Expansion is not built into this plan because this will be the central work area of the library and should be completed at the outset. It may be advisable to install dedicated electrical, telephone, and speaker wire conduits from this point to the services coming into the building from outside as well as to the children's and multipurpose rooms.

AREA DESIGNATION Bookstacks

Activities: Select books, read briefly.

| Occupancy - Public 10 (at one time) | Staff (at one time) None |

Furniture and Equipment Description Quantity Dimensions Area

9 ranges double-faced steel bracket shelving 90" high, 8" deep. Each range to consist of 6 sections 3' long. Each range 18' long.

Ranges should be spaced 5' on centers allowing a 44" aisle.

Ranges should be braced from the top with UL approved raceways that will also carry wiring for the stack lights. These top braces should extend to the structure of the building on both sides. End panels should be wood with signs indicating book subjects and Dewey Decimal number of books at the end of each stack. These signs should be lighted and should be easily changed. Electrical receptacles should be provided in each end panel. Stack lighting should be single flourescent tubes suspended from inverted U-brackets mounted on top of the stack to support electrical raceways. Lamps should be shielded with paddles or parawedge louvers to prevent glare.

2 ranges single-faced steel bracket wall shelving 90" high, 8" wide. Each range to consist of 6 sections 3' long attached to walls on each side of the free-standing double-faced set of ranges above.

Avoid placing books near radiators.

Close Proximity Desired	Close Proximity NOT Desired
Card catalog, Reference area	
Area required (Total) 1,200 square feet	Proportions - Dimensions 24' × 50'
Book Capacity 18,000 books	Seating Capacity none

Other materials
none

Architectural Features - Ambience - Environment

Orderly, well-lighted but no glare. Carpeting or some kind of quiet, resilient floor covering. If stacks are installed after floor covering, the floor covering job will be simpler, but it will be difficult to replace the floor covering if it wears out. If carpet is not used, avoid floor covering that requires buffing machines, which will be difficult to operate in narrow stack aisles.

Stacks should be an unobtrusive, neutral off-white or gray color that will not show dirt and will not compete with the colorful book jackets. Select a color that is standard with the manufacturer so that later stack additions will match and scratches can be easily painted over. Avoid black, which looks shabby soon and shows dirt easily. The large quantity of books in this stack must be in one sequence of arrangement for easy self-service access.

The stacks should be initially set up with a base shelf and five widely spaced additional shelves, so that tall books can be shelved in their correct sequence. As the stacks become crowded, the sixth shelf, stored in compact knocked-down fashion, can be set up, and the base shelf used, but tall books will then have to be put on the lower shelf.

AREA DESIGNATION Children

Activities: Children will select books, read, study, and listen to stories.

Occupancy - Public 25   Staff (at one time) 1
(at one time)

Furniture and Equipment Description Quantity Dimensions Area

3 triple book bins for children's books, 49" long, 23" wide, 23" high. Each book bin will hold 250 books for a total of 750 books.

20 floor cushions, each 21" in diameter and 3" thick.

2 cushion holders for 10 cushions each, 30" high, 24" in diameter.

4 ranges single-faced wall shelving 60" high, 8" wide, 6 sections each range. These ranges will hold about 2,600 children's books.

1 range double-faced free-standing steel bracket shelving 6 sections, 60" high, 10" wide, anchored to the floor by some careful method. 1,300 books.

The above free-standing range to separate the story-hour and picture book area for small children up to 8 years old from the library-study area for older children, with the equipment described below.

2 round tables, 27" high and 48" in diameter.

8 side chairs with upholstered seats and backs.

Display bulletin board area above the wall shelving for childrens art. This display should have lighting for its special illumination.

1 paperback book rack for 600 books.

1 movie-mover or videodisc player for children to see carefully selected films. To be located in story area. Speakers should be built-in.

20 drawer card catalog.

Close Proximity Desired	Close Proximity NOT Desired
Entry-Display	Reference and Reading
Area required (Total) 400 square feet	Proportions - Dimensions
Book Capacity 5,250	Seating Capacity 20 cushions, 8 chairs

Other materials
Videodiscs or 16 mm films
borrowed from State Library

Architectural Features - Ambience - Environment There are two basic areas. The one for smaller children may be noisier and will be equipped for stories, film, or shows. It will be defined by the picture book bins and the cushion holders and should be separated by the free-standing range of bookstacks from the more conventional table and chair area. Although this children's area is now quite small, provisions should be made for almost doubling the area in the future if population trends change. Sound separation of these areas from one another and from adult areas requires careful consideration, since a small staff will serve both adults and children and therefore must have visual and sound control over all these areas. No provision has been made for a separate children's toilet. The adult toilets should have some provision for children's use, and toilet locations should be planned so that children do not have to pass through the adult areas to use them. 15 low coat hooks.

AREA DESIGNATION Young Adult

Activities: Young people age 13-17 will study and discuss.

Occupancy - Public 6 (at one time)	Staff (at one time) None (1 future)

Furniture and Equipment Description Quantity Dimensions Area
2 carrels.
     2 chairs.
     1 round table.
     4 chairs.
     Bulletin board.
     Casette players with headphones.
     1 paperback book displayer.

Close Proximity Desired	Close Proximity NOT Desired
Staff control - Reference	Reading
Area required (Total) 150 square feet	Proportions - Dimensions
Book Capacity 600	Seating Capacity 6

Other materials
100 audio-casettes

Architectural Features - Ambience - Environment
This area ideally would be integrated into the reference area but sound isolated from it. It should be informal, comfortable and designed to absorb hard usage without evidence. Lighting should be high-level, glare free light.

AREA DESIGNATION Staff workroom and office

Activities: Books will be ordered, catalogued, and processed, public suggestions will be discussed, staff will eat meals, take coffee breaks; materials waiting for processing will be stored. overdues will be typed.

Occupancy - Public 1 or 2 (at one time)	Staff (at one time) 1 or 2

Furniture and Equipment Description Quantity Dimensions Area
Double pedestal desk with file drawers and locks.
Upholstered swivel chair on carpet casters with good lumbar support.
2 side chairs with upholstered seats and backs.
1 range 3-4 sections of metal single-faced wall shelving, 90" high.
1 storage cabinet, 6' high with lock.
1 table, 30" high, 48" long.
4 chairs.
1 compact kitchen unit with stove, refrigerator, sink, and storage. This unit should be available to staff and for public functions.
2 staff lockers for handbags and coats.
1 typing stand on carpet casters.
1 processing counter, 9' long with cabinets or shelves above and below.
2-4 drawer letter vertical file or side file.
8 coat hooks.
1 4-drawer letter-size file for library association business.

Close Proximity Desired	Close Proximity NOT Desired
Check-out, return, and reference desks	
Area required (Total) 250 square feet	Proportions - Dimensions
Book Capacity 450	Seating Capacity 7
Other materials	

Since the staff is small, this area should have visual access to all other library areas. It can be one large room separated by furnishings or two smaller rooms separated by glass partitions. These glass partitions do not have to be completely soundproof, but should reduce sound levels. The rooms should have excellent lighting levels without glare since they may be used for long periods of time.

Doors should be carefully planned to give quick access to public areas. A small staff toilet would be a much appreciated amenity.

The kitchen unit should be near the multipurpose room so that it can be used for both areas, but it should be capable of being locked off from the staff area when the multipurpose room is in use.

AREA DESIGNATION Multipurpose room

Activities: Listen to lectures, hold meetings, listen to music, see films, look at art exhibits. This room should be capable of being used as an extension of the reading room, temporarily, or it may be converted to reading room use permanently

---

Occupancy - Public 50 (at one time)	Staff (at one time) None

Furniture and Equipment Description Quantity Dimensions Area

50 comfortable chairs with upholstered seats and backs that glide on carpet and are stackable.

Stage platform.

Built-in speaker system.

Microphone with several jacks on stage and in audience.

Exhibit panels - Brewster Sho-Walls, Track lighting.

6 sections, 42" high, 10" deep, single-faced wood shelving with sliding glass doors and locks (to house future special collections).

4 folding tables to seat four people each (future 10). These should be able to be stored somewhere in this room when not in use.

5 Sections, 90" high, 10" deep, double-faced wood shelving with sliding, lockable doors.

Close Proximity Desired Reading Area	Close Proximity NOT Desired
Controlled access from library	Information/Circulation
Area required (Total) 700 square feet	Proportions - Dimensions
Book Capacity 1,500	Seating Capacity 50

Other materials

Architectural Features - Ambience - Environment
This area must be controllable from the library when the library is open by the use of glass or closed-circuit TV. It should also be capable of separate use when the library is closed. There will be *no* stage lighting, dressing rooms, or theatrical requirements. There should be a small separate projection room sound isolated from the audience with a glass window and a table underneath the window for a portable 16 mm sound projector. Speakers mounted behind a permanent perforated screen should be connected to the projector. There should be a curtain to protect the screen. The projector should be mounted above the audience to prevent audience interference with the images. Lighting should be on three circuits—aisles, audience, stage. This area should be specified for bidding both as a shell and as a finished area in addition to being bid as an additive alternate. Walls should be planned for art exhibits with off-white color and few vertical mullions. Exhibit lighting should be separate from the other lighting and can be track lighting in the center as well as sides. There should be a storage area for the chairs and for exhibit panels.
Storage for 50 stack chairs and 10 folding tables.

AREA DESIGNATION Nonassignable

Activities: Heating and air-handling equipment, custodial storage, passageways, garbage, service entrance, deliveries.

Occupancy - Public (at one time) None	Staff (at one time) None

Furniture and Equipment Description Quantity Dimensions Area
Vacuum cleaner.
Mops and pails.
Custodial locker.
Heating boiler and ductwork.
Cooling fans.
Filters.
Light bulb, paper product, and filter storage shelves.
Garbage cans.

Close Proximity Desired	Close Proximity NOT Desired
Area required (Total) 300-500 square feet	Proportions - Dimensions
Book Capacity	Seating Capacity
Other materials	

Architectural Features - Ambience - Environment
These areas should be minimal construction cost. Outside shed type location should be considered, especially for the initial building phase. Careful analysis should be made of the trade-off between local and central units in initial cost, maintenance, operating cost, and ease of control, as well as flexibility for building additions. (HVAC)

Site Plan Critique

    (See the accompanying illustrations. The first shows the site at time of purchase.)

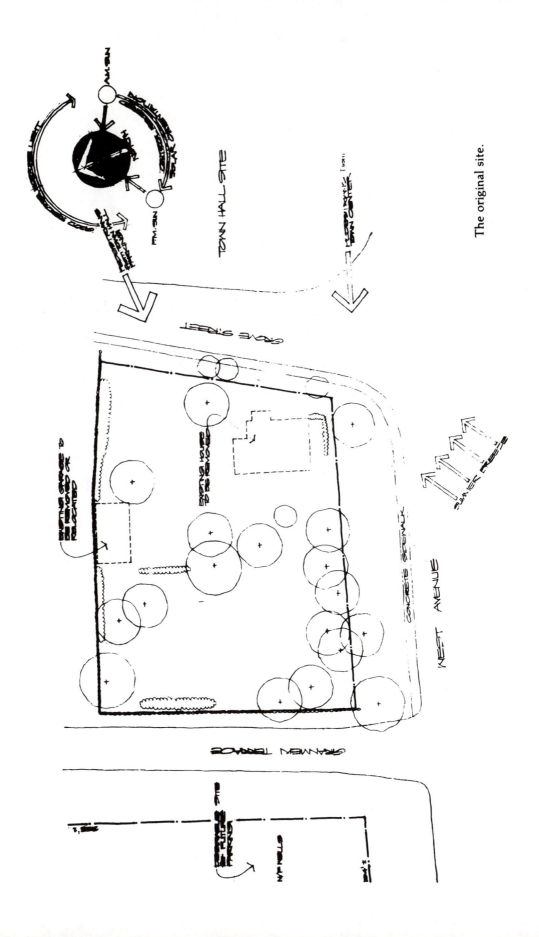

The original site.

A. In this plan, the traffic can flow easily around the building with a convenient drop off point near a library parking entrance. Parking is slightly closer to the library entrance, and a central control point in the building could handle both pedestrian and automobile entrances. In addition, access from Town Hall parking would be more convenient.

Site plan A.

B. This plan shows less connection between Town Hall and library parking. The building is not oriented toward the main street. It is more difficult to coordinate a control point with pedestrian and automobile access. But there is a better opportunity for building expansion in one direction. It is a good solution if additional parking to the west is obtained.

Site plan B.

Schematic Critique: Site Plan A

A-1. *Advantages:*-Multipurpose area convenient to adult reading or children's expansion if necessary. Central control area with good control over all functions. Entry convenient to pedestrians and Town Hall across the street. Orderly, easy to use and control bookstack area.

Disadvantages: Entrance not convenient to rear parking.

A-2. *Advantages:* Entry and control convenient to both parking and pedestrian entry. Children and multipurpose spaces can expand as needed and work together flexibly. Orderly, easy to use and control bookstack area.

Disadvantages: - Multipurpose area cannot be used for adult reading at busy times. Rear parking entrance, which will be used by most people, is too narrow and is not open to other library functions.

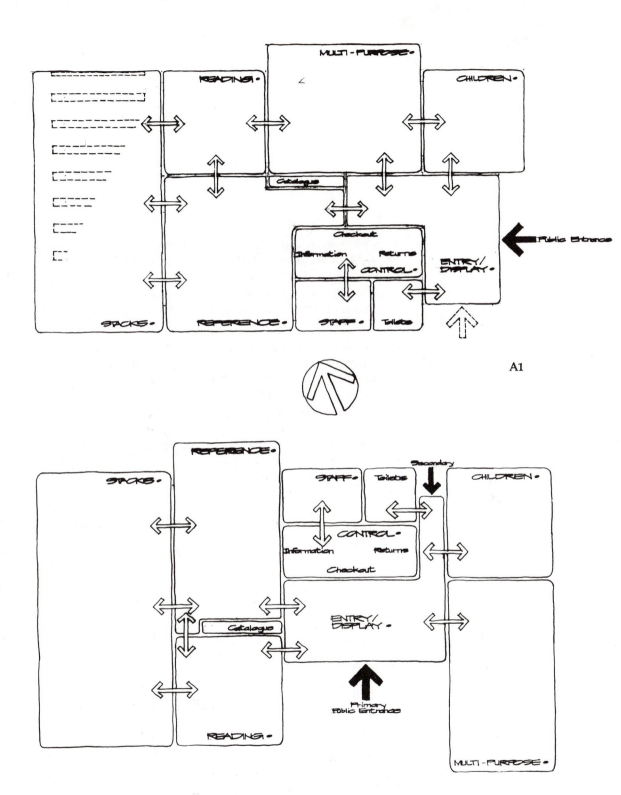

A1

A2

A-3. *Advantages:* Children and adult reading can use multipurpose area when necessary. Centralized control, single entrance.

Disadvantages: No entry from parking area. Bookstacks may be difficult to supervise because staff will not have visibility down all bookstack aisles.

A-4. *Advantages:* Noise isolation of multipurpose room. Entrance convenient to Town Hall parking lot. Control point has good, compact supervision over all library activities.

Disadvantages: Two-level library presents supervision problems and less convenient public access. Multipurpose room less readily available for expansion of adult reading or children's functions. No convenient parking entrance.

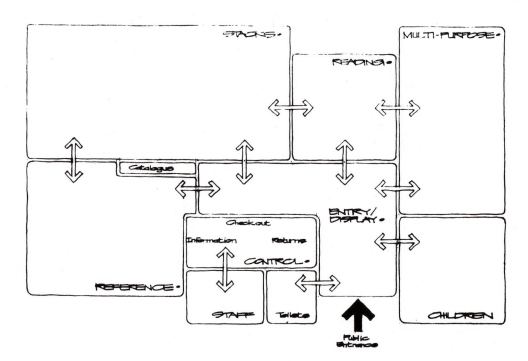

A3

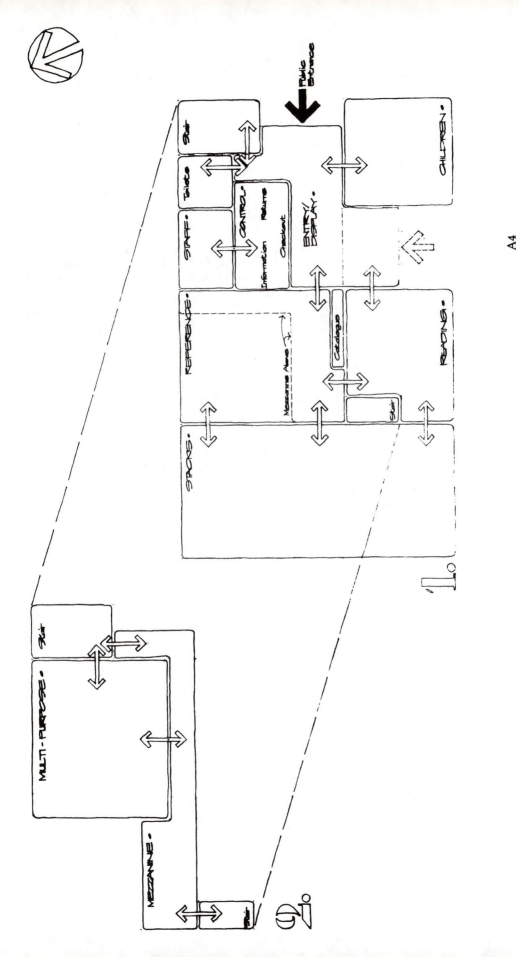

Public Entrance

CHILDREN·

Stair

Toilets

STAFF·

CONTROL·
Returns
Checkout
Information

ENTRY/
DISPLAY·

REFERENCE·

Mezzanine Above

Catalogue

READING·

Stair

STACKS·

MULTI · PURPOSE ·

Stair

MEZZANINE·

Stair

A4

Schematic Critique: Site Plan B

B-1. *Advantages:* Convenient entry from pedestrian main street and Town Hall parking. Good control over all functions. Expansion of adult reading and children into multipurpose space when necessary.

Disadvantages: No convenient entry from library parking lot. Reading and reference areas not visible from entrance.

B-2. *Advantages:* Convenient entry from library and Town Hall parking lots. Good central control of all functions. Multipurpose room can be easily used as part of children's.

Disadvantages: No pedestrian entry and poor orientation of building to main street. No expansion of reading into multipurpose space.

Designed by Galliher and Schoenhardt.

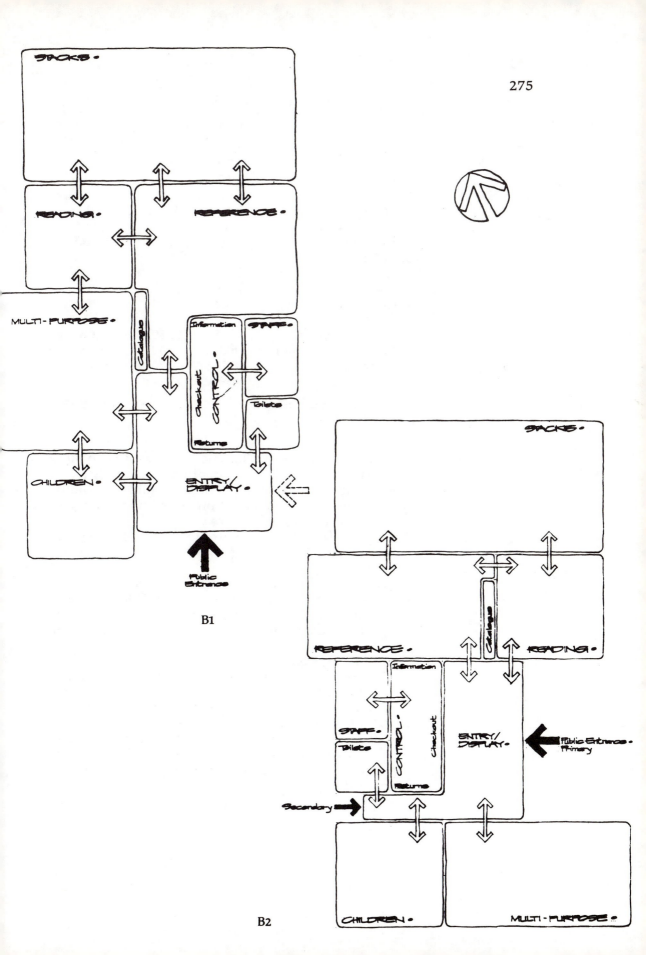

275

B1

B2

Architectural
Design-Program Analysis:Crane Library

Area	Design versus Program	Differential
1. Gross total	6,299	—
Without basement	5,190	—
2. Net total	5,998 4,180	+ 1,818
Without basement	5,128 3,880	+ 1,248
3. Entry-Display	814 300	+ 514
4. Reading	463 280	+ 183
5. Reference/Young Adult	1,380 600/150	+ 630
6. Bookstacks	1,135 1,200	- 65
7. Children	522 400	+ 122
8. Staff workroom/Office	187 250	- 63
9. Multipurpose room	627 700	- 73
10. Nonassignable	870 300	+ 570
Seat Total:	39 29–44	

Commentary:

1. *Expansion-Reduction:* No significant expansion possible on site due to limit on site depth and saving of trees. Reduction would be by deletion of Children's/Multipurpose section and relocation of Children to one end corner of the bookstack area.
2. *Entry-Display:* 12-foot counter instead of 18-foot, paperback rack in reading area; periodical seating area is extra.
3. *Reading area:* Reference table shown within area.
4. *Reference:* Young adult area included. One range is missing. One card catalog section added.
5. *Bookstacks:* One double range relocated to exterior wall.
6. *Children:* One book bin shown instead of three. 3-foot diameter tables instead of 4-foot 10 sections short. Shortage of space requirements must be filled by use of multipurpose especially for story-telling.
7. *Staff workroom and office:* 7-foot shelving versus 9 to 12 foot. Closet substituted for storage cabinet and lockers. 3-foot table instead of 4-foot table. 2 side chairs short. Access to basement storage provides relief for space shortage here.

8. *Multipurpose:* Use for reading expansion is somewhat questionable. No projection room provided. 8 sections of 10-inch deep shelving instead of 10. 40 seats shown, 50 are possible.
9. *Nonassignable:* A custodial locker will be provided in the toilet room or chimney area.

Development Critique 1

Here are some considerations that may be helpfull in continuing design development:

1. Staff control: In a one person library of this size, great care must be taken to provide maximum opportunity for visual control.
   a. Larger glass in office/workroom.
   b. Better visibility to children's and multipurpose.
   c. A general effort to make the entire interior space seem more like a single integrated space rather than four separate buildings as is now the case.
   d. Provide a three-sided island counter instead of an excessively long counter so that one staff member can give better service with fewer steps and still control entries and service areas.

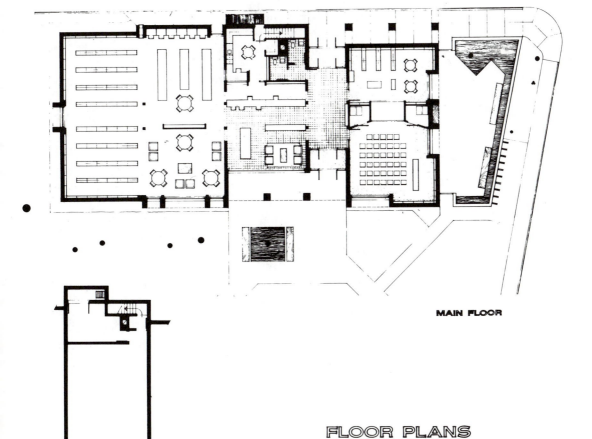

MAIN FLOOR

BASEMENT

FLOOR PLANS

Development Plan 1.

2. Nonusable space: Front and rear outside verandas and long entry vestibule provide excessive, costly, inconvenient, and unsupervisable areas that would be more useful if incorporated into the functioning parts of the building. In the case of the front area, this is the design feature that breaks up the building and reduces accessiblity and flexibility.

3. Expansion: This is a minimal building for a growing community. If expansion cannot be accommodated because of lot size restrictions, setbacks, and proper siting, and because of roof design, then careful consideration should be given to vertical future expansion including consideration of an elevator for the handicapped (at least an elevator location) and an access point that the public can use and the staff can control. I note that the attic area is huge and the large cellar area already designed is not accessible to the public.

4. Flexibility of children/multipurpose could be improved by relocation of chair closets.

5. Some details -
   a. How will light from outside be controlled in multipurpose?
   b. Initial entry impact is zero as far as library function is concerned.
   c. No projection area.
   d. Can multipurpose be used when the rest of the library is closed?
   e. Stone plaza in front will be impossible to shovel snow.
   f. What floor covering in vestibule and reading? Noisy?

Development Critique 2

1. Expansion: This plan requires a difficult and expensive expansion decision, since expansion is at both ends of the building, thus requiring a choice between additional book space and a multipurpose room.

2. There are many expensive nonfunctional design elements. The front entrance could be enclosed, baffled, and brought forward at little additional expense. There are many exterior corners not strictly necessary for functional purposes that in some cases reduce the functional size of the building while adding to the cost. The bookstack area could, for example, be

increased in size while being reduced in cost by carrying the building straight out in that direction rather than indenting to create a distinction from the reading area.

3. The chair storage area in the childrens room should be constructed with easily movable partitions for future children's room expansion. I assume it is not a structural element in the building.

4. Childrens area formality is perhaps misleading. This area will inevitably be changed and rearranged on a daily basis. We should assume that the functions of story hour, reading, and learning activities will be constantly changing, requiring an open casual space with movable furniture, partitions on wheels, floor cushions, etc.

5. Magazine and newspaper shelving?

6. Future design: As you know, I am concerned about many of the final elements in the design not shown in any drawings produced thus far. The various ceiling heights and the variety of functions that will take place in this building will make lighting a crucial design element. Natural and artificial lighting should blend together unobtrusively; this may be difficult to accomplish in some of the higher ceiling areas.

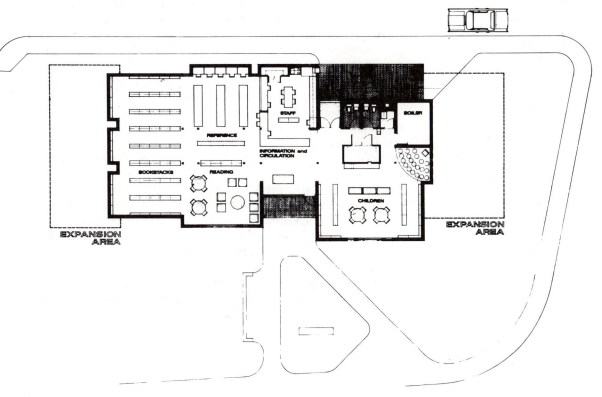

FLOOR PLAN

Development plan 2.

a. Task lighting suitable for the function performed.

b. Minimal reflected glare to reduce veiled reflectance.

c. Louvered lighting to minimize direct reflectance.

d. Reduction in the brightness of luminaires to eliminate high contrast.

e. Low noise ballasts.

f. Satisfying color performance of lamps.

g. Easy bulb replacement, cool long-life bulb installation.

h. Energy conserving specification of low wattage lamps.

i. Standardized lamps, 4-foot tubes.

7. In mechanical design I hope we can strive for maximum local control of heating, cooling, and ventilation. Although the general public should not have access to controls, the location of thermostats and fans should be such that a careful balance of uniform conditions can be maintained in each functional area of the library. In this connection, I am especially concerned about the variation in ceiling heights that could result in a difficult temperature control situation in the reading room. Windows in this area may also cause temperature control difficulties.

8. Large attic: This space resulting from the high-pitched roof design is one of the most attractive and expensive features of the building. It would appear that the building will include several hundred feet of usable space in the attic, yet there is no access to this space. At the very least there should be future provision for an elevator to gain access to this location, and the client should understand that the extra high ceiling in the reading room effectively prevents future expansion into this area.

9. Where will the historical materials be located? In the staff area?

10. Furniture design and selection will be exceedingly important in the functioning of this building, which is very large compared to the size of the present staff. The information/circulation desk should have 30-inch and 39-inch high sections and a wide variety of adjustable shelves, drawers of several sizes, and lockable storage areas. The browsing/display unit should have interior lighting and flexibility to accommodate books, records, pamphlets, and art objects.

11. Would it be possible to install windows in the east wall of the staff area so there could be some supervision of the vestibule and outside waiting areas?
12. There should be a gate to prevent public access to the staff area from the entrance.
13. Book capacities—21,400 (program called for 26,650).
    Bookstack area—15,300 books
    Reference—1,125 plus 100 at counter.
    Reading—800 books or 120 magazine titles.
    Display—200 books.
    Children—3,000 books (assuming 60-inch shelving height)
    900 picture books in bins.
14. Seating—54.
    Adult—5 carrels.
    7 lounge chairs.
    6 counter chairs (only 2 shown).
    8 table chairs.
    Children—8 table chairs.
    20 cushions.
15. Energy conservation: The fact that there are relatively few windows and a large insulating attic space will result in lower fuel consumption, as will the careful sheltering of the north side of the building from window penetration. However, the south entrance is alarmingly close to the staff station and without a vestibule or wind baffle may be a major source of heat loss if it is used to any extent. The high ceilinged reading room may also be expensive to heat and cool.

Manross branch, Bristol,
Connecticut, Public Library,
designed by Willis N. Mills, Jr.

Bibliography

Bruno Bettelheim, *A Home For The Heart*. New York: Knopf, 1974

Michael Brawne, *Libraries - Architecture and Equipment*. New York: Praeger, 1970

Aaron and Elaine Cohen, *Designing and Space Planning for Libraries:* A Behavioral Guide. New York: Bowker 1979

CRC *Performance Guidelines for Planning Community Resource Centers*. Washington, D. C.: Researchitects, 1976

Ernest R. DeProspro, Ellen Altman and Kenneth E. Beasley, *Performance Measures for Public Libraries*. Chicago: PLA/American Library Association, 1973

Albert James Diaz, *Microforms in Libraries*. Microform Review, 1975

John E. Flynn and Arthur W. Segill, *Architectural Interior Systems*. New York: Van Nostrand/Reinhold, 1970

Edward T. Hall, *The Hidden Dimension*. Garden City: Doubleday, 1966

Richard B. Hall, "The Library Space Utilization Methodology" in *Library Journal*, December 1, 1978

Albert Mehrabian, *Public Places and Private Spaces*. New York: Basic Books, 1976

Keyes Metcalf, *Library Lighting*. Washington, D. C.: Association of Research Libraries, 1970

Werner Mevissen, *Public Library Building*. Essen: Ernst Heyer, 1958

Rolf Myller, *The Design of the Small Public Library*. New York: Bowker, 1966

O. Newman, *Defensible Space*. New York: Macmillan, 1973

Dorothy Pollet and Peter C. Haskell, editors, *Sign Systems for Libraries: Solving the Wayfinding Problem*. New York: Bowker, 1979

Nikolaus Pevsner, *A History of Building Types*. Princeton: Princeton University Press, 1976

Robert Sommer, *Design Awareness*. New York: Rinehart, 1972

Robert Sommer, *Personal Space*. Englewood: Prentice-Hall, 1969

Richard G. Stein, *Architecture and Energy*. Garden City: Doubleday, 1977

Godfrey Thompson, *Planning and Design of Library Buildings*. New York: Nichols Publishing Co. 1978

Joseph L. Wheeler and Alfred M. Githens, *The American Public Library Building*. New York: Scribners, 1941

Index

\